PLUNDERING PARADISE

PLUNDERING PARADISE

The Struggle for the Environment in the Philippines

ROBIN BROAD

WITH

JOHN CAVANAGH

UNIVERSITY OF CALIFORNIA PRESS
BERKELEY   LOS ANGELES   OXFORD

University of California Press
Berkeley and Los Angeles, California

University of California Press, Ltd.
Oxford, England

Library of Congress Cataloging-in-Publication Data

Broad, Robin.
    Plundering paradise : the struggle for the environ-
ment in the Philippines / Robin Broad, with John
Cavanagh.
        p.   cm.
    Includes bibliographical references and index.
    ISBN 0-520-08081-5 (alk. paper)
    1. Human ecology—Philippines.   2. Environmental
policy—Philippines.   3. Environmental protection—
Philippines.   4. Philippines—Social conditions.   5.
Philippines—Economic conditions.   I. Cavanagh, John.
II. Title.
GF669.4.B75   1993
363.7'009599—dc20   92-27742
                                                                    CIP

Printed in the United States of America
9 8 7 6 5 4 3 2 1

The paper used in this publication meets the minimum requirements of American National Standard for Information Sci-
ences—Permanence of Paper for Printed Library Materials,
ANSI Z39.48-1984. ∞

For our parents

Contents

Foreword

There is an all-too-easy, aesthetic quality to environmentalism as commonly practiced in the United States. We worry about pandas; we recycle Perrier bottles; we eat an ice cream named Rainforest Crunch. Environmentalism tends to become a lifestyle issue, a matter of what you choose to eat or buy or do on your vacation. It is a sign both of the success of environmentalism and of its failure that it has been so readily absorbed by the upper-middle class, but largely as a matter of gesture and taste. In the conventional stereotype, a concern with the environment is almost a defining feature of affluence—i.e., of the absence of more pressing concerns.

But if environmentalism can be trivialized, commodified, and tamed, this is no longer true of the root concerns that motivate the movement. What may once have seemed to be merely aesthetic worries have grown into a generalized, well-justified dread. Every week brings us horrifying new glimpses of a planet in torment—buckling under the load of its human freight, littered with garbage, overheated, gasping for air. Just as the central issue of the last four decades was the Cold War and the threat of nuclear annihilation, the central challenge of the "New World Order" is the preservation of our habitat and of earthly life itself. Good intentions, individual gestures, and politically correct ice creams will no longer suffice.

Fortunately, a new kind of environmentalism is beginning to emerge from the people who might least be expected to embrace it—the literal wretched of the earth. In the United States, the starting point is the unequal distribution of waste. Studies have shown what many communities had long suspected: toxic wastes

tend to end up in localities where incomes are low and skin colors
dark. In the southeastern states, for example, three-quarters of all
toxic-waste landfills are located in low-income, black neighborhoods. Nationwide, more than half of all African and Latino Americans live in communities that contain at least one toxic-waste site.

Globally, the inequities are even sharper. From the vantage
point of the industrial North, the South is often viewed as a vaca-
tionland, where even poverty is brightened by sunshine and readily available fish and fruit. But such postcard images are further
from the truth than they ever were. The Third World, home of
most of the world's poor, is also the site of the most life-threatening
environmental damage. One reason is that northern countries have
exploited the Third World's economic vulnerability by using the
South as a dumping ground, a run-off site for toxic wastes and
equally toxic industries. At the same time, population pressures
force many of the Third World peasantry to squeeze still more from
their depleted fields and fisheries and their remaining forests. And
then there is the effect of sheer plunder, as local elites and multinational corporations scramble to extract what is left of the Third
World's great natural wealth.

Plundering Paradise is one of the first, and certainly one of the
most engaging, books to chronicle both the environmental devastation of the Third World and the ongoing movement of resistance.
In the Philippines, environmentalism is not a matter of opting to
recycle or to conserve bits of nature for recreational purposes. The
"scenery" all turns out to be functional: rainforests that provide fuel
and keep a group on the fertile soil, coral reefs that sustain fish and
shelter coastal villages from tidal waves, mangrove forests that
nourish water birds and fish. All of this "paradise" is being ravaged
at a furious pace by mining companies, logging companies, and
agribusiness—backed up by one of the most callous and corrupt
military establishments on earth.

The story of the destruction of this island nation as a human habitat would be unbearable without the counterpoint of another story,
one of human resistance and hope. In their often frightening, sometimes funny, travels throughout the Philippines, Broad and Cavanagh met dozens of activists—not always literate and probably unaware, in most cases, of environmentalism as a cause for the
affluent. For these peasant environmentalists, saving the land, the
trees, the fish, is a matter of personal and community survival.

It is also infinitely more dangerous than, say, deciding to recycle one's newspapers. American readers will be disturbed to learn how little the rule of law prevails in Cory Aquino's (and her successor's) Philippines, where the military make little distinction between Communist insurgents and nonviolent community-based organizations. Peasants who block logging trucks or protest toxic mining operations face arrest, detention, or even "salvaging"—the peculiar local term for being "disappeared" or extralegally killed. One such activist you will meet in these pages is Ely de la Rosa, a forty-three-year-old father of five and a leader of a fishers' organization. For his efforts to democratize marine resources and halt the destruction of coastal mangrove trees, he was assassinated in January of 1990.

In this desperate context, Broad and Cavanagh's prescription for ecological reform makes perfect sense: Ordinary people—farmers and fishers—need to regain control over the land and other resources. To the corporate plunderers, the land and its wealth are mere "factors of production," entirely instrumental to the bottom line. The Third World peasantry sees things differently: They know that their children have no future unless the land and the forests and the seas can be preserved for them.

An American cannot travel along with Broad and Cavanagh, even vicariously, without wanting to reach out and exchange addresses with the brave, indigenous environmentalists to whom they introduce us. Somehow the link must be forged between First World concern and Third World activism, between those who are still only worried and those who are already living at the very margins of a sustainable habitat. Knowing that *their* rainforests affect *our* air, that *our* wastes and *our* consumption affect *their* farms and homes, makes a new global environmental alliance both natural and urgently necessary.

To quote someone who spoke in a very different context, an American cattle rancher threatened by industrial wastes: "I was one of those guys who used to think that what happens on the other side of the fence is no concern to me and what happens on my side is no concern to them. But when it's coming over the fence and under the fence, I decided to do something about it." In the world as a whole, there are no longer any fences that hold.

Barbara Ehrenreich

Acknowledgments

News of the Philippines over the past few years has been filled with devastating natural disasters: earthquakes, volcanic eruptions, violent tropical storms. These make arresting copy on the six o'clock news. This book is about a far more important and hopeful story that is unfolding beyond the scrutiny of press and TV cameras. It is the story of millions of ordinary Filipinos who are acting together to fight the plunder of their forests, fisheries, and fertile lands. In an era of United Nations earth summits and spreading global environmental awareness, these Filipinos are a vital part of the answer to environmental destruction.

We recount their stories after extensive travels, research, and interviews across the Philippines, much of it conducted between August, 1988, and August, 1989, when we were based in Manila, and a subsequent May–July, 1991, research trip. (The book also builds on understandings gained from numerous earlier sojourns in the Philippines, dating back to 1977.) In our recent trips, as in previous ones, we undertook considerable fieldwork outside Manila, including journeys to Bataan (February–March, 1989, June, 1989, July, 1989, and May, 1991), Benguet (January, 1989, and June, 1991), Mindanao (May, 1989), Mindoro (October, 1988), Palawan (April, 1989), and Siquijor (December, 1988). Most of the research for the book was conducted during the six-year term of Corazon Aquino, but the dynamic of resource plunder and citizen action continues under her hand-picked successor to the presidency, General Fidel Ramos.

A word on style: throughout the book, we recount these 1988–

1991 interviews in the present tense regardless of when they occurred. We also identify people by the title they held at the time of the interview; many now have new titles in the new Philippine administration.

Now, the words of acknowledgment. Overall, we single out two individuals who made this book happen. Chip Fay, former Asia representative of the Friends of the Earth, helped in so many ways with our trips, interviews, research, photographs, and general education on environmental issues that he practically could be listed as a third author. Isagani Serrano of the Philippine Rural Reconstruction Movement was our inspiration, guide, and teacher through his native province of Bataan, the setting for the second half of the book. If we have simply shared a bit of the vast wisdom of these two, then we have in these pages accomplished something worthwhile.

Hundreds of other special individuals, families, and organizations helped us plan, guided us, housed us not as guests but as friends, and shared a slice of their lives. We cannot possibly list them all, but we are sincerely grateful. We would like to thank individually here some who helped over extended periods of time for this project:

In Bataan: Lisa Dacanay, Ernie Adrañeda, and the rest of the Bataan branch of the Philippine Rural Reconstruction Movement, Ditas Consunji, Rudy Pascua, and Carling Serrano.

In Benguet: Gerry Fiagoy and the Cordillera Resource Center for Indigenous Peoples' Rights.

In Manila: Marilen Abesamis, Chat Canlas and family, Noel de Dios, the Diokno family, Larry Henares, Junie Kalaw, Fe and Roger Mangahas, Bong Mendoza, Helen Mendoza, Boying Pimentel, Odie Santos, Ed Villegas, the Freedom from Debt Coalition, Friends of the Earth–Philippines, Haribon, Ibon Databank, the Legal Rights and Natural Resources Center, MASAI, the Philippine Center for Investigative Journalism, the Philippine Center for Policy Studies, and the Philippine Rural Reconstruction Movement. The University of the Philippines School of Economics provided institutional and collegial support for both of us during our 1988–89 tenure as visiting research associates.

In Mindanao: the dela Cerna family, Boy Ferrer, Karl Gaspar,

Pat Kelly, the Alternate Resource Center, the Mindanao Interfaith People's Conference Secretariat, and PSK.

In Palawan: Lito Alisuag, Len Jos (whose life was sadly cut short by cancer), Louie Oliva, and the rest of Haribon-Palawan.

In Pampanga: the women of BUKLOD.

In Siquijor: the family of Eliseo Rocamora.

In Tarlac: the management of Hacienda Luisita.

As the writing proceeded, several individuals offered their critical eye and comments. Five read the entire manuscript, and we have benefited enormously from their detailed reactions: Sheldon Annis, James Boyce, Chip Fay, David Korten, and Fran Korten. Others read portions of the manuscript and also offered invaluable comments: Lito Alisuag, Walden Bello, Joe Collins, Dan Connell, Ditas Consunji, Doug Cunningham, Cony Dangpa-Subagan, Jorge Emmanuel, Sergy Floro, Karl Gaspar, Eugene Gonzales, Pat Kelly, Owen Lynch, Sean McDonagh, Butch Montes, Joel Rocamora, Nonette Royo, Isagani Serrano, Dinky Soliman, and Marites Vitug. We thank them profusely and absolve them of responsibility for anything that remains with which they disagree or find to be in error.

In the United States, we received support, insights, and sustenance from our families and from our colleagues at the School of International Service at The American University, the Institute for Policy Studies, the Philippine Development Forum, and, in Amsterdam, the Transnational Institute.

We are honored to have the work of five others within these covers. To Barbara Ehrenreich, who first alerted us to a number of issues surrounding women in the global assembly line, we remain forever grateful for the time and energy put into the Foreword. On photographs, the talents of Chip Fay, Debbie Hird, the Scarboro Missions, and Paul Tañedo have captured in images more powerful than our words much of what we saw.

None of this would have been possible without a grant for the first year and a half of our research and writing provided by the John D. and Catherine T. MacArthur Foundation, whose visionary redefinition of what constitutes security is to be applauded. A second trip in 1991 was supported by the Southeast Asia Council of the Association for Asian Studies through its Small Grants to Isolated

Southeast Asian Scholars Program, funded by the Luce Foundation.

Last, and in many ways most, our thanks to the University of California Press. Project editor Mark Pentecost expertly oversaw production. Jane-Ellen Long, copy editor extraordinaire, lent her considerable talents. We also benefited from the skills of editorial assistant Valeurie Friedman and senior designer Barbara Jellow. Finally, very special thanks to our editor, Naomi Schneider. It was Naomi who enjoyed our letters from the Philippines enough to encourage us to expand them into a book. Along the way, she has provided the soundest of guidance.

All of these individuals and organizations have enriched our lives and contributed to experiences we will cherish for a long, long time. The pages that follow are a small repayment for all they have given to us.

Robin Broad
John Cavanagh
Washington, D.C.
September, 1992

The Beauty of the Philippines. . . . A world you didn't think still existed. But it does, right here in the island paradise. . . . Where tropical nights rain stars. Dazzling blue waters beckon to the pristine white sands bleached even whiter by the sun. And coconut trees bend to listen to the waves. Where life is an idyll and smiles are dreamy.
Philippine Airlines advertisement

A plunder economy, that's the post World War II Philippine history . . . plunder of seas, plunder of mines, plunder of forests.
Father Sean McDonagh, Irish Columban Missionary, formerly based in the Philippines

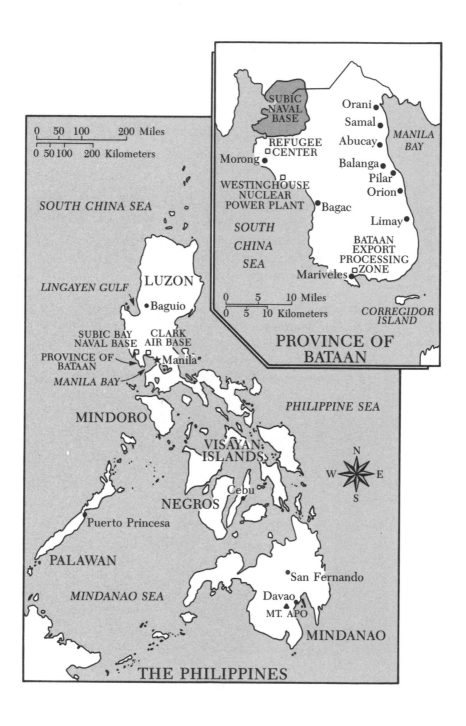

0   50   100   200 Miles

0 50 100   200 Kilometers

SOUTH CHINA SEA

LINGAYEN GULF

LUZON

• Baguio

SUBIC BAY
NAVAL BASE

CLARK
AIR BASE

PROVINCE OF
BATAAN

★ Manila

MANILA BAY

MINDORO

PHILIPPINE SEA

VISAYAN
ISLANDS

Cebu

NEGROS

Puerto Princesa

PALAWAN

MINDANAO SEA

San Fernando

Davao
MT. APO

MINDANAO

THE PHILIPPINES

N
W   E
S

SUBIC
NAVAL
BASE

Orani •

Samal •

Abucay •

Balanga •

Pilar •

Orion •

MANILA
BAY

REFUGEE
□ CENTER

Morong •

WESTINGHOUSE
NUCLEAR
POWER PLANT

• Bagac

SOUTH

CHINA

SEA

Limay •

BATAAN
EXPORT
PROCESSING
□ ZONE

Mariveles •

CORREGIDOR
ISLAND

PROVINCE OF
BATAAN

Chapter One

Generation Lost

The ultimate aim and measure of . . . real development is the enhancement of the capacities of the poorest, their health and nutrition, their education and skills, their abilities to control their own lives, and their opportunities to earn a fair reward for their labours. This is the kind of development which the majority of people in the poor world seek.
UNICEF, *The State of the World's Children 1989* (New York: Oxford University Press, 1989), p. 36

I am terrified for the future of my children. How can they survive in this kind of situation? What can they look forward to? . . . But in the end, we must keep on hoping and working.
Dr. Leonor Briones, president of the Freedom from Debt Coalition and professor at the University of the Philippines, personal communication

We travel to the Philippines to learn what has become of one of the world's most bountiful paradises, a country that recently boasted spectacular tropical rainforests and coral reefs teeming with colorful exotic fish. We come to spend time with participants in a new brand of environmentalism that is springing up here as the natural resources are being torn down.

We leave our native United States at a moment when an increasingly vocal and powerful environmental movement is stimulating widespread concern over greenhouse-gas emissions, ozone depletion, toxic wastes, species extinction, and, ultimately, the fate of the planet. We are traveling to a country where another environmental movement—of poorer people whose very existence depends on forests, fisheries, and fertile lands—is on the ascent.

We are entering a country of environmental ruin, a country where the lives of peasants, fishers, and others are being altered drastically by the sudden human devastation of millennia-old environments. And this devastation is also uniting its victims to act in

1

defense of nature and, ultimately, in defense of their children's future.

Our goal is to learn about these actions and to share the lessons from them with others in the United States. But understanding the actions first requires understanding the people and some of the obstacles they hurdle daily in their efforts to survive.

It is the children of the Philippines we notice immediately as we drive from Manila's Benigno Aquino International Airport into the city. And it is their images that haunt us most when we leave. As we wend our way through the narrow, noisy, fetid streets, we see children everywhere. Children bathe in public faucets. Nude and nearly nude toddlers scamper around. Brothers and sisters little older than the babies chase after their younger siblings, scooping them up and carrying them back to the small shacks that line so many of Manila's streets, shacks built of old wood planks or pieces of cardboard or scraps of indefinable origin.

The children's images haunt us because so many of them are doing what children should not have to do: they are at work. The stoplights at Manila's grimy intersections have become a popular children's workplace. At a minute-long red light, children swarm onto the road. A small boy sells cigarettes by the stick: Philip Morris, Marlboro, and the rougher local brands Champion and Hope. He carries them in a homemade wooden box, almost as big as he, that has other small compartments for the Wrigley's chewing gum and menthol candies he also sells by the piece. He and a handful of other boys laden with candy, cigarettes, or a few of the country's two-dozen-odd newspapers race from vehicle to vehicle to hawk their wares at each window.

Still another boy jumps onto an automobile hood and begins to wipe the soot off the windshield, hoping that if he acts quickly enough the driver will feel obliged to give him a few coins. Some girls stand between the lanes of traffic selling scraps of cloth stitched together into multicolored, pancake-sized circles, used by drivers to wipe sweat from bodies and grime from steering wheels. Three circles can be bought for a peso (just under 5 cents in the late 1980s; around 4 cents in the early 1990s).[1]

Young girls hawk wreaths of fragrant *sampaguita* flowers, to be hung from rearview mirrors in an attempt to camouflage the suffocating fumes of low-grade diesel fuel: three wreaths for 5 pesos. "Please, ma'am, I'm tired," becomes the sad plea late at night as the traffic snarl slows and the price goes down. "Two more sales and I can go home."

The steady workers at the intersection half a block from where we live in Manila slowly become etched into our consciousness. Day in and day out, a girl who cannot be more than nine leads her blind father to the vehicles stopped at the red light. He keeps one hand on her shoulder; the other hand, guided by hers, silently reaches out to the vehicle windows. Just as silently the young girl, her eyes mournfully beseeching, patiently positions and repositions the begging hand from driver to passenger, vehicle to vehicle.

Three scrawny, ragged children who appear to be a family team work on the other side of our street corner. The oldest one, certainly under ten years of age and perhaps no older than seven, is the mastermind of the enterprise. He generally stays on the side of the road. Understanding that there will be more sympathy for the smallest, he pushes his younger brother and an even younger sister, a toddler still, onto the teeming street as the cars stop at the red light. As the light turns green, the two scurry back to him. He puts his arm around them, assessing that red light's pickings and psyching them up for the next one.

The only significant change in the red-light economy occurs at Christmas time. Then the regular inhabitants are joined by migrants from the outlying provinces. Withered, dusty women carry sleeping infants. The woven fabric draped around their waists as skirts identifies them as indigenous Filipinos from the north. Each woman cradles an infant who seems never to wake in the noise and tropical heat; each holds out her free hand, hoping for charity. With their sunken cheeks and sagging bodies, the women look as if they have lived far too many years to be the mothers of the children; but they claim they are. Aggressive sales pitches, vital to success at the intersection, are foreign to the Philippine culture. Yet the women somehow muster their courage again and again, at times not merely extending their begging hand but actually poking the people in the vehicles.

One day we go around Manila trying to estimate the number of children who work at the intersections. We soon give up: too many to count, and too much pollution. Other researchers' estimates of the number of street children vary widely, from a conservative figure of 75,000 in Manila to as many as 1.2 million found nationally.[2]

We are haunted by the children because their lives and prospects constitute for us the most damning indictment of the development strategy followed by the Philippines. In brief, the majority of Filipino children have no choice but to spend their childhoods denied most of the pleasures of youth; instead, they must work in employment that is more often than not undignified, demeaning, dangerous, or all three together. An eleven-year-old sugarcane cutter in the central Philippine island of Negros, when asked if he found time to play, put it starkly: "Play is only for rich children."[3]

As these child workers mature into adult workers, they will find few opportunities to shift to more meaningful, less demeaning, and less dangerous work in their own country. And those children who survive childhoods of sacrifice—of disease, hunger, and long hours of work—face another threat that has only recently entered the national consciousness: the plunder of the environment. In other words, not only are they living in a perilous present, they are being robbed of their future.

Whether or not they live on the streets, the majority of Filipino children must enter the labor market, despite an official ban on child labor. As Pratima Kale, UNICEF's representative in the Philippines during much of the 1980s, explains to us: "During the economic crisis [in the mid-1980s] and until now, the labor force has been swollen by women and kids. This is unprecedented in Philippine history." An estimated two-thirds of Philippine children work. Some are our street-corner hawkers and beggars. Some are self-proclaimed car-watchers, who will guard your parked car for a peso or so. Others stitch and embroider. Still others are domestic "helpers," the *katulongs*, *labanderas*, and *yayas*, who clean houses, prepare meals, wash clothes, and care for younger children.

We have also tried to calculate the earnings of the children at our street corner. A day's take varies widely, but it is clear that, be they beggars or sellers of wares, the children earn barely enough to survive. One study contended that children working as vendors and scavengers earn an average of the peso-equivalent of 50 cents daily. Another estimated that the approximately 5–7 million Filipinos between the ages of five and fourteen who work as hired hands on farms or in factories and sweatshops bring in as little as the peso-equivalent of 5 cents a day. Although such wages are only a fraction of the minimum wage for adults, the contributions of the children in the family can add up to some 30–60 percent of family income.[4]

When these children are at work or on the streets, their education suffers heavily. One government study acknowledged that 240,000 students, out of an average enrollment of 1,000,000 first graders, drop out during the four-year primary education course—in other words, 25 percent do not complete even those crucial first four years of schooling. One-fifth of these drop-outs revert to illiteracy. Another government agency calculated that 40 percent of students drop out before they reach high school.[5]

Outside Manila, intersections with traffic lights are few and traffic is sparse. Yet, wherever we go, we find children at work. Perhaps we should not be surprised. After all, the Philippines is a poor country. As the first sentence in a confidential version of a 1988 World Bank report on Philippine poverty stated: "The Philippines is the only [Southeast Asian] country where the average living standard is declining and the number of people living in poverty is increasing."[6] If you randomly select ten Filipinos, you will find that somewhere between five and seven of them have incomes below the poverty line.[7] In addition, the Philippines is a land of children: five of the ten will be under twenty years of age.[8] This combination of poverty and youth accounts for the number of working children.

We travel north from Manila to Baguio, the so-called summer capital of the Philippines.[9] Baguio's location high in the mountains makes it cool enough to support pine trees and to offer a welcome respite from Manila's stifling heat—although the pine trees are disappearing as the city expands. Those few Manilans who can afford it have second homes in this "City of Pines," to which they retreat during the steamy tropical summers. (It was U.S. colonial officials stationed in Manila who conceived of Baguio; it was Americans who engineered the steep road that winds around the mountain to reach the city; and it was an American who designed the city—although it was Filipinos who built, and whose taxes paid for large parts of, the enterprise.)[10]

In Baguio, we go to Mine's View Park for a stunning view of the majestic Cordillera Mountains, marred only by several barren patches that are the legacy of decades of logging and mining. But as we join other foreign and Filipino tourists at the park's crowded circular viewing stand, we find it hard to concentrate on the admittedly grand panorama. We, the tourists, gather at the edge of a steep cliff, well protected by guardrails. On the rocky cliff below the guardrails stand a dozen or so of Baguio's young children; safety precautions are meant for tourists only. The sport at Mine's View Park is this: a tourist throws a coin (typically a 25-centavo piece, worth about a penny) over the guardrail, and the youngsters dash across the rocky ledges to catch it in a handmade, mitt-like cardboard container at the end of a long pole. Tourists, both foreign and Filipino, watch as if observing elephants at a zoo catching peanuts thrown by the crowd. The tourists appear to take delight in flinging coins to the most precarious part of the cliff. They cheer as the first child scampers to the spot in time to catch the falling coin.

Various permutations of this scene greet us at tourist spots throughout the country. As we head south from Manila to the island of Mindoro, we come to realize that at least a touch of danger seems to be key in devising employment opportunities that transform children into tourist attractions. To get to Mindoro, you take a bus to the port of Batangas, and then a boat to the tourist town of Puerto Galera. In Batangas, the interval between bus and boat has given rise to another child-intensive service. "Throw coins, Joe?" A young boy tugs at our sleeve. (To many Filipinos, all Westerners are "Joe," a remnant of World War II's G.I. Joe.) The child points to the murky ocean waters beside the pier, the stage for the Batangas version of the Baguio sport. Tourists throw coins into the sea and he and his companions dive for them, holding their breath for impressive stretches of time.

On the other end of the boat ride from Batangas, another type of child labor awaits us. Puerto Galera's beautiful natural harbor once sheltered Spanish galleons from typhoons. Today it is frequented by tourists for its beautiful white sand beaches—one complete with a floating bar. John takes a walk on another of the beaches. A boy of ten or so approaches him, smiles, and sits down on his lap. It is a slightly forward gesture for a Filipino child, yet the little boy is laughing a cute child's laugh and shyly asking where John is from. The two of them chat a bit in Tagalog: How old are you? What's your name? Where do you live? Idle chatter until a chilling realization hits: this youngster is propositioning John. This sweet little boy is one of as many as 20,000 Filipino youngsters who survive by selling their bodies as child prostitutes.[11]

The prostitution of the "hospitality girls" who work in Manila's tourist district and for decades conducted business in the towns adjacent to the two large U.S. military bases in the Philippines has been well chronicled. (At this writing, the U.S. government has closed one base and announced that all troops will be out of the other by the end of 1992.) Still, we are not quite prepared for the sight of what has been called the "biggest brothel in the world."

Subic Naval Base, a couple of hours' drive northwest of Manila, has long been the main repair facility of the U.S. Pacific Fleet. A local women's center in Olongapo, the town adjacent to Subic, sets up our visit. Tetchie (not her real name), our guide, is a bargirl who, like most of the women in Olongapo's entertainment industry, comes from a poor rural family. She has the night off from the bar; in such "spare" time she volunteers at the women's center, explaining Olongapo to visiting students, social activists, and researchers like ourselves. The first stop on tonight's alternative tour of Olongapo is The Runway, the bar where Tetchie works as a waitress. How the bar got its name becomes obvious once we step inside: a dozen or so Filipinas stand on a low-budget version of a Miss-America-pageant runway at the center of the bar. They sway sadly and self-consciously to the blare of the music, tugging on their skimpy bathing suits in a hopeless attempt to cover themselves.

Like Tetchie, these are among Olongapo's 15,000–17,000 "hospitality girls" (prostitutes)—waitresses, cashiers, go-go dancers, and entertainers—who work in and around more than three hundred bars, massage parlors, and entertainment centers.[12] Some, such as the go-go dancers, receive a minimal wage. Many do not. Most of their earnings are made through their cut of the "bar fine" that customers who are interested in services beyond drinks and dancing pay to the bar owner. The law says hospitality girls must be at least eighteen years of age. Yet, it is not unusual to find girls who admit to being in their mid-teens.

Sometimes they are even younger. Two twenty-ish young men—stereotypic clean-cut U.S. farm boys, blonde crew cuts, blue eyes, freckles—are perched on bar stools in front of us at The Runway. Between them sits a young Filipina with hair that cascades over her chair and falls nearly to the ground. As we watch we realize she is a

mere child—twelve, maybe thirteen. Little attempt has been
made to camouflage her youth. She wears rubber thongs, patched
shorts, and a T-shirt that is much too big without being stylishly
oversized. These are the clothes of a poor rural child. Her body,
too, is that of a child; it has scarcely begun to develop curves.

But the two sailors amuse themselves with her there in the bar.
One twists her hair into a knot and kisses her aggressively. She
recoils in shamed laughter, as if she has never kissed this way before. His friend takes a turn, then the first grabs her again. They
continue passing her back and forth until they somehow reach an
agreement about whose she will be for the night. The loser walks
away, and somewhat later the other two leave as a couple.

Tetchie, in her late twenties, tells us that there are about 3,000
abandoned street children in Olongapo, some of whom are Amera-
sian—referred to as "souvenir babies." Many of Olongapo's abandoned children become child prostitutes. Tetchie reminds us of a
well-publicized case: in 1987, a twelve-year-old child prostitute
from Olongapo died after an ovary became infected from a broken
tip of a vibrator one of her foreign clients had inserted months before.

When people-power toppled Ferdinand Marcos and brought Corazon Aquino to power in February of 1986, hope was engendered
that life would improve for the children of the Philippines. Aquino
had wooed crowds with promises of social justice and an end to
corruption in this land of persistent poverty. For many of the 60–
70 percent of Filipinos who still live and die in the countryside, it
was Aquino's campaign pledge to land reform that inspired the
most optimism. As U.S. government land-reform advisor Roy Prosterman said of the situation: "The Philippines has one of the worst
land-tenure problems still found on our planet. Two and one-half
million out of the Philippines' four million agricultural families
make their living primarily on land that they do not own, as either
tenant farmers or agricultural laborers."[13] In other words, as a
World Bank study on the Philippines concluded: "A fundamental
cause of rural poverty is the distribution of land."[14]

You need only drive an hour and a half north of Manila to understand why public cynicism about Aquino's commitment to social

reform grew over the course of her six-year term. Here, in the province of Tarlac, is the sprawling, over 6,000-hectare sugar plantation of Corazon Aquino's family, the Cojuangcos' Hacienda Luisita. In 1987 a vastly watered-down land-reform provision passed the Philippine legislature, a body more than three-quarters of the members of which are peso-millionaires and many are large landowners.[15] The land-reform bill that emerged is biased in favor of landowners, as is reflected in one of its numerous loopholes: the corporate stock-sharing program allows landowners to avoid selling their land by instead distributing corporate stock to their workers over a thirty-year period. As time for implementation of the reform arrived, all eyes turned to Hacienda Luisita. Following the letter of this loophole, the Cojuangcos finessed Hacienda Luisita's reform so that the 7,000 regular workers would, over the thirty-year period, receive only one-third of the shares. The Cojuangco family would be left with the majority share—and guaranteed control of the estate.

In mid–1989, we visit the plantation's migrant sugarcane cutters in their living quarters, hot, cramped, cardboard-partitioned pens in huge, open barracks. Children wearing rags and the vacant stares of malnutrition gather around us. The Hacienda Luisita Corporation provides us with a guide to help us understand what we see. Now our guide explains why the children's pathetic state is not the Cojuangcos' fault. The approximately 3,000 cane cutters are casual laborers, imported from the poorer parts of the Philippines for four to five months a year to augment the labor of the "regular" workers at the plantation. The plantation contracts and pays for the migrant husband's labor. The wage, our guide explains, is enough for the husband's subsistence; the plantation owners should not be blamed if the casual worker breaks the rules by bringing along a wife and kids.

Life for the regular workers is slightly better, for they receive higher wages and more than temporary employment (and, of course, that corporate stock). Even then, however, the wages are barely adequate to support their families. "Nutrition here is still below par," admits a plantation doctor. The doctor shares with us the results of a nutritional survey that weighed 65 percent of the preschool population of five barrios where the regular workers live.

Over half of these children suffered from serious malnutrition that will stunt the mental development of many, crippling them throughout their lives.

We drive around the cane fields and watch the workers toil. We spot some small figures carrying huge loads of sugarcane under the broiling sun. "Do the children work in the fields?" we ask the plantation official. "Some younger members of the family might be helping," he replies, but they "are not formally on the payroll."

Nearby, the quarters of the Cojuangco family's forty-odd race horses and the eighteen-hole golf course ("only the best," we are told) appear grotesquely plush by comparison. Imelda Marcos's infamous 1,200 pairs of shoes find their counterpart in the 6,000 fighting cocks (cockfighting is a leading legal gambling activity in the Philippine countryside) of Aquino's brother, each cock living under its own tiny roof on the hacienda's grounds. Our guide brightens as we change the conversation from the children's hunger to the cocks' health. "We feed 'em vitamins," he says proudly, "Ben Johnson–style." These contrasting images sum up the priorities of Philippine development—well-fed, muscular fighting cocks and hungry, overworked children.

Corazon Aquino also promised the Philippines peace; she vowed to bring an end to the two-decade civil war with the nation's well-established insurgency. As she insightfully phrased it early in her administration: "The roots of the insurgency are in the economic condition of the people and the social structures that oppress them."[16] Indeed, during a short-lived ceasefire in late 1986 and early 1987, the two sides sat down to discuss paths to peace.

But not all were happy with the peace talks. To demonstrate their dissatisfaction with Aquino's pursuit of such a "soft line," segments of the government military attempted a series of coups against her administration. Six attempts failed to dislodge Aquino, but they succeeded in teaching her a lesson and changing the course of her administration. Among other de facto concessions to appease the disgruntled military, the government stepped up its counter-insurgency efforts in the countryside. Aquino rationalized her about-face in a speech to the Philippine Military Academy in early 1987: "The answer to terrorism of the left and the right is not social and economic reform but police and military action. . . . I told you when we were discussing the peace initiatives that when they fail, as we feared they would, and when it becomes necessary to take out the sword of war, that I want a string of honorable military victories. I want this victory."[17]

One of the most visible of Aquino's all-out military campaigns took place in April, 1989, on the central Philippine island of Negros, an island whose sugar haciendas and gross inequalities have made it a microcosm of the yawning gap between rich and poor found throughout the archipelago—and an insurgent stronghold. On one side are the rich of Negros: the sugar *hacenderos*, who drive dazzling white Mercedes-Benzes and have buying habits that put Negros near the top of the country's charts for up-market Electrolux appliance sales. The hospitals of Manila are often deemed not good enough by the rich of Negros; some travel to the United States to give birth. On the other side, 90 percent of the people of Negros fall below the poverty line. Most of them will never see a doctor. Hunger and disease are all-pervasive. A United Nations Children's Fund (UNICEF) publication reported that, on the average, at least one child dies before the age of five in every sugarworker's family in Negros; nearly one-third (29 percent) of the families lose two or more children.[18]

"Operation Thunderbolt," the April military assault, made matters even worse for the children and their parents. To avoid the massive bombings and helicopter gunship strafing of fields and villages, some 35,000 civilians were forced to evacuate their homes and settle temporarily in makeshift refugee centers. Although this form of "strategic hamletting" had been practiced regularly during the Marcos years, Operation Thunderbolt under the Aquino administration produced the single largest civilian evacuation in the Philippines since World War II. Measles, pneumonia, and gastroenteritis flourished in the crowded and unsanitary evacuation sites. Of the civilians in the temporary shelters, 280—mostly children—were dead within three months, the majority of them victims of malnutrition and disease. By mid–1990, a team of investigative reporters placed the number of children who had died at Operation Thunderbolt's evacuation centers at 257. Families buried one, two, sometimes three children. One grandmother buried five of her grandchildren. Journalist Malou Mangahas wrote, "The children of Negros, they were dying three years ago from malnutrition and disease bred by poverty. Now, they are dying still from malnutrition and disease bred by poverty, but also by war."[19]

The children's deaths, the government claimed, were a "necessary social cost" of war.[20] But, even by the government's own count, Operation Thunderbolt killed more children than insurgents. It was, one evacuee sobs to us as she spoke of the numbness that set in as they saw tiny cardboard coffins lined up day after day, hard to "believe that Cory is on our side."

A UNICEF poster seems custom-made for the children we encounter during our travels in the Philippines. The poster, with a photograph of a wide-eyed young child, asks, "What would you like to be when you grow up?" The answer, in bold letters across the breadth of the poster, is jolting: "Alive." In our travels and conversations with poor Filipinos (who, remember, are the majority of the country's citizens) we ask that poster's question whenever we can.

And a slight variant: What do you hope your children will be when they grow up? With no pretensions of having carried out a scientific survey, we can relate the following: Farmers expect their children to be farmers. Fishers expect their children to fish. And workers hope their children will be able to find jobs. If they allow themselves the luxury of a wish for their progeny, it is hardly what one would term frivolous musing; if they dream, it is typically of schooling for their children and grandchildren.

Sometimes we cannot get a specific answer. "It depends," a woman in a rural town tells us as she adds another twig to the wood fire over which she is cooking rice for her family of five. One of us is holding her four-month-old on our lap. The other is on the dirt floor, playing with her toddler. Neither child wears diapers. (Even cloth diapers, we discover, are a luxury for the majority of Filipinos.) "Depends on what?" we ask. She chuckles. "On *suerte* [good luck] and *malas* [bad luck], of course." She laughs as she adds, "We all believe in *malas* and *suerte*. But if you don't work, you don't get *suerte*."

The problem is that you need *suerte* in order to find a job, the niece of a friend of ours laments. She is in her twenties and has just received her degree as a medical technician. She is smart and energetic and wants to work—and has a skill that presumably she could use productively in the Philippines. She would, on the surface, appear to be one of the lucky ones, one of those with *suerte*. And yet, she tells us, she is not. The problem is that she wants to stay and work in the Philippines. "I am from this country; my family is here; I want to work here." But she feels as if she is being pushed to leave her homeland in search of employment overseas—or, at least, that she has little choice. Her parents are not rich. In her initial years as a medical technician in the Philippines, her annual salary would be but a third of the amount she needs to repay one year of the debt she incurred for her schooling. And because so few jobs are available, it is next to impossible to get even such a low-paying one without the assistance of someone with influence—"a backer," as they say in the Philippines.

Like our friend's niece, some of today's children have *suerte* enough to be getting training that will enable them to become professionals: doctors and nurses, lawyers and teachers, engineers. Yet, ironically, like her, they are likely to find the jobs open to them so poorly paid or so scarce that many will join the 1.5–2.5 million Filipinos working overseas. The Philippine Nurses Association, for example, estimates that of 150,000 registered Filipino nurses, 90,000 are working overseas. This confers on the Philippines the dubious distinction of being the number one exporter of nurses in the world—and it is the number two exporter of doctors. Medical professionals are being forced out of the country, despite a desperate health crisis in the Philippines in which 30–40 percent of the need for nursing personnel is unmet, and despite the astounding fact that the majority of Filipinos live and die without receiving any kind of professional health care at all.[21]

It is not only the Philippine health-care system that suffers from this export of professional and high-skilled workers. We meet female college students who are majoring in education, not with dreams of one day becoming a teacher but because such a degree will be a useful credential in securing a job in Hong Kong—as a maid. We often hear stories of college-educated teachers who now work in Hong Kong and elsewhere as domestic servants and chambermaids. It is understandable, since they can earn over three times as much cleaning in Hong Kong as they can teaching in the Philippines. Yet, partially as a result of this brain-drain, the Philippine Department of Education, Culture, and Sports noted that it was short nearly 45,000 elementary and secondary school teachers for the 1989 school year.[22]

Indeed, overseas work is perceived by many of the people we interview as the surest path to *suerte*. This becomes very clear to us during our stay in Bataan, a province a few hours' drive northwest of Manila. As the governor of that province tells us, "If you see a house of concrete [rather than wood, bamboo, or thatched palm leaves], you can be sure someone in the family is in Saudi Arabia or the United States." Or, as a mayor explains in response to our question about how any poor fisher in his town is able to afford one of the small but expensive wooden boats, "You know, there are many unemployed here, engineers, nurses, and many recent [college] graduates. But some are lucky, some have sons and daughters working abroad."

The people of Bataan who have such *suerte* are understandably proud to display it. "I ♥ Saudi Arabia," proclaims a bumper sticker on a passenger mini-bus. "Petro-Engineering International Saudi Arabia," brags the T-shirt of one of its passengers. Most common of all are decorative rugs hung on living-room walls. These rugs, brought home by workers from the Middle East, almost always depict a dog and a cat; a minority show mountains and lakes. But whatever they depict, they demonstrate that that particular household is lucky enough to have someone working in the Middle East.

Every year more than 700,000 new job-seekers are added to a Philippine labor force that already has some 6,000,000 underemployed and unemployed workers.[23] In the late 1980s, the many Filipinos working overseas were concentrated in Saudi Arabia, Japan, Hong Kong, the United Arab Emirates, Kuwait, Taiwan, Australia, and the United States. The exodus to the Middle East started in the mid–1970s, when oil-rich countries imported labor to build roads, hotels, homes, industrial complexes, and the like. By 1986, labor had become the Philippines' number one earner of foreign exchange, as overseas workers sent back remittances of over one billion dollars a year. The Filipinos who work abroad, then, are not only easing the domestic unemployment situation somewhat; they are also a key source of the foreign exchange the government desperately needs to repay its onerous $28 billion foreign debt. So vital

are they to the economy that President Aquino herself lauded overseas workers as the "new heroes of the Republic."[24]

Overseas work may bring a temporary increase in income that
buys a color television and perhaps even schooling for one's kids,
but the Philippines' "new heroes" have their own sets of problems,
their own *malas*. We hear stories of horror at the hands of employ-
ers overseas: young women who travel to Japan thinking they will
be entertainers only to find themselves prostitutes and virtual pris-
oners, a maid in Kuwait who died after having been beaten by her
employer, men and women returning psychologically scarred. We
meet pained husbands who, having spent years overseas, return to
discover that they and their almost-grown children are near-
strangers. We meet Filipinos whose spouses went overseas so long
ago to provide for their families that their marriages are by now, for
all intents and purposes, over.

In Bataan, we become friends with a young father of two who has
recently returned from working six years in the Middle East. He is
fairly typical of the Philippines overseas workers: the majority per-
form manual labor in the Middle East, and 75 percent are twenty-
five to forty-four years old.[25] And, like other skilled construction
workers in the Middle East, he earned more than $500 per month,
whereas in the Philippines he would probably have earned the
peso-equivalent of around $75.[26] Our friend and his wife are from
families of modest means, but his new concrete, three-bedroom
home tells of his recent *suerte*. Inside are a color television, a tiled
bathroom with indoor plumbing, and a kitchen with an electric
range and other modern appliances—all *katas ng Saudi*, fruit of
Saudi Arabian employment.

Though his children had more toys than most of their playmates
and more financial security, they were lacking a father. So, when
his Saudi Arabian contract expired, he returned home, willing to
sacrifice a decent salary for a poorer-paying job that would allow
him to be with his wife and children. The problem, he confides to
us with great frustration, is that he has not found a job at all. His
savings dwindling, he finds himself sadly contemplating a return to
the Middle East to support his family.

He sends us to visit his older sister. She and her husband run a
small eatery in a nearby town. Displaying typical Filipino hospital-

ity, they welcome us like family, feed us their local delicacies (vehemently refusing payment), and insist we spend the night. Late in the evening, the wife takes out a photo album and tells us her story. Her father was killed when she was twelve, and she had to stop her schooling to become a "helper," a maid, for a local Bataan family. The one dollar per month that she earned she promptly brought to her mother. Years later, she married and had two daughters, one of whom was bedridden. She and her husband worked hard to make ends meet, but they could not. After a number of jobs in the Philippines, the couple decided that there was no other option: one of them had to seek work overseas. For two years, the wife worked as a maid for a Brazilian diplomat living in Australia. Her employee was good to her, but the years were not. Her sickly daughter died while she was away; she returned home for the funeral. In a corner of the bedroom are all she has to show for those two years: a pair of winter boots and a large blonde doll.

You cannot travel anywhere in the Philippines without hearing tales of life as an overseas contract worker. The brother-in-law of a friend shares his. He is an assistant principal at a public high school in Manila, but, in the late 1980s, he makes the peso-equivalent of only $5.75 a day. That is hardly enough to support his family. (It has been estimated that the peso-equivalent of between $6 and $9 was needed to keep a family of six above the poverty line in the late 1980s.)[27] Because of this situation, some years ago he went to the Middle East to work for two lonely years. On his return, he used his savings to buy a "jeepney," one of the colorfully painted, elongated descendants of a World War II jeep that ply Manila's streets as public mini-buses into which can be squeezed 16–20 riders. Now, he comes home for dinner after a full day of work at the high school, then goes out and drives his jeepney route twice, netting enough to more than double his salary each month.

If temporary contract work in the Middle East is a much-sought-after commodity, work in the United States is coveted even more; it is perceived as the ideal place to live. Filipinos often tell us that if they could just get to the United States, their problems would be solved. Secretaries, barbers, children of our friends, even one of the mayors we interview: all want us to bring them back with us to "the States," and, if not, to help them get visas to travel there alone. "Everyone is rich in Utah, aren't they?" a clerical worker asks as if confident of an affirmative response, adding that she recently became a Mormon and is hopeful that she will be able to emigrate to Utah soon—and therefore become rich herself. On occasion, when we ask a child what he or she wants to be when grown, we get the answer "American." (When asked in a 1982 survey what nationality they would want to be, only 10 out of 207 Filipino elementary students chose Filipino.)[28] "At a young age, my ambition was to be an American," a Filipino movie director, who has garnered worldwide acclaim for his nationalist movies, admitted to historian Stanley Karnow.[29]

In our conversations with Filipinos about their dreams and hopes and their children's prospects, they often raise on their own the topic that we have come to study: the future of the country's natural resources.

"What will your children be when they grow up?" we ask a poor fisherman in Bataan. He sighs. "My father was a fisherman and so I too am a fisherman. I was born a fisherman. But the fish are dying. So there will be no fish for my son to catch. He will not even be able to be a fisherman like I am." Elsewhere in the Philippines, we talk with a peasant woman whose family grows rice on a small plot of land. She gives us a strikingly similar answer: "The forests are disappearing, and so the soil of our rice field is being washed to the sea. There will be no soil left by the time our children are grown. What, I wonder, will become of them? How will they grow rice?"

We are reminded of these statements some months later in Manila as we sit in the plush, wood-paneled waiting room of the country's Secretary of the Department of Environment and Natural Resources. A large painting that hangs over the sofa dominates the room. The picture depicts a barren, clear-cut hillside, littered with brown tree stumps. Nothing lives in the painting; it is a scene of total plunder and of no hope.

One of the questions we raise in subsequent chapters concerns the extent to which this painting and these prognoses about fish, soil, and other natural resources reflect the situation across the country. How fast are the natural resources being depleted, and what impact does this have on the people? How much of the destruction is caused by the poorer victims (and their rapid population growth) and how much by the privileged few?

Is there really no hope?

In many of the places where we are guided through plundered landscapes—scenes reminiscent of the barren painting—we see people acting together to counter the destruction and to build a better life for their children. In the provinces we visit, we discover that, as options have narrowed for the next generation and as resources have been depleted, very ordinary Filipinos have begun to fight back. Indeed, the intensity of their actions seems related to the extent of the destruction. They have blockaded logging roads to halt commercial loggers. They have replanted trees. They have fought the destruction of coastal mangrove forests. They have taken over vacant lands on which they have cultivated traditional varieties of rice using little or no chemical fertilizer and pesticide.

Consciously or unconsciously, they have become environmentalists.

And if we are to grasp why, underneath the plunder and the despair, there is hope for the children of the Philippines, we have to listen to what gives their parents inspiration and motivation. We have to try to understand their brand of environmentalism.

In the remote community of San Fernando in the southern province of Bukidnon, a young peasant woman explains how and why she and other rice and corn farmers who live near rapidly balding mountains became activists against the government's logging policies. She has never heard of global warming, but she knows well why her life and that of her children depend on these trees: "Without trees, there is no food, and without food, no life," she tells us in the local dialect. To motivate others, she and some of her fellow residents of San Fernando wrote a letter about their battle to save the forests and had the letter put away with instructions that it be reread in fifteen years. It was a time capsule of sorts—but one to spur them to action. When the letter is read again, the young woman explained to others, your children will ask you: What did you do when the forests were being destroyed? Did you fight for my future or were you silent?

This anecdote is but one of many that suggest that the central development issues that will determine the future of the Philippines' children are also in large part environmental issues. By the same token, we run into few purely environmental issues; most environmental problems demand broad developmental responses.

This book is about environment and development and people like the woman in San Fernando, people who form the backbone of the new citizens' movement for environmentally sustainable development in a country where that movement is particularly dynamic and promising. Through citizens' organizations, they are asking questions, making connections, and initiating actions—in brief, making their own history.

In this book, we offer their stories and some of their insights, much as they were offered to us throughout our travels. We attempt to piece together the various strands of the new environmentalism and to answer the questions: How do ordinary Filipinos perceive the environment and development problem? Can poor people be the catalysts of a new brand of environmentalism? What kinds of organizations have they constructed to reverse the resource plunder? What kinds of actions are they launching? Under what circumstances have citizens' groups gained ground in their attempts to replant forests and to manage natural resources sustainably? In short: Who is behind the plunder; who is organizing against it; and what are the strategies to address the problem and to launch development alternatives that can create a better future?

In the pages that follow, we move from Baguio in the north to Mindanao in the south, from Palawan in the west back to Bataan, site of the infamous battles of World War II. In each of these places we discover ingredients of a new approach to development. In each of these places we find that, out of the plunder, citizens' groups are working to rebuild their paradise. This process of rebuilding offers lessons, ideas, and hope for individuals and organizations the world over who are trying to construct a more participatory, equitable, and sustainable future.

Chapter Two

Nature's Revenge

Others get rich on nature, while we get nature's revenge.
Peasant in San Fernando, Bukidnon, Mindanao

To understand the rapid growth of Philippine grass-roots environmentalism over the last few years, we travel through the country's main ecosystems: its uplands and lowlands, its freshwater and coastal areas.

We start, as do most visitors to the Philippines, in Manila, an urban ecosystem which today ranks among the most polluted on earth, and among the most congested as well. Inhabited by some eight to ten million Filipinos, Manila is bursting at its seams with people who struggle daily with an urban infrastructure in decay.

That mix of congestion and pollution makes itself felt constantly. Several times a week, for instance, we travel by public transport through Quiapo, Manila's traditional market center, which overflows with people and vehicles almost 24 hours a day. Most people are in Quiapo as are we—simply to pass from one part of metropolitan Manila to another. Others come as devotees of the Black Nazarene, a seventeenth-century life-size figurine housed in Quiapo's old Catholic church. Some are more interested in the small stalls outside the church doors, where women sell various medicinal herbs and amulets that are reputed to enhance sex drive or induce menstruation, as the need may be. Still others head for the plaza next to the church, where for decades rallies of every conceivable political hue have been held.

None of the transients in Quiapo except us seems at all interested in a structure at the side of the plaza, just across from the church and the vendors. The structure resembles a baseball scoreboard, but words on it proclaim it to be an "Air Quality Meter" and a "Project of the National Pollution Control Commission." The board, once green, is now black with soot. No lights flash to indicate whether the air has reached unsafe levels; no numbers appear.

An official in the Department of Environment and Natural Resources subsequently tells us that the meter has not worked for
years and, indeed, that Manila's air quality has not been measured
since 1983.

These days, the best gauge of air quality is the number of people
who hold a handkerchief over nose and mouth as they pass through
places like Quiapo, in a crude and inadequate attempt to filter out
the pollution. These makeshift masks alone are enough to dispute
the contention advanced by some Westerners that only rich people
in rich countries care about air quality.[1]

Faces half-hidden by these handkerchiefs, millions of commuters queue up along Manila's streets in Quiapo and elsewhere during morning and evening rush hours. The throngs fill the sidewalks
and spill out far into the streets, like spectators expecting Macy's
Thanksgiving Day parade. But, in reality, they are anxiously awaiting a ride—and that is not easy to get in Manila. Even with thousands of buses, tens of thousands of jeepneys, one aboveground
metro-rail system, numerous taxis, and an ever-increasing number
of private cars, the available transport is not enough for the city's
burgeoning population. As a result, rush hour has expanded to
three hours in the morning and another three at night. A government "spot survey" reported that the average wait for a ride during
peak hours doubled over the 1980s, reaching a full hour. In certain
parts of the city we find ourselves stranded even longer, frantically
trying to squeeze into anything on wheels that passes. Considering
our frustration and anxiety on those occasions, it does not totally
surprise us to read newspaper accounts of murders that occur in
the frenzy of rush hours as people fight for a seat.[2]

Waiting, with or without handkerchief, it is impossible to filter
out the big black clouds of exhaust many of the vehicles leave in
their wake. "Smoke-belchers," Filipinos call them, referring rather
unscientifically to any vehicle whose exhaust chokes bystanders.
The government's Department of Environment and Natural Resources (DENR) reports that more than 50 percent of Manila's vehicles are "smoke-belchers," by which they mean vehicles violating
emission standards on air pollution.

These statistics help to explain why asthma and other respiratory
diseases run rampant in Manila, as do several varieties of eye ailments. The children of Manila, and particularly those who work on

its streets, are especially vulnerable. We conduct another informal poll: more than half of our friends' children suffer from some respiratory disease. Like many Manilans, we spend much of our time in the city bathing our stinging eyes with eye-drops and battling various eye infections.

Although experts attribute 60–70 percent of Manila's air pollution to motor vehicles, other environmental nightmares compound the problem. During our initial few months in Manila, the city's main garbage dump ("Smokey Mountain") is closed: it simply cannot accommodate any more garbage, we are told. Informal garbage heaps appear on nearly every street. Some households become exasperated and torch the fetid fly-ridden piles, sending nauseating fumes of burning plastic into the air. Other households simply let the heaps build up. As a result, typhoid and other water- and foodborne diseases are said to be on the rise. The rainy season exacerbates the problem. During typhoons, silt from denuded hills combines with the ubiquitous rancid garbage to jam sewers, on one occasion leaving a section of Metro-Manila up to ten feet below flooding waters.

In Manila, as we discover, action to combat this pollution is stymied neither by a lack of public concern nor by an absence of laws. Both exist in abundance. Consider the transport sector again. For over a decade now, it has been unlawful for any owner or operator to allow a motor vehicle to discharge above a set level of air pollutants. Consumer groups spring up regularly to fight the pollution of Manila's air; they sport such colorful acronyms as GASP (Groups Against Smoke Pollution) and GAS MASC (Groups Against Smoke-Belching to Make Air Safe and Clean). And, as the president of one of the jeepney drivers' unions explains, the drivers themselves would like nothing more than to have nonpolluting vehicles: "We know that smoke-belching is bad. After all, we're the ones hurt most by it. You travel to and from work in the pollution. But we're the ones who have to suffer in it for fourteen hours a day."

Old diesel engines, many imported secondhand from countries like Japan, are part of the problem. Pollution is further aggravated by cheap, low-grade petroleum that produces high levels of sulfur dioxide (which can cause bronchitis and irritation of mucus membranes) and contains dangerous amounts of lead (particularly harmful to children). Philippine gasoline brands, as a top DENR official readily admits, are among the "dirtiest in the world." But, he explains, this is all a poor country like the Philippines can afford.

To shift to low-sulphur and unleaded fuel would, first of all, mean redesigning Philippine refineries, which would, in turn, increase fuel prices. It would also require new engines. And how the public transport sector could cope is hard to imagine. Most jeepneys, for instance, are owned by individuals or small entrepreneurs whose earnings are insufficient to purchase newer, cleaner engines. To yank offending vehicles off the road would be to strand even more commuters. And even were enforcement of air quality standards desirable, the government frankly acknowledges that it lacks the funds to do a decent job.

Outlaw jeepneys? Get foreign funds for new buses and metro-rails to crisscross the metropolitan area cleanly? More complications here—for, pollution-ridden as the current transportation system is, it is probably the largest employer in a city where unemployment is a serious problem. Beyond the 100,000 or so jeepney drivers, hundreds of thousands more earn their livelihood from this form of transport. Aside from the dependence of the street children on this traffic, thousands service the jeepneys, sell spare parts, repair tires, paint the jeepneys, or sell colorful jeepney decals proclaiming everything from a pious "God, protect this trip" to a racy "Driver by day; screw-driver by night."

No easy answers, we begin to discover. As long as the Philippines and the majority of Filipinos are locked into a grinding cycle of poverty and inequality, pollution in the cities will flourish. And most of the Filipinos who live in Manila will find life difficult to bear.

But anyone who listens to the various dialects being spoken on Manila's street corners comes to realize that many of the city's inhabitants are not native Manileños. They, like the majority of Filipinos, began their lives in the outlying provinces, where most live at or below subsistence level. In the provinces, most people depend for their livelihoods directly on the country's forests, fishing grounds, minerals, and once-fertile lands. The degradation of these natural resources is leaving growing numbers of Filipinos even poorer—and with little choice but to migrate to Manila and add to its burgeoning population.

To witness this "push factor" for ourselves, we leave Manila's pollution and crowds behind and travel into the countryside. There we see that Manila's pollution represents but a small part of the Philippine environmental crisis. And there we begin to catch glimpses of a fundamental difference between the environmental problems in Manila and those in the countryside, a difference that parallels one between Third and First World countries overall. As we venture outside Manila, we discover that most environmental problems involve the depletion and degradation of natural resources at the *start* of the production chain. Forests and fishing grounds, for most rural Filipinos, are sources of livelihood, not places of recreation or spots for an idyllic vacation. Countries like the Philippines are generally primary producers, with large subsistence sectors totally dependent on natural resources. To live, people eat and sell the fish they catch or the crops they grow—and typically these people exist at the margin. For them, the ecological crisis involves the fate of resources at the start of the development pipeline. Natural-resource degradation becomes an immediate, and life- and livelihood-threatening, crisis.

This concern is quite different from the air and water pollution and waste-disposal problems that most city-dwellers and most Western environmentalists think of as the ecological challenge. These problems occur at the *end* of the production chain, at the end of the development pipeline. They have to do with the disposal and assimilation of what is left over—the waste—after something is produced. They are the bulk of the environmental crisis in richer countries but make up a minority of the environmental problems in a country like the Philippines. It is a simple point, yet crucial for understanding where the Philippine ecological crisis and its environmental movement are, and where they are not. Celso Roque, then president of the Philippine environmental group Haribon, captured some of this difference in 1986:

Western environmentalism as an ideology and as technology must be adapted and revised to suit the unique Philippine conditions. Our social and ecological landscape is almost in direct contrast with that of the west. It is tropical rather than temperate. The economy is agricultural rather than industrial. There is general poverty rather than affluence. The population is rapidly growing rather than stable. The system of access to natural resources is feudal rather than democratic.[3]

These differences are dramatized as we journey by bus to places such as the province of Benguet, a half-dozen hours and a world away from the urban pollution and congestion of Manila. There, we travel in a rented jeepney from Baguio City to the municipality of Itogon. The climb over narrow mountain roads strewn with rocks is slow, bumpy, and perilous. But the spectacular view from a small barrio at the top makes the trip seem worthwhile. Across a deep valley rise other towering peaks of the Cordillera Mountain Range of northern Luzon, where indigenous Igorot ("people of the mountains") have lived for centuries. Hours by bus north of here are the awe-inspiring rice terraces, some built by Igorot ancestors two thousand years ago—rice terraces so impressively and intricately sculpted on the mountainsides that they have been called the eighth wonder of the world. There, Igorot women and men practice organic rice production using typhoon-resistant native varieties that provide stable yields.

But the Cordillera is also gold country, and Benguet province offers a window into the dynamics of the mining sector. As we clamber out of the jeepney and the driver turns off the engine, we are greeted by a persistent droning of heavy machinery far below. The sound directs our gaze down into the heart of the valley. There, on the facing mountainside, dozens of bulldozers, cranes, and trucks weave their way up deep man-made gashes. We are looking at an enormous open-pit mine. A large slice of the mountain has already been carved away by these earth-eating machines. Without its tree-cover, the exposed slope of the mountain facing us looks unstable: nothing holds it together any longer. The view brings to mind the glass side of one of those ant-farms that fascinate children, but here heavy machinery replaces the ants. And, as we remind ourselves with a shock, the ant-farm's sand is in this case the inside of a mountain, its topsoil and trees stripped and its rock blasted and leveled.

"This is the Grand Antamok open-pit mine," says one of the Igorot residents of Itogon, whose stories we have traveled up into these Cordillera Mountains to hear.[4]

Our Igorot guides help us decipher what we are seeing. At the foot of the mine stand long rows of bunkhouses where, we are told, hundreds of miners (many of them also Igorot) sleep, despite the constant noise and dust of the twenty-four-hour mining operation. Just below the barracks, at the lowest point of the valley, a wide brown riverbed winds its way out of sight. It has been a long, hot summer and the rainy season is late in arriving, which explains why there is no water in the riverbed. But, near the mine site, enor-

mous piles of rocky waste from the open pit ("muck-waste," the locals call it) have been bulldozed into the riverbed, a convenient and
cheap waste-disposal method.

Our Igorot hosts are, they inform us, also gold-miners. They call
themselves "pocket-miners." As several tell us with pride, they descend from many generations of Igorot pocket-miners who, long
before the days of mining companies, found themselves sitting on
some of the Philippines' richest gold veins. Indeed, seventeenth-
century Spanish conquistadores, whose interest in the Philippines
derived at least partially from its minerals, made note of the small-
scale mining in the Cordilleras.[5]

The technology of small-scale mining has not changed much
since then. "We mine as did our grandfathers before us," explains
one of the pocket-miners, directing our attention away from the
huge open pit to several small holes in an adjacent slope. From this
far away, the holes look like small round caves. These are the "pockets," where teams of five or six people have tediously hammered
and chiseled their way up to 50 meters inside the mountain. "We
are not engineers. But we can spit into a stone and tell where
there's gold," an old man tells us with pride. "No one in the company can do that."

After the pocket-miners manually chisel away enough stone,
they carry it in sacks to a small nearby mill. Like the pocket-mining
itself, the milling operation is low on technology and high on sweat.
Again like the pocket-mining, the mill's technology has changed
little, we are told, from the time of the miners' grandparents. At
the mill site, women and children hammer the gold-bearing rocks
into nuggets the size of corn kernels. The nuggets are then crushed
even finer in the mill's big metal container (run by a small motor).
Finally, the crushed rock is flushed with water and sluiced and
panned to remove the minuscule grains of gold.

Most are second- to fifth-generation pocket-miners and, over the
years, have been able to feed families, build simple but sturdy
homes, and even send their children to school. "We are not edu-
cated; small-scale mining is the only viable job for us," one miner
explains. Another echoes him: "We chose this work because, even
though we do not have an education, it is possible to live well."

Or, at least, it *was* possible.

One of our Igorot hosts points to the left, to a nearby ridge. A slice of mountain has been torn away, an enormous bite taken out of one side of the peak. It is another of the Benguet Corporation's open-pit mines in the Grand Antamok Project region, this one in an area referred to as Keystone West. Our hosts have brought us up to this mountain peak to see these two scars in the Cordilleras, these two parts of the Grand Antamok Project. For the open pits have changed these people's lives dramatically.

The people of Itogon trace their troubles back to the early 1980s, when Benguet Corporation, whose vast gold-mining concession from the Philippine government now covers subsoil rights to most of what we see, began bulldozing open-pit mines in this area without consulting the Itogon community. Soon thereafter the residents of Keystone started to notice some disturbing changes.

One woman, a former schoolteacher and wife of a pocket-miner, points to her three small children. They are on the ground playing a game with two toys of the sort that entertain children in poor families everywhere in the Philippines—in this case, a small, nondescript stone and a somewhat rusty San Miguel beer-bottle cap. "The children are dirty," she says quietly. "They can't take baths here because there's no water. And they all have skin rashes. There used to be a spring nearby—just there." She indicates an area below the sliced-off ridge of Keystone West. But as the land was leveled, she continues, and "the open-pit mining began, it disrupted the water flow, and the spring just disappeared. We now have to go to the other side of the mountain to get water." As a result, there is not enough water either for bathing or for drinking.

As we are told time and time again by people with similar stories, on this mountain and elsewhere, water means life. Migration flows, settlements, and people's lives are built around water. As the water dries up, so do the people's possibilities. "We used to plant rice and bananas right over there," another woman tells us. "But now we can't because there is no water."

Water is a major problem. But the open-pit mine has brought other ecological problems to the long-time residents of this area. There is also the pollution—including the constant noise pollution of Benguet's machinery. And there is the omnipresent thick dust that covers everything during the long dry season.

As if those were not problems enough, instead of using water as the Igorot in this area do, Benguet uses toxic chemicals to separate the gold from the rest of the rock. (In certain other parts of the Philippines and elsewhere in the Third World, some small-scale miners also use chemicals such as mercury in the processing of the minerals.) Then, one pocket-miner explains, Benguet simply flushes those toxics down the river with the left-over mine tailings. "We used to have a lot of cows here—almost fifty. But they drank the water with the tailings and died." Benguet, he says, refused pleas for compensation.

As Benguet intensified its open-pit operations, other problems arose for the Igorot pocket-miners. Would the pocket-miners simply move out as Benguet decided to expand its operations into the area of the pocket-mines? Where would they go? Whose land was this? Whose tunnels? Whose gold? We hear the common refrain: "This area is owned by the whole community. If we lose our water, if we lose our source of livelihood, how can we live? What will happen to our children?" As many as 20,000 people may be affected as small-scale miners in the area lose their work.[6]

In early 1990, the problems came to a head; the pocket-miners decided to act. One day, they tell us, to stop Benguet from mining their lands they set up a small barricade on the lone road heading up the lucrative Keystone Vein. The blockade, coordinated with similar actions by pocket-miners in two other nearby veins of Benguet's open-pit expansion, succeeded in closing the Grand Antamok Project sites for three full months. After three months the government intervened, and Benguet signed an agreement with leaders from the two other sites. The agreement committed the company to a number of environmental actions, including improvement of water supplies and a halt on dumping their toxic and other wastes into the river. But, after their previous experiences with Benguet Corporation, the Keystone blockaders doubted Benguet's sincerity. More than one year later, at the time of our visit, the promises remain unfulfilled and the blockade by the Keystone pocket-miners continues.

We walk back to the two-story wooden house of one of the pocket-miners and sit in the shade of a large mango tree. An older man speaks up: "The company is powerful with the government. But we're also people even though we're poor. They can pay big taxes to the government. But what happens to our world here? It becomes dust. It's in our blood as Igorot not to want to see our brothers in hardship. But that's what we're seeing now."

Cynicism about Benguet Corporation runs deep, and the doubts extend to the Philippine government, which controls mining licenses and actually owns about a third of the shares of Benguet Corporation. The cynicism partially explains the residents' reluctance to believe in paper promises. The pocket-miners show us recent photos they have taken of Benguet dumping tailings in the river, in clear violation of the 1990 agreement. They have brought the photos to the attention of the relevant government officials but, they emphasize with frustration in their voices, the government has not acted.

In the nearby city of Baguio, researchers from the[Cordillera Resource Center for Indigenous Peoples' Rights]tell us more about the Benguet Corporation and provide us with voluminous background materials. Started by U.S. investors in 1903, later sold to one of the wealthiest Philippine families, and now owned in approximately equal thirds by wealthy Filipinos, the Philippine government, and U.S. investors, the company spearheaded the Philippines' ascendance to become the world's ninth largest gold producer, and it turned gold and copper concentrates into two of the country's leading exports.

For eight decades the company operated underground mines to extract the area's high-grade gold deposits. The spread of the underground mines, which used the abundant pine trees of the Cordilleras as internal buttresses, contributed significantly to the deforestation. Benguet did well over the years, becoming one of the Philippines' top twenty corporations, its largest primary-gold producer, and the seventh largest gold producer in the world.[7]

But the very success of the underground mines, the very efficiency of the plunder, limited the life of the operations. By the 1980s, Benguet found itself confronting a consequence of its large-scale mining of a nonrenewable resource: profits began to fall as the underground mines exhausted the richer veins. In addition, labor costs rose as miners increasingly unionized.

Open-pit mining offered a lucrative way to use less labor while pursuing "optimization in the exploration of available mineral resources," as Benguet Corporation phrased it. Indeed, Benguet's

gold subsidiary forecasts more than doubling its revenues from
1989 levels within a few years in its Grand Antamok Project as
mines are shifted to open-pit operations. Using Benguet's own pro-
jections of potential gold reserves, the Cordillera Resource Center
has calculated that the Grand Antamok Project will yield the corporation more than $400 million in revenues over a thirteen-year
period. Given such high dollar earnings, the Keystone residents
tell us, they doubt a Philippine government so heavily indebted to
foreign banks will clamp down—even if after that thirteen-year period the gold, and the entire mountain, will be gone.[8]

There are still other facets of the story of the Benguet mines. As
a basic law of ecology has it, everything is connected to everything
else. The effects of open-pit mining are not confined to the Cordillera Mountains, for the river basin in which we saw the waste from
the Grand Antamok Project winds down through the central Luzon
rice-bowl to the vast Lingayen Gulf from which, some half a century ago, the Japanese dramatically invaded the Philippines in the
wake of Pearl Harbor.

A local environmental group in 1989 "followed the tailings" to
learn of the devastation wrought by these gold and copper mine
tailings, which often contain traces of the mercury or cyanide used
by Benguet and the area's other big mining companies in processing the minerals. Rice farmers in the two provinces served by the
rivers from the Cordilleras complain that, as the quantity of the
tailings in their irrigated fields has risen, rice yields have plummeted. Mining wastes and tailings damage lowland irrigation canals
too. And fishers in the Lingayen Gulf report a substantial reduction
in catch as siltation from the tailings smothers coral reefs. Nationwide, according to the Center for Environmental Concerns in Manila, around 160,000 tons of such chemical-laced tailings find their
way into Philippine rivers and lakes every day. These tailings are
partly to blame for the fact that about a third of the country's largest
132 rivers are biologically dead, and most of the rest are badly polluted.[9]

To cull the basics of the mining story: For centuries, indigenous
miners worked many rich mineral veins in small-scale operations
that offered a livelihood and did not threaten the area's ecology.
Over this last century, a few giant mining firms—many with significant foreign ownership—received government concessions and

began large-scale operations with much of the output destined for export. The two communities of miners, large-scale and small-scale, coexisted relatively peacefully until the large-scale companies began to encroach on the areas of the indigenous miners and the adverse ecological impact of large-scale mining spread. Today Itogon is experiencing crisis and confrontation: a growing movement is challenging the right of the few to mine in a fashion so detrimental to the many. And although a Benguet vice-president assures us that "we are concerned with sustainable development; this is the [Benguet] corporate philosophy," what others see is plunder.

We recount the story of the Itogon pocket-miners in some detail as an introduction to the Philippines' environmental problems and its environmentalists. We do so in part to provide a contrast to Manila's end-of-the-pipeline urban pollution. And we do so also because it bears similarities to stories we hear that involve ecosystems in other parts of the Philippine archipelago.

As recently as World War II, the more than 7,000 Philippine islands were lavishly endowed with rainforests, fish, fertile lowlands, and extensive mineral deposits. Since then, by some estimates, the plunder of these resources has been taking place at a rate that is among the fastest in the world.[10] Fragile ecosystems have been pushed to their limit. As we discover firsthand, there are few places you can go in the Philippines without meeting some sort of ecological disaster. Some of these encounters begin to help us understand the forces behind the destruction as well as those fighting it.

Farmers hike with us up bare mountaintops they recall as covered with dense forests only half a generation ago. And they show us their fields, where we can actually see the path taken by their precious topsoil as recent heavy floods from the clear-cut hills above carried it off and deposited it in riverbeds below. Fishers paddle us to coral reefs, once deserving of their Tagalog name *bahay ng isda* ("fish homes"), now white and dying, no longer inhabited by an abundance of fish. As the trees and reefs fall, our guides explain, so do their harvests, be they of fish, corn, or rice.

In short, nature is taking its revenge.

At times we can judge the extent of the plunder for ourselves. The plight of the forests, for example, is clear.

We travel to what was considered the Philippines' last frontier in the early post–World War II period, to Mindanao, the southernmost island. In order to discover what has become of Mindanao's forests, we retrace a journey Robin took fifteen years ago when she first lived in Mindanao: beginning in the north, we ride a series of rickety old buses and jeepneys into the central province of Bukidnon and then on toward the southern port city of Davao.

The views from these mountain roads offer ample testimony to the efficiency of the late-twentieth-century technology of large-scale commercial logging, even in a poor country. Some fifteen years ago, when there was little more than a steep, rock-strewn dirt path across these mountains, this part of central Mindanao was passable only with a four-wheel-drive vehicle. The forests were thick, and the people few. Now, thanks to the greed of the big commercial logging companies and the need of the small agriculturalists (who move into the forests only after the loggers have built roads and chopped down the biggest trees), the mountains are almost bare. Hardly a tree is in sight; in many places, the only trees left standing are those that do not float and therefore cannot be transported down rivers to the sawmills closer to Mindanao's ports. The deforestation is a crime that has already contributed to a series of droughts which some of Bukidnon's inhabitants fear will turn one of the most fertile areas in Asia into a desert.

Bukidnon is a microcosm of processes at work in the country as a whole. When Ferdinand Magellan claimed the Philippine Islands for Spain in 1521, the archipelago was perhaps 90 percent forested. One hundred years ago, when the United States barged in on the tail end of the Philippines' near-completed revolution for independence from Spain and claimed the islands as a U.S. colony, some 70 percent was blanketed with trees. By the time of independence after World War II, forest cover was down to somewhere around 60 percent—and had decreased to around 35 percent by the time Ferdinand Marcos won his second presidential election in 1969. Today only about 20 percent of the country is still forested, less than half of the 54 percent forest cover that the Department of Environment and Natural Resources says the country needs to maintain a stable ecosystem.[11]

Of the 6–7 million or so hectares of forest that remain, only about 600,000 are primary (virgin) rainforest. Some 120,000 to

200,000 hectares of the remaining forest are disappearing each year. To transfer these numbers to a different context: A country whose total land-mass is only the size of Nevada is *every year* losing forest on an area equal to three-quarters of Rhode Island.

Today over 18 million Filipinos who live in the overlogged uplands are directly affected by this loss of forest cover. Among them are most of the approximately 3.5–4.5 million indigenous peoples of the Philippines, peoples like the Igorot of northern Luzon.[12] Indeed, the majority of the remaining forests are located on lands these communities claim as ancestral domain.[13] Through the centuries, lowlander migrants—first, commercial loggers and big corporations, and then, in their wake, subsistence farmers—pushed many of the indigenous occupants onto more and more marginal lands in more and more fragile ecosystems. But it is these indigenous Filipinos who have traditionally lived sustainably in the forest.

Today, many of them are struggling for survival, demanding recognition of their ancestral-domain rights, which includes rights to lands lost. Throughout the Philippines, where indigenous people still live on ancestral land, they are trying to protect the last remaining rainforests from the plunder that has followed the invasion of the lowlanders.

One of the most dramatic instances of such resistance to the destruction of age-old forests is unfolding about 100 kilometers south of the bald Bukidnon mountains, at the foot of the Philippines' highest peak. This is Mount Apo, a dormant volcano and site of the last major forest cover in southcentral Mindanao. Mount Apo's forested slopes and foothills are home to the Bagobo, one of Mindanao's many indigenous groups who are collectively known as the Lumad ("born of the soil").[14] Mount Apo is the Bagobo ancestral land, their place of worship; it is where their supreme god and common ancestor, Apo Sandawa, lives. In brief, the mountain is sacred. And over the centuries, they explain, Apo Sandawa has been good to them: the mountain has been a source of water, food, and shelter.

In 1936 the Philippine government declared Mount Apo a national park, and decades later the Association of Southeast Asian Nations classified it as one of the region's "heritage sites"—which together should certainly have been enough to guarantee that Apo Sandawa would not be disturbed. To the contrary, however, in 1985 the government-owned Philippine National Oil Company (PNOC) began exploratory drilling at the base of Mount Apo to test the potential for geothermal energy development. The government's own DENR raised concerns, denying the project a permit for exploration in 1988. But PNOC decided to ignore such interference. By 1989, two test wells (each more than 2,000 meters deep and 20 centimeters in diameter) and a 8.5-kilometer road had been built; Mount Apo's Blue Lake, where Bagobo went to worship, had turned brown and muddy; trees in the area were said to be dying; erosion near the road was reported; and PNOC made clear its intention to build new roads and expand the number of geothermal wells to as many as thirty-five or forty.

At that point, the resistance of the Bagobo and other Lumad—and the confrontation—escalated. Two thousand Lumad from nine tribes met and signed a *d'yandi*, an intertribal blood compact to defend their area from the project. It was an historic occasion: only the third Lumad *d'yandi* since the thirteenth century, and the first time in history for all nine tribes here to gather as one. Their solemn words made the event all the more momentous: "For us . . . the land is our life; a loving gift of [The Creator] to our race. We will die to defend it, even to the last drop of blood."[15] One year later, as PNOC persisted, the Lumad leaders issued an even stronger pledge as part of a ceremony during which three trees were planted: "We are ready to take up arms, if necessary, to defend . . . our rights to survive as a people of the mother earth."[16] In an attempt to explain the resistance to others in this predominantly Catholic country, one of the elders asks rhetorically, "How would the people of Manila like it if someone dug giant holes in your Manila Cathedral?"

For their concern for the fate of their forests, many Lumad leaders are being termed Communists, detained by paramilitary forces, and harassed, and their ancestral domains are being bombed by the government military. The geothermal project continues, as does the Bagobo's life-and-death struggle to protect their ancestral domain.

For the Lumad, the Mount Apo geothermal project is not simply an environmental issue; it is inextricably linked to larger questions of development. As one elder expounds: "We do not oppose development . . . we are for it: for the improvement of humanity, not the opposite."[17] Or, as a young Lumad leader, Edtami Mansayagan, queries: "For whose development is this?"[18]

We learn in Manila that Mount Apo is also one of the last remaining habitats of the endangered Philippine monkey-eating eagle (*Pithecaphaga jefferyi*)—undoubtedly the most famous of Philippine animals, thanks to the interest Charles Lindbergh took in saving it from extinction. Today perhaps three hundred of these eagles are left in the wild. The Philippine eagle, like Mount Apo's flying lemur and the Philippine tarsier, represent the country's abundance of plant and animal species (its "biodiversity") and should be tallied as part of its natural wealth. Instead, however, the eagle, the lemur, the tarsier, and others are likely to be among the silent victims of the country's forest destruction on Mount Apo and elsewhere.

No one knows just how many such species were or are found in the Philippine forests. It is known that island nations tend to have greater numbers of unique species. In the Philippines, one survey of just over a hectare of forest reserve uncovered more than one hundred species of trees. On one mountain alone, Mount Makiling, more woody plant species exist than in the entire continental United States. Yet, considering the extent of the country's forest destruction, some experts have concluded that half of the species unique to the Philippines—its endemic life forms—have already been lost. The Philippines, concludes a report prepared for the U.S. government Agency for International Development, represents "the single worst case scenario . . . of loss of biological diversity in tropical Southeast Asia."[19]

In travels to other parts of Mindanao, we follow the destructive path of deforestation into the arable lowlands. For generations, the mainstay of the Philippine diet has been rice and, in some areas, corn. In recent years, we are told, yields have been declining in fields beneath overlogged hills. Without the tree cover, rain and mud rush unimpeded down the slopes, leading to flooding and erosion. Overall, throughout the Philippines, around a billion cubic meters of agricultural topsoil (the equivalent of 100,000 hectares of land one meter deep) are lost to erosion each year.[20] Deforestation deserves a good deal of the blame for wiping out in a century natural resources that had been created over thousands upon thousands of years.

The loss of topsoil is compounded by unrestrained use of agricultural chemicals. Decades ago, Mindanao's fertile lowlands attracted such large agribusiness firms as Del Monte and Dole, and they have made huge profits off pineapple and banana plantations there. Today, these companies control fully half of Mindanao's arable land. South of Mount Apo, we descend from the hills into vast tropical-fruit plantations. At some of these, workers without gloves or masks use dangerous—and, in at least one instance, banned—pesticides and other chemicals. They complain to us of skin rashes, respiratory diseases, pregnancy complications, sterility, and even death.[21]

The land, too, is suffering from the corporations' abuse. At a large Dole pineapple plantation on the southern coast, we view the complete denudation of miles and miles of land between the mountains and the sea. "The plantation looks quite modern and efficient," a worker confides. "But there are real problems when it rains. The original creeks were bulldozed by the company to flatten the area and diverted into big creeks and then into rivers. So when you have heavy rains, it is really flooded." Now, when it rains, the rivers simply rush with enormous force into the sea, bringing substantial amounts of eroded soil with them.

If we start to grasp the extent of the destruction of the Philippine ecosystems as we travel through Mindanao, we begin to appreciate what it feels like to be among its victims only when we journey to a small fishing community in Mindoro, the island just southwest of Luzon. We visit, in part, to learn about fish and coral reefs and mangrove forests. But nature has different plans for us, including a taste of the helplessness and fear that the degradation of a natural-resource base can bring to the recipients of nature's revenge.

What happens is this: As we prepare to leave Mindoro for Manila, a "signal 3" typhoon—that is, the strongest—brings torrential rains and powerful winds, marooning us for several days. Typhoons are a way of life in the Philippines; such inconveniences as being stranded for a day or two are to be expected.

What is not expected is what happens *after* the height of the typhoon passes: an angry sea begins to move inshore. As the waves grow fiercer and taller over the next two days, the sea inundates the beach area where we are staying, uprooting trees, collapsing bamboo huts, and, with shocking ease, eating away at cement foundations of other buildings in its path until they too crumble. We look to our local host for reassurance, for a statement that we should not worry, that this happens in every big typhoon. But his eyes tell of fear and of the unknown. "This is the first time I've experienced anything like this," he says quietly, as the water and sand invade the room.

We sit with legs raised on bamboo chairs to avoid the incoming water. We watch helplessly as the waves grow bigger, and we listen to the sounds of destruction around us. There is no evacuation team to whisk us to safety, no radio broadcast to advise us what to do. The radio (once we gather enough batteries to turn it on) reports only what is happening in Manila, miles away. We discuss putting together our own evacuation plan. But the unpaved road to the nearest town now resembles a river; it is impassable. The hills behind us would offer safety from the oncoming waters but, steep and eroded as they are, they present their own set of dangers.

So we sit and wait, powerless against the sea—until finally the waves grow smaller, the ocean recedes, and the destruction stops.

Days later, safely back in Manila, we discuss our experience with marine-resource experts. "You must have experienced a 'storm surge,'" they surmise, explaining that giant waves can be generated in the wake of typhoon winds when the storm moves out into open sea. But why wouldn't the fishers along Mindoro's coast have experienced something like this before? we ask. And why would it have such force?

The answer they suggest shows us another instance of plunder: such waves used to be weakened by coral reefs that encircled islands like Mindoro. In addition to serving as breakwalls against storm surges, coral reefs are also where fish live, eat, and congregate. But in the past fifteen years, 70 percent of the Philippine reefs have been destroyed—thanks to a combination of siltation from denuded mountains, tailings from mines, and harmful fishing techniques. These last include gargantuan drift nets used by foreign fishing fleets, dynamite blasting by fishers in search of quick-and-easy catches, and cyanide squirted into the reefs to stun and catch the exotic tropical fish about half of which will end up inhabiting aquariums in U.S. homes. Foreign demand for pieces of the coral reef takes its toll as well, and the U.S. market also accounts for more than half of these illegal exports of ornamental coral.[22]

Plunder of this magnitude—massacred reefs, eroded soil, degraded forest land—is numbing enough to be almost incomprehensible. But after seeing the destruction and strain on these ecosystems, we begin to understand the constant inflow of people from the countryside to the city. If your minerals were being depleted, your forests chopped, your soil eroded, your fish caught by others, where else would you go? The inescapable conclusion is that the pollution and the congestion of Manila will never be solved without first halting the depletion of the country's natural resources.

Yet really to understand how to reverse that degradation, we need to grapple in more depth with some key questions: Whose resources are these? Who is really responsible for the plunder? How is this destruction related to a development path that has transferred control of these resources from millions of farmers, fishers, and indigenous peoples to the government and a few large Filipino and foreign firms?

To answer these and other questions, we decide to look in more detail at the Philippines' tropical rainforests, a resource whose destruction throughout Asia, Africa, and Latin America has captured the attention of people globally as one major contributor to global warming.

Chapter Three

The Last Rainforests

Our environmental problem is not a problem of trees and of
water. It's a problem of politics, of economics.

> Dr. Delfin Ganapin, Jr., Assistant Secretary, Republic of
> the Philippines Department of Environment and Natural
> Resources

About 22,000 years ago, Palawan was already inhabited by
man. This is proven by the discovery of fossil remains. . . .
Where he came from . . . is not known. . . . [P]erhaps he was
one of those born in the Garden of Eden and wandered to
Palawan. Or it could have been that the Garden of Eden was
right here in Palawan instead of in the valley of the Tigris-
Euphrates as supposed.

> Province of Palawan, National Census and Statistics Office,
> *Facts and Figures About Palawan*, 1985, p. 1

As recently as 1900, lush tropical rainforests carpeted most of the
Philippine archipelago. At the current rate of deforestation, however, the country will enter the twenty-first century a barren landscape, with nearly all of its rainforests destroyed. No province
better illustrates why the Philippine tropical rainforests are disappearing than the long, narrow island of Palawan, some 350 nautical
miles southwest of Manila. There, an unfolding drama of people,
power, and politics has turned Palawan into a microcosm of the rapidly vanishing tropical rainforests throughout the country and in
many parts of the world.

Palawan is the Philippines' last frontier. Its relative isolation from
the rest of the archipelago spared many of its resources from the
systematic exploitation practiced elsewhere. As the planning and
development coordinator for the province phrases it to us, "Palawan has been thrown out into the China Sea." Indeed, its closest
neighbor is not even another Philippine island, but the Malaysian
state of Sabah on the island of Borneo. It is said you can use a five-

39

battery flashlight to signal between Palawan and Borneo. In fact, we are told, in the Pleistocene period a land bridge linked the two islands.

Until recent decades, the rest of the Philippines viewed Palawan simply in terms of its isolation; the island has long hosted a leper community and a convict colony. As transport costs fell, however, and as the other islands were increasingly overlogged and overfished, it became only a matter of time before Palawan was "discovered" by thousands of poor farmers and fishers from other islands—and by big commercial loggers.

Today, Palawan is covered with one of the Philippines' largest continuous tracts of tropical rainforest. But the forest's days are numbered if the present rate of logging continues. As a result, Palawan has become the center of one of the fiercest environmental battles in Southeast Asia, a battle taken up in early 1988 by one of the Philippines' most influential environmental groups, Haribon (a contraction of the Tagalog words *haring ibon*, meaning "king bird," in reference to the endangered Philippine eagle).

Among the first Palaweños we interview are a group of local environmentalists, who in 1989 are in the process of setting up in Palawan Haribon's sixth chapter. But they defer answering many of our questions; they insist that the only way to understand what is happening to Palawan is first to hike into its rainforests. We agree to do just that, with some of these local environmentalists as guides.

A hike into Palawan's rainforests requires both time and patience. We wake up early to catch the one daily jeepney that runs from the provincial capital of Puerto Princesa to our first stop, Baheli. Jeepneys in the province are just like jeepneys in Manila—except that they are often several times more crowded. Initially we perch on a thin piece of wood that is balanced across the back of the vehicle, where passengers get on and off. Luck is with us, however: after about half an hour we get seats inside the jeepney. True, the jeepney is a bit crowded: there are eight people on each side, as is usual, but added to that are three young children standing in the center, two women who replace us on the board, and three men who dangle rather precariously off the back, their feet balanced on the running board, plus several live chickens (feet tied) and one very scared, squealing piglet in an old rice sack. On the roof, rattling around with the baskets of food and wares, cling another twenty or so men and boys who enjoy the view and endure the blaring tropical sun.

After a couple of hot, dusty hours (roads in the provinces are seldom paved), we arrive at Baheli, a small fishing village on a river. Here the jeepney route ends. Now we are confronted with a typical Palawan problem: no more roads. We talk the owner of a *banca*—a fishing boat, in this case, small and motorized—into carrying us on our journey's next leg, down the river. A young boy stands at the boat's bow, a long bamboo pole in hand, to help guide us along the narrow, shallow river. Exchanging constant banter, he and the driver maneuver the boat between the incredibly thick mangroves that line the river on both sides.

We have read of such mangrove forests, which once bordered much of the Philippines' coastal areas, creating rich breeding grounds and shelters for fish. These days, however, it is unusual to find such dense mangroves in the Philippines. According to Philippine government statistics, 92 percent of the virgin mangrove swamps that existed in 1920 had been destroyed by 1985: victims of coastal development, local demand for firewood, and, increasingly, "fish-pondification," that is, conversion to commercial fishponds and prawn farms.[1]

After an hour we reach the point where the river spills into a spectacular bay that feeds the South China Sea. We hug the northern coast of the bay, gliding over transparent water, until we reach another mangrove-lined river and turn inland.

Soon thereafter, at a grouping of a few huts, we disembark. An old logging road runs from this community to the area where we will spend the night. But the noontime tropical sun is fierce, forcing us to respect *siesta* hours. We stop at the open hut of an old farmer (whom, out of respect, we call *tatay*, "father") and ask if we can take refuge until the heat subsides.

When we begin our hike, we do so accompanied by a sled-like cart drawn by a *carabao* (water buffalo), rented for the peso-equivalent of $2.50 from *tatay*'s neighbor to pull our food and belongings. *Carabao* are the main work animals and the only technology most Philippine peasants ever dream of owning. (At a cost of about the equivalent of $250 per animal, however, even *carabao* remain an unaffordable dream for many.) They are said to be very dependable animals. But, as we discover, because they do not sweat and therefore have to be bathed every few hours, be it in a river or a mud puddle, as a means of transport they are slow.

As the sun sets, we stop for the night in a small barrio nestled between two mountains. The next day, we hike in the morning and then board another fishing boat for the final leg of our journey. The scene from the water looking landward is magnificent. Tall mountains, blanketed by lush forests, plunge dramatically to the shimmering sea. It is, we remark, much like the scenes all around the country that would have greeted Spanish explorers in the sixteenth century or the Chinese traders centuries before.

As we trek, we see few signs of civilization. Virgin forests of *ipil*, *almaciga*, *balete*, and other majestic trees surround us, peak after peak. Monkeys chatter over our heads, stopping to stare in silence when they spot us, as interested by us as we by them. At intervals, narrow waterfalls cascade from limestone cliffs into the emerald waters below. We pause occasionally to pay our respects to trees so huge that when three adults circle the trunks, arms outstretched, fingers barely touch. Underneath an enormous mountain, with a cathedral-like dome so grand it has acquired the name of St. Paul's, we paddle a small *banca* up a long underground river, its caves illuminated solely by the light of our kerosene lantern. Thousands of bats and swifts soar and dive overhead.

The surrounding forests, as one of our Palawan-born guides proudly tells us, are "one of the world's last living libraries of ecology." Yet, as we hike, the singing of the birds is often disturbed by the roar of chain saws, even as we enter areas near the underground river that have been declared part of the Philippine national park system and therefore officially off-limits to logging.

At one point, our guides point to thin green saplings growing alongside the trail. These are falcata (*Albizzia falcataria*), fast-growing non-native softwoods planted as part of the logging concessionaire's reforestation program to replace native hardwood (Dipterocarp) species that have been cut down. One guide silently motions us to follow him off the logging road and into the falcata. We find that the falcata replanting simply hugs the trail. About ten feet off the road, the reforestation ceases abruptly. The reforested strip is designed to give the impression that, as is required by the logging concessionaires' license agreement with the Philippine government, which "owns" this forest land, reforestation has been accomplished.

Instead, nestled between that reforested strip and mountainsides still green with hardwood forests lies a large, flat expanse that has been clear-cut. Scruffy green bushes dot a field scarred with tree trunks and brown debris, dead branches and leaves. Here and there, felled but unwanted logs crisscross it. (The scene reminds us of a statistic cited by Nicholas Guppy, who has studied tropical rainforests the world over for more than thirty-five years: "Frequently 90–98 percent of trees are left unused when an area of rain forest is logged. . . . Where 10 percent of trees are extracted, around 55 percent are usually irreparably damaged.")[2] "This area was clear-cut in the early 1980s," says one of our guides, adding that it worries him, because it is the source of water for the underground river.

The major fear of Palaweños such as our guides, as they watch their forests disappear, is not the loss of beauty. Nor is it the global-warming effect, of which many have no knowledge. In a country where the majority of people live close to the margin of survival, the main concern is more immediate. According to the Palaweños, the rampant logging is drying up the island's watersheds, threatening municipal drinking-water systems as well as irrigation for lowland farmers. Palawan is encircled by the nation's richest fishing grounds; we are told that approximately two out of three fish sold in Manila come from its waters. Yet, silt from denuded mountains is flowing down rivers into the sea, smothering coral reefs and thus depleting fish resources. The deforestation has also threatened the survival of the Batak, indigenous Filipinos who live by gathering resin from *almaciga* trees. They are being driven into extinction as that giant of hardwoods—supposedly a protected species—is hauled out of Palawan's forests.[3]

Later, as the sunset brings a surreal glow of reddish pink to the mountains, we ask our guides more questions about the forests of Palawan. They know the statistics well: Although forests still cover an estimated 54 percent of Palawan, some 19,000 hectares of trees are being torn down every year. The main culprit, we are told, is Palawan's biggest logging company, Pagdanan Timber Products, owned by Filipino timber baron and businessman Jose "Pepito" Alvarez. A man who became rich exporting timber from Indonesia in the 1970s, Alvarez owns two logging companies with concessions in

Palawan. His forest concessions are estimated to cover about 61 percent of Palawan's productive forest, with as much as two-thirds of the concessions in virgin rainforest. Most of Alvarez's harvest is exported to Japan, Taiwan, and South Korea, nations which now carefully control the cutting of their own forests.[4]

Ultimately, however, the problem is not just Alvarez. Like all logging and mining concessionaires in the Philippines, Alvarez is beholden to the Philippine government since, by Philippine law, all lands above eighteen degrees of slope (and all minerals found within) belong to the state and are managed by the Department of Environment and Natural Resources. This has turned fully one-half of the Philippines' 30 million hectares into so-called "public land," including almost all its forests and most of the ancestral domains of the indigenous peoples of the Philippines. As a Philippine indigenous-peoples' support group notes: "Simply put, lands of the public domain include mineral and forest lands, public parks and reservations, as well as other lands which the government has failed to classify. All in all, these constitute some fifty-three percent of the total Philippine land mass, making the State the greatest landlord in the country."[5]

In return for what have historically been some of the world's lowest logging fees and flimsy promises to reforest cut lands, the government has granted such loggers as Pepito Alvarez concessions to log specified areas for a specific period of time. To say that the power to distribute forest concessions gives DENR (and the president, if she or he wants it) a great deal of clout is an understatement. For a government that is chronically short of cash, forest and mineral concessions become a prime government instrument for rewarding allies and engendering patronage. As Haribon's president Maximo "Junie" Kalaw, Jr., notes, "Forest resources and land resources were given as political patronage and as a source of resources to keep people in power and to buy electoral votes."[6] Not surprisingly, timber and mining concessionaires have historically been some of the main electoral financiers of the candidates.[7]

Alvarez is a player in this patronage game. His Palawan concessions, Pagdanan and a sister timber company, were granted in the early 1980s by then-president Ferdinand Marcos. As Pagdanan's executive vice-president tells us, the firms began to "log in earnest in 1981" in Palawan. By one account, "the logging companies are cutting round the clock so the forest continues to dwindle as each month passes."[8] According to Haribon calculations, Alvarez's Palawan operations provide him annual revenues of some $24 million.[9] That figure by itself may not immediately convey a sense of Alvarez's power in Palawan, but two comparisons put it in better perspective: it is equivalent to three-quarters of the total income of this entire province of about 500,000 people, and it is 24 times the provincial government's annual budget of $1 million.[10]

These comparisons are important, our guides stress, in understanding who is and who is not to blame for the deforestation in these last rainforests. Both the Philippine government and the big loggers have long placed most of the blame on the millions of Filipino peasants who now inhabit the country's upland areas. Through forms of shifting (commonly but pejoratively known as "slash-and-burn") agriculture and tree-cutting for fuel, the argument goes, these upland farmers have been chopping down the Philippine forest. In other words, poverty is blamed for the deforestation. According to Pagdanan's full-page advertisements in the nation's leading daily newspapers, the blame for the disappearance of Palawan's forests lies at the door of "slash-and-burn farmers, settlers, and illegal loggers who indiscriminately cut the trees."[11] Indeed, the logging company claims that it actually protects the forests; 120 Pagdanan guards are armed with high-powered rifles to keep Palawan's 21,000 shifting agriculturalists from clearing portions of the forests to plant subsistence crops.

This argument angers our guides. "The biggest *kainginero* [slash-and-burn agriculturalist] is Pepito Alvarez," one says. He reminds us that the clear-cut area we saw earlier in the day was cut down by Pagdanan. That area is not an isolated case, the guides say. Indeed, we later meet a number of former Pagdanan workers who have lodged a complaint with DENR, charging that Pagdanan practices illegal logging (including clear-cutting and cutting of undersized logs) and that its reforestation program is a showcase limited to the sides of the roads. The workers show us dozens of photos to prove the charges.

Alvarez's indiscriminate logging practices are not the only rebuttal our guides provide to the *kaingineros'* defense. It is, they emphasize, a case of blaming the victim. To understand why poor shifting agriculturalists exist and why many no longer practice the

traditional sustainable methods of farming requires a look at the
whole picture. As Haribon president Junie Kalaw explains in an
interview with the Berkeley, California–based Philippine Resource
Center:

> In the past 15 years we have had only 470 logging concessionaires [in the
> Philippines] who [have been given the right to exploit] all the resources
> of the forests. . . . The average profit on logging is 100,000 pesos per hec-
> tare after you've paid all expenses. When you total this, it would amount
> to about $42 billion, more than our foreign debt, that came from the forest
> and this money went to 470 people. The process created poverty for 17
> million people around the forest areas.[12]

More concisely, as Kalaw himself phrases it time and time again to
Philippine audiences: "The fundamental thing is that the greed created the need." Gareth Porter and Delfin Ganapin, Jr., call it "the
politics of natural resources," by which they mean that "the Philippine political system has concentrated control of natural resources
in the hands of the few at the expense of the economically disadvan-
taged and [has] put a premium on the short-term exploitation of
resources."[13] In other words, as with Palawan's one huge commercial logger versus its thousands of shifting agriculturalists, unequal
control of resources, not poverty, is the chief culprit. Inequality,
not poverty, leaves the very poor with no choice but to dig their
own graves environmentally.[14]

In addition, our guides and other Philippine-based environmentalists explain, it is precisely because of big loggers like Alvarez that
most farmers can enter the forests in the first place. Only loggers
have the equipment to build roads into the heart of the forest. Once
the big commercial loggers have chopped down the commercially
viable trees, they abandon the area. But they leave logging roads
that, in the words of one Philippine forester, serve as "the arteries
of forest destruction."[15] As we are told by a farmer elsewhere in the
Philippines, poor shifting agriculturalists "will only penetrate into
areas that loggers have opened up because of the roads. How could
[the farmers] cut all the big trees by themselves?"[16]

In Palawan we learn not simply that a few individuals control the
resources. We learn how such a system is maintained. Palawan is
testimony to the fact that the environmental issue in the Philip-

pines and in much of the Third World is primarily a question of power. Palaweños often refer to Pagdanan as people did to the legendary banana companies in Central America at the turn of the century: as El Compañia ("the company"). For all intents and purposes, Palawan is a company island. Control of natural resources—forest, minerals, fishing grounds, or agricultural land—gives economic power. That "economic power," as one of the few local politicians who is willing to meet with us explains, "is always political power if you know how to use it."

Alvarez understands the connection well. A 1988 exposé in the well-respected *Far Eastern Economic Review* presented evidence that Alvarez has cultivated close ties with Palawan's two congressmen (one of whom is Ramon Mitra, Aquino's ambitious speaker of the House of Representatives). As we discover in Palawan, almost all local politicians, from the governor down to the mayors, are "connected" to this logger. The church hierarchy, an outspoken critic of natural-resource destruction in other parts of the country, remains noticeably silent in Palawan. The *Far Eastern Economic Review* reported that Palawan's bishop "is alleged to receive free lumber from Alvarez." [17]

Our trip to Palawan comes at an historic moment: electoral democracy has returned to the Philippines after two decades of the Marcos dictatorship. Corazon Aquino is in power; elections have been held for local, provincial, and national offices. Yet, the island of Palawan feels eerily like the Philippines during the days of martial law. There are politicians opposed to Alvarez, but most are circumspect in voicing their opposition. Says one to us in reference to the rule of the logger and his political allies, "Theirs is a reign of terror."

That reign includes attempts to censor opposing views. The province's two newspapers and single radio station are controlled by politicians close to Alvarez. An application by an opposition group for a second radio station, we are told, was turned down by the national government. Around the time of our visit, copies of a Manila newspaper carrying an article critical of Palawan's power structure mysteriously disappear. Days later, copies of the article are distributed clandestinely, in the belief that mere possession of the copied page could bring down reprisals. Subsequently, a person quoted in that article is physically assaulted. At least one civil servant with Haribon connections is reportedly threatened with dismissal.

In Palawan, environmentalists talk quietly in restaurants, changing the subject quickly if someone passes nearby. They often look over their shoulder as they walk. Says one Manila-based environmentalist who visited Palawan a couple of months after we were there, "I know I was followed during my last trip there."

A reporter who co-authored the *Far Eastern Economic Review* article about Palawan and Alvarez not only was slapped with a large libel suit but also received a death threat. Both presumably are attempts to frighten other reporters away from the story.

The former Pagdanan workers who lodged the complaint against Alvarez with DENR also brought a case against him with the Department of Labor, citing unfair labor practices and violation of labor law. They filed yet another with the Commission on Human Rights, charging that the Philippine military gave training to Pagdanan's guards who, in turn, have murdered several individuals. These workers too have felt Alvarez's power. According to one former Pagdanan worker, Alvarez initially laughed at the workers' case, boasting to some of them that he could buy off any lawyer they found. It was a threat he appears to have been able to follow through on three times—until leading human-rights lawyer Augusto "Bobbit" Sanchez (Aquino's first labor minister) offered to represent them. More personal threats of reprisals against them and their families have forced the labor leaders to leave Palawan. A battle is now pending in the lethargic and often corrupt Philippine courts. As the worker tells us: "It is very hard to win if your opponent is a rich person. . . . This is a government of the rich. We are poor, so there is nothing for us."

In this context of extreme inequity of resource access and control and of political power, well-meaning reforestation programs can easily backfire. What we learn about reforestation in Palawan reminds us of stories told of inequality in another context: Some years ago, U.S. researchers Betsy Hartmann and James Boyce wrote an insightful book about Bangladesh. The authors studied foreign-funded tubewells, an aid project intended to bring irrigation water to Bangladesh's small farmers. Time and time again, however, the tubewells ended up owned by the richest people in the village—

effectively making them richer and more powerful, and leaving others (including the targeted beneficiaries) even poorer and less powerful than before.[18]

Financial aid and other forms of assistance poured into a community dominated by a few wealthy individuals are likely to reinforce, if not exacerbate, the unequal power relations. This is as true for reforestation as it was for tubewells. (And it is as true for projects of nongovernmental environmental organizations as it is for those of Western aid agencies.)

Indeed, Hartmann and Boyce's tubewell story is replayed in Palawan, only this time it is about trees, not irrigation facilities. The executive vice-president of Alvarez's Pagdanan Timber Products informs us that Alvarez's company is among those applying to DENR for some of the money from an Asian Development Bank loan for Philippine reforestation: "We intend to avail [ourselves] of the ADB reforestry loan. We want to get a big portion." The Asian Development Bank and the other multilateral development banks have billed this and other reforestation loans as part of their answer to complaints by Western environmental groups that they do not lend enough for environmental projects. But the on-the-ground reality is somewhat different, as longtime Philippine-based Irish Columban missionary and ecologist Sean McDonagh elaborates to us: "When you say the Asian Development Bank is going to replant trees, everyone claps. But [the ADB loan] isn't for real reforestation of hardwood forests. It is to put plantations on the hills, which will be monocropped. And the very people who replant it will be the loggers who took the original forest down," who will then, of course, get richer taking it down again.

Pagdanan's concern is not hardwood forests for Palawan's future generations. Rather, as that top executive of Pagdanan readily admits to us during an interview in Manila, Alvarez's plan for the ADB loan is to plant fast-growing softwood trees for his plywood plant, thereby ensuring his own economic future after the natural forests have disappeared: "Sooner or later, we'll be going into processed woods. Lumber may be a thing of the past later on." The idea is to prepare for that eventuality: "When our leases run out, our industrial tree plantations will tide us over."

The lesson of Hartmann and Boyce's tubewells and of Alvarez's reforestation is simple, as the Friends of the Earth representative

in Asia, Paul "Chip" Fay, explains to us: "You cannot have a technical solution without addressing access to resources. Investing into
the existing resource allocation system is investing into a structure
that is unsustainable." David Kummer reaches a similar conclusion
in his work on post–World War II Philippine deforestation: "The
process of deforestation described for the Philippines is not ame-
nable to a technical solution. . . . Rather, the fundamental issue is,
who has the right to use the forest resource? In the Philippines, the
answer has invariably been that the forest belongs to loggers and
their allies." [19]

This lesson is particularly important now that many Western environmentalists are highlighting how deforestation contributes to
the emission of greenhouse gases and hence to global warming. The
understandable initial impulse of many environmentalists without
firsthand exposure to the "politics of natural resources" is to steer
money toward massive reforestation projects and the like. In 1988,
for example, the World Wildlife Fund signed a "debt-for-nature
swap" agreement with Haribon and the government's DENR. The
World Wildlife Fund agreed to purchase up to $2 million of Philip-
pine external debt papers and, through DENR and Haribon, to use
that amount for environmental projects in the Philippines, with
priority placed on St. Paul's and one other stunning national park
in Palawan, El Nido. [20]

Haribon members to whom we talk are excited about the swap
but caution extreme care in moving forward with similar undertakings. The swap was announced before meaningful discussions could
be carried out with intended beneficiaries about how the money
could best be used and managed. Indeed, there seems to have
been neither time for such discussions nor a realistic plan as to who
would initiate them. Logging interests in Palawan capitalized on
this by telling small-scale fishers that the swap would deny them
access to their fishing grounds. The charge was untrue, but the
damage difficult to undo.

This incident underscores the necessity of carrying on extensive
discussions with local people to define such programs. As we learn
in Palawan, to reverse deforestation requires consciously taking the
side of those who are battling against timber tycoons like Alvarez
and for the democratization and redistribution of forest resources
to the people who live there. As long as they keep these basics of

power and politics constantly in mind, Western and poor-country environmentalists together represent a strong force in reversing the destruction of natural resources.

Sometimes the stories of life with El Compañia seem almost humorous. Haribon president Junie Kalaw tells of being invited to speak before the Palawan provincial board: "One member of the board invited me. But after I spoke, a resolution to 'thank Haribon' [for speaking] became such a contentious issue that the board had to recess." Eventually the resolution was voted down, seven to four. For a time, Haribon was notified that it was banned from Palawan. The Pagdanan executive vice-president explains to us that, among other things, "Haribon would like Palawan to stay in the iron age."

To be an environmentalist in Palawan these days is to court harassment, threats, and even death. A local official in Palawan who tried to stop illegal logging was murdered, allegedly by bodyguards of one of Palawan's biggest politicians.[21] Merely saying the word *environment* out loud in Palawan can get you in trouble. That, one shaken local-government official who has no involvement with Haribon relates to us, is all he and some friends did one night over beers in a Palawan bar. "Four drunk men, big men, approached our table. One threatened: 'You, Haribon, you get out of Palawan.' They ignored our denials. We left quickly. . . . 'We'll remember your faces,' they shouted after us."

Palawan's trees and Alvarez are participants in what Sean McDonagh calls a "plunder economy." Like McDonagh, many local environmentalists believe that the current environmental crisis and the inequity that breeds it are endemic to the Philippine development strategy. Dating as far back as the Spanish and U.S. colonial periods, that strategy has been to grant a near-monopoly over natural resources to a few individuals and firms. For decades, gold, copper, timber, and agribusiness firms—both foreign and, more recently, Filipino—have been offered incentives to extract the maximum amount of resources at the minimum cost, with most of the resources earmarked for export. Facing virtually no environmental controls, firms have torn up the soil, the forests, and the coral reefs with little regard for anything beyond their own short-term profits.

Forest destruction began under the Spanish, Philippine colonial rulers from 1565 to 1898, who sought lumber for shipbuilding and who deforested land for huge sugar, coconut, and abaca plantations. The destruction accelerated under U.S. colonial rule (1898–1946), which marked the start of modern commercial logging on the islands. U.S. lumber companies joined with Philippine businessmen to cut trees on Negros, in Bataan, and in other areas. Within a decade of independence, the Philippine government began a system of one-to-ten-year concessions wherein the lumber company was supposed to replant some of its logged-over areas. Corruption, inadequate enforcement, and an interlocking of interests (as well as, on many occasions, of directorates) between loggers and government officials made a joke of this requirement.[22]

The 1920s through the 1960s marked the heyday of Philippine log exports; the Philippines was, during that period, tropical Asia's top exporter of tropical rainforest timber. As demand for wood in Japan grew rapidly in the 1960s, quick and easy money was made. In 1969, for example, Philippine raw log exports accounted for 16.8 percent of world log exports (by value), second only to the United States's 23.5 percent.[23]

As we saw in the case of Alvarez, Marcos transformed the concession system into a way to reward close associates (whose concession contracts were, at times, simply handwritten notes from him).[24] By the mid–1970s, cronies such as Marcos's defense minister, Juan Ponce Enrile (subsequently one of the main protagonists on the anti-Marcos side of the Philippines' people-power revolution, then Aquino's first minister of defense, and later a senator in an anti-Aquino political party), controlled a large share of the then few hundred companies with timber leases.[25] By 1976, almost all the easily accessible lowland forests of the Philippines had been felled, increasing the appeal of more inaccessible forests such as Palawan's.[26]

Under President Aquino, DENR has reduced the number of concessionaires and has attempted to press them to replant more forests. And it has increased government taxes on cut timber and rents for the holders of timber licensing agreements. But the charges are still far below reforestation costs and still encourage maximum exploitation in the shortest period possible.[27] The reforms have not changed the overall system in any significant way.

As one environmentalist explains to us, "We're still subsidizing the loggers."

If the Philippine executive branch were able to transcend its own special interests, the Philippine Congress would present the next obstacle. For if Alvarez is a king-maker in Palawan, wielding economic power that dwarfs that of local political, military, and environmental forces, so too, in their own areas, are most of the country's other big loggers. Like Alvarez, many of these loggers have shifted their allegiance and economic backing from Marcos to politicians in Aquino's camp—and will do the same with Aquino's successor. Meaningful environmental legislation, like the countrywide logging ban debated ad nauseam in Congress in the late 1980s and early 1990s, is difficult to pass through a Congress made up of the nation's elite. And even should a logging ban eventually pass, as the World Bank notes in one of its masterful understatements, "government sanctions of any kind are not notably successful in the Philippines."[28]

The plunder economy has been fueled in recent years by the financial pressures of the debt crisis. Because the Marcos government borrowed heavily to finance this resource-destructive form of development and to pad private bank accounts, the Philippine government now channels approximately two-fifths of government expenditures into servicing a large domestic debt and its approximately $28 billion foreign debt. This leaves few resources for government ministries that are supposed to look after the health and education of Filipinos, let alone for the part of DENR that is supposed to protect the environment (as opposed to the part of DENR that makes money from the forest concessions). Indeed, the Philippines budget allocation for total debt service is about double the amount for all social services (education, health, housing, community development, and the like).[29]

The more than $3 billion now paid annually as service on the foreign debt exceeds the amount that comes into the country as new aid and loans. The resulting negative net resource flow—a reverse Marshall Plan of sorts—puts the Aquino government in a constant frenzy to generate more dollars to repay its creditors. The burning question is, How to get ahead of those debt repayments? International development experts and creditors (including the

World Bank, the International Monetary Fund, and the United States' Agency for International Development) prescribe a certain solution, which the Aquino government continues to follow: Spend less and export more.[30] That means, Ship out more wood products, minerals, fish, prawns, and cash crops such as pineapples and bananas, as well as such manufactured goods as garments and electronic parts—all already among the top exports.

The export frenzy to earn foreign exchange to repay the Marcos debt reinforces the activities of Alvarez and others involved in the extraction or destruction of natural resources. (In 1988, official export earnings from timber were $200 million.)[31] Debt did not cause the Philippines to become a plunder economy; the country had started on its path to plunder long before. What the debt burden did was add one more reason to allow the plunder to continue.

But the people of Palawan are fighting back.

We extend our stay in the capital city of Puerto Princesa to witness a congress held by Palawan's local environmentalists. Attending the meeting are delegates representing a wide cross-section of Philippine society: former Pagdanan workers, small farmers, bird watchers, lawyers, schoolteachers, government employees, a member of the military. A month later, in May of 1989, 250 of Palawan's environmentalists gather for a formal launching of their local chapter of Haribon. Chapter members are already involved in a campaign to preserve the watershed of Palawan's capital city and in an effort to stop the export of rare animal species. Within a matter of months, they begin an artificial reef project in Puerto Princesa and a livelihood project with the Batak.

Those at the launching are well aware that their mere presence is a serious statement. And no one there contests the fundamental reality of Palawan inequality: one logger is far more powerful than all of them in terms of political connections, financial resources, and sheer force—"goons, guns, and gold," as the Philippine cliché goes. Yet, the participants tell us, they are confident they can stop the plunder; they are confident of being able to organize others on the island and then link them to broader national and international campaigns to save the last rainforests here and elsewhere. "Palawan," one of them says with conviction, "is important to the whole world."

The environmental activists of Palawan represent a new breed.

Rooted among farmers, fishers, and workers, their network includes allies in the middle and professional classes. The phenomenon is not unique to the Philippines' last frontier. Such groups are cropping up all over the country. As in Palawan, despite growing repression, their ranks are swelling, as are their connections to broader campaigns for sustainable development.

Chapter Four

"The First Environmentalists"

> *One night, while [Chico] Mendes watched television at the union hall with some friends and a reporter, a documentary described the greenhouse effect and the carbon dioxide that was spewing from the burning forests of the Amazon. Suddenly, there was Chico Mendes, the Amazon's own ecologist, depicted as fighting to save the "lungs of the world." In a rare display of frustration, Mendes jumped up and yelled at the television, "I'm not protecting the forest because I'm worried that in 20 years the world will be affected. I'm worried about it because there are thousands of people living here who depend on the forest—and their lives are in danger every day."*
>
> Andrew Revkin, *The Burning Season: The Murder of Chico Mendes and the Fight for the Amazon Rain Forest* (Boston: Houghton Mifflin, 1990), pp. 260–61

"One hundred sixty-seven logs. One hundred sixty-seven illegally cut logs that the people of San Fernando confiscated as they floated down the river." The man speaks in the local dialect, but he says the numbers in slow, careful English, as if wanting to be certain we do not misunderstand. He crouches down low as rural Filipinos are accustomed to do when there are no chairs. His feet are shoeless, with the flattened, wide soles and cracked toenails of someone who has farmed barefoot for decades, without the benefit of mechanized tools and tractors. He puckers his lips and points with his chin to a few dozen long, beautifully straight hardwood logs piled high in an open shed on the bank of the Tigua River in this community of small farmers in the landlocked province of Bukidnon on the southern island of Mindanao. We mentally measure the logs' average length and girth—perhaps twelve feet long and a couple of feet in diameter. Then he directs our attention outside, where more are piled. "One hundred sixty-seven logs," he repeats, this time looking over our shoulders to make sure we write the figure in our notebooks.

The farmer points up the river toward the mountains from

whence the logs came. The date is May, 1989, a couple of years into San Fernando's logging battles, and the national government in Manila has recently ordered that the two big commercial logging companies here close down operations in this area. Yet, we are told that illegal loggers, said to pay 30 percent of their take to the logging companies who hold the concessions, take no heed. According to one observer, "Anywhere from two to 30 rafts, each carrying 6 logs, float down the . . . river every other day," headed for illegal sawmills below.[1]

That was true until the farmers of this barrio in the municipality of San Fernando decided to step in—or, more literally, wade in. Thus this community came to have these 167 logs under its care. Proud of their successful confiscation, the barrio residents contacted the provincial branch of the government's Department of Environment and Natural Resources "for word on what to do with these logs which are really public property," the man explains. Months pass and there is no reply. "We are frustrated and confused. Will we get an answer? What if we do not get a reply? Is it up to us to decide what to do with these logs?"

It would be difficult to pinpoint a single event that pushed the farmers of San Fernando to start the blockade of trucks hauling logs out of their forests in 1987. Nor is there one leader or group that emboldened them to expand their campaign over the next years until it brought thirteen of them to a face-to-face negotiating meeting with President Corazon Aquino in 1990. Instead, a steady succession of events in this poor municipality moved people to act—and led them to discover the difference between government promises and concerted citizen action.

It is such people as the peasants of San Fernando whom Haribon president Junie Kalaw terms the "first environmentalists" of the Philippines. In developed countries, people often assume that environmentalism is a luxury item, that its most active proponents come from the middle- to upper-class strata of society. People in an underdeveloped country like the Philippines, it is said, need food, jobs, clothes. We assume they cannot possibly be aware of their need for trees, or perhaps that they will not feel the need for trees until after they have education, jobs, savings accounts, VCRs—that is, after they have become "developed" like us. In addition, some in developed countries talk about a "trade-off" facing developing countries in terms of environmental issues, suggesting that environmental protection forces the sacrifice of growth and development.

This is not what we find in San Fernando; it is certainly not what the residents in San Fernando describe to us.

We decided to go to San Fernando to hear the participants tell their own story. The trip itself speaks volumes about the problems that beset a poor country like the Philippines. First, we fly from Manila over the rest of the island of Luzon, then over the cluster of islands in the middle of the Philippines known collectively as the Visayas. We land in northern Mindanao, on an airstrip so nestled into the mountains that in the rainy season pilots at times fail to spot it beneath the cloud cover (and are left with no choice but to return plane and passengers to the north).

The rest of our journey is over land, not an easy endeavor on an island whose landscape is dominated by mountains running north to south. We go to the marketplace to catch a bus that will take us on the main north-south road leading into Bukidnon. Climbing onto an old, crowded vehicle, we find no seats and little standing room. We follow the friendly suggestion of some other passengers and settle down with pieces of luggage that have been piled atop a large spare tire at the back of the bus. Sharing our tire are a mother and her three small children, one holding a sack that keeps wiggling. "A puppy," the mother explains, noticing our curiosity.

The bus turns southward and begins slowly to climb a steep hill. The road has been paved in the last decade, but still it is dusty. Almost every passenger on the bus swaddles his or her head with whatever happens to be available: a kerchief, a towel, an extra T-shirt. Some shroud their faces. Thin boards could be pulled up to cover the windows and keep dust out, but then the heat would become unbearable.

When the bus stops at various small communities along the way to pick up passengers, we are surrounded by vendors hawking bus food. "*Maize, maize, maize*," cry children who hold out ears of yellow corn, roasted over charcoal fires. "*Chicharon, chicharon*," beseech women carrying straw baskets filled with fried pork skin. Others offer peanuts or small pineapples (which, we are told by another passenger, are either rejects from the Bukidnon Del Monte plantation or else ones that have fallen off the Del Monte trucks).

To wash it all down is the ubiquitous Coke, sold in plastic bags, a rubber band serving the dual purpose of closing the bag and holding a straw in place. And to fit the pocketbooks of the clientele, almost all are sold in portions that cost a couple of pesos or less.

The bus continues on, past a colorful sign that welcomes us to Bukidnon and depicts corn fields, cattle ranches, and pineapple plantations. Bukidnon, literally "land of the mountains," is often referred to as the watershed of Mindanao; six of the major rivers on the island originate in its mountains. We are now traversing a plateau; in many areas, fields planted to pineapple for Del Monte stretch to the foot of the mountains. Where the plateau turns into hillsides grow small fields of yellow corn—some undoubtedly to grill and sell, some for animal feed, and much to grind into corn grits, the staple food of most Filipinos too poor to eat rice. Beyond the corn fields, the hills and mountains are bare except for an occasional lone tree.

We chug along until we come to a sudden stop. This time it is an unscheduled one. Engine problems, the word spreads through the bus. The passengers climb over each other—and over luggage and chickens (feet tied) and cardboard boxes of groceries and supplies—to get out of the bus. Once outside, they patiently settle down in whatever shade they can find to escape the sweltering tropical sun. We seem to be the only passengers anxious to know what the problem is. After all, as the mother indicates to us with a shrug of her shoulders, no matter what the problem, we passengers can only wait and see what happens. So we find a bit of shade and sit and wait—and try hard to learn the art of patience. "Roll," yells the bus driver after an hour or so.

We get off in a town another hour down the road and find the street corner from which, we are told, jeepneys travel eastward to San Fernando. We are in luck, we think: a jeepney, motor running, is parked in front of a small bakery. "When is this jeepney scheduled to leave?" we ask the driver, and receive one of our many lessons in cross-cultural differences. "*Alas puno*," he replies with a friendly smile, meaning "When it's full" but turning the phrase into a joke by saying literally "At full o'clock."

"Full o'clock" comes more than two hours later—after the driver has slowly circled around town several times, honking his horn to entice passengers, and has loaded some galvanized-iron sheets and plastic pipes on the roof. There now seem to be about two people for every seat (including the driver's, where a passenger squeezes in on his left). Even the front hood of the jeep is occupied, by a woman holding a somewhat leaky plastic bag containing a slab of raw meat.

"How long does the trip to San Fernando take?" we ask. "It depends," the driver responds with another smile. One of the wooden bridges was washed out by recent heavy rains, he explains; it may or may not have been reconstructed by now. If not, we will have to get off the jeepney, wade across the river, and wait for another jeepney to fetch us on the other side. Other passengers smile at our concern; they know that the trip may take three hours, or it may take the whole day. That is life here.

A few blocks out of town, the pavement disappears; on this stage of the journey there is no way to avoid the dust, no matter how ingenious you are about covering yourself. We bump along, stopping for water whenever possible, both for the jeepney's steaming engine and for its dusty passengers. There are no stops for food on this kind of road, no women and children offering local products for a peso or so.

Somewhere on a rather steep incline, we stop quite suddenly: a flat tire. We two Americans are the only passengers who disembark as the driver replaces the blown tire with one whose last treads disappeared long ago. "The road is in very bad shape now," sighs one of the passengers, explaining that the lone road to San Fernando was built by a logging company and used to be maintained by the loggers.

Still, we are fortunate: the bridge has been repaired, and only a few hours later we coast into the town center of San Fernando. The main street is unpaved, bordered by a few one- and two-story weathered wooden homes and shops, some separated by fields of tall green grasses with a few banana trees. We say goodbye to our fellow jeepney passengers and approach a small *sari-sari* store (actually, a window opening into a tiny single room sparsely stocked with supplies) in hopes of finding a 7-Up to soothe our gritty throats. Alas, delivery, we are told, has not come through yet this week.

Like most rural Philippine municipalities, San Fernando covers a large land area, with a population dispersed over wide-flung communities called barrios or *barangays*. So our journey to hear the story of San Fernando is not yet over. For the next few days, we hike across corn fields, walk carefully along the dirt embankments separating rice paddies, climb over dusty, nearly barren hills, and wade across rivers to the far-lying barrios of San Fernando to meet the actors in this story.

Almost everyone with whom we speak is a self-described "poor peasant who grows corn" or rice. The majority are lowland Filipinos who migrated south to Mindanao, a place whose resources have served as a magnet for settlers from the middle of this century onward. The migrants were mostly interested in the fertile lands of this, the Philippines' second largest island. But Mindanao also had rich fishing banks, and minerals galore: iron, copper, silver, gold, and limestone. The Filipinos migrated for many of the same reasons American settlers had pushed westward: they were encouraged by homesteading laws and were going in search of land to farm and a future for their children. And, just as U.S. settlers brutally pushed Native Americans off their ancestral lands, so too did lowland Filipino migrants displace the indigenous inhabitants from theirs. By the mid–1980s, nearly 25 percent of the Philippine population lived in Mindanao.[2]

Most who resettled in San Fernando remained poor peasants. They lived in simple huts of bamboo, thatched palm leaves, and *cogon*-grass. Most grew rice or corn on land they did not own; 90 percent of San Fernando's 33,000 inhabitants, even today, are small farmers without title to the land they till.[3] They had few, if any, savings, and they worked hard, as they had done almost since birth. Life is never easy for a Filipino peasant; but, decades ago, here in San Fernando, an old man tells us, "Food was plentiful. There was plenty of fish, plenty of corn, and plenty of rice."

Then, we are told, problems began to appear.

We are resting at a cluster of houses. It is late in the day and the peasants are returning home from their fields. A young mother, perhaps in her twenties, and an elderly couple do most of the talking.

For years, the younger woman explains, "ever we since started seeing big logging trucks" pass through San Fernando, the peasants watched the rivers change shape, turn muddier, less deep, yet more violent during the big rains. In formerly flood-free areas, the river would now overflow its banks, inundating adjacent fields with mud from the increasingly barren hills around them. And, the old man interjects, the river would sometimes even swallow the edges of the fertile fields along its side. In the last five years, one peasant who cultivated land on the banks of the Tigua lost nearly half of the land he had farmed.[4]

There were other changes, too. Creeks nourished by once-forested watersheds disappeared during the dry season; landslides became common during the rainy season. And the rat population, which had previously found food in the forests and had been kept in check by forest predators, now ravaged farmers' fields at night. "People are hungry because the rats are eating everything," continues the young woman solemnly. Today, more than four out of five children suffer from some degree of malnutrition.[5]

The problems, the people say they came intuitively to understand, could be summed up in one word: *trees*. The forests that had still been lush in the 1970s were disappearing by the 1980s. Mindanao's riches not only had attracted poor settlers; they also had lured agricultural plantations (Del Monte and Dole, for example), miners—and loggers. Commercial logging interests have operated in Bukidnon for decades, but the major logging drive came in the wake of martial law in 1972. By the late 1980s, it was estimated that only 17 percent of Bukidnon's forests were still intact (and some say this figure is too high).[6]

The old man with whom we speak points to left and right, at bald hills scarred with tree stumps. "In 1963, when I came here, those were still forests, so thick that even a *carabao* could not go there. When the forests were still there, the water was plentiful. Even if it did not rain for two months, a small child could not cross the river. Now, even with rain, a child can cross easily." His wife sighs and points to the mountains behind us. "Now, without the forests, there is more and more soil erosion," she says. "It is so strong it even forms a mark on the hill" when the rains rush down the bare slopes above and wash the topsoil away.

These are "big, serious problems," interjects her husband, as if wanting to be sure we foreign visitors grasp the implications for agricultural productivity. San Fernando's rice and corn fields depend on rainwater; there is no irrigation here. "Before, even if it did not rain for two months, my field would not dry up. Now it dries up after two days without rain, and it becomes very hard to plow. It is much harder to farm now than before. And our topsoil has become thin because of the erosion." Some harvests fell by more than 50 percent.[7]

We nod in agreement. In the late 1970s, when Robin first came to Bukidnon and lived with peasants like these, the mountains were green and lush; they looked much like Palawan's do today. Robin often found herself mesmerized by the province's relatively untouched beauty. Few people talked about trees then. And although, like many of Bukidnon's inhabitants then, she often hitched rides on logging trucks, she never realized that the forests were being cut as rapidly as they clearly must have been.

"Who taught you about these things?" we ask. "Did the priests teach you these things?" The old man looks somewhat insulted. "It was our own thinking that saw these connections and we asked the [church] to set up seminars to help us understand further." In 1987, at the people's request, the Redemptorists, an order of Philippine missionaries who were based in San Fernando at the time, led ecology workshops to help put the people's observations in a larger context. "Actually," admits Redemptorist brother Karl Gaspar, "we were not experts in ecology; we were not planning to have studies or meetings about ecology. But that was the issue the people were most interested in."

Many of the San Fernando residents who participated in these workshops were already environmental activists of a sort, having belonged to a local church-based environmental group (Pagbugtaw sa Kamatuoran, or PSK, meaning "to be awakened to the truth"). PSK had been organized in the early 1980s to oppose the Marcos government's plan to dam Bukidnon's Pulangi River. The dam, which would have been the second largest in Asia, would have flooded much of San Fernando. After the dam was postponed, PSK became dormant, but the issue of the trees reactivated it.[8]

The 1987 discussions about the trees had begun in an atmosphere of hope. Corazon Aquino had recently come to power, and though Manila politics often seem too far away from the day-to-day reality of Mindanao to have much relevance here, the residents of San Fernando thought the change of government would make a difference. If the authoritarian government of Ferdinand Marcos had given way to the people-powered Aquino, certainly the new government would listen to what San Fernando people-power had to say.

So they decided to do what you do in a feudal society: you ask your patron for help. The farmers wrote to President Aquino asking that logging be stopped in the area. They focused on one logging company, which had been operating in the area for over twenty years and whose trucks passed through San Fernando: the Caridad C. Almendras Logging Enterprises. Almendras's story was not dissimilar to those of the country's other big loggers. The scion of the Almendras family was a former senator, said to have been a good friend of Ferdinand Marcos. Almendras's timber license granted him logging rights to nearly 43,000 hectares of forest.[9]

The farmers documented their legal case against the logger, complaining that the company was not only logging in critical watershed areas but was also cutting undersized logs. They cited Almendras's use of high-powered machines called "yarders" or "wreckers," which are banned throughout the Philippines because they knock down smaller trees as they haul out big, heavy trees. In addition, they argued that the logging company had violated its obligations under the licensing agreement by failing to plant new trees.

About nine hundred residents of San Fernando signed the petition to President Aquino and then waited for an answer—which, says the young woman with a smile, "we thought we would get."

After months with no reply, the petitioners came to the painful realization that they might never receive an answer. After much thought, they concluded that they had waited long enough. People-power, they agreed, meant action. One day in July of 1987, they held a mass. And then they acted. In the middle of the single dirt road passing from the hills through San Fernando's town proper, several hundred of them sat down. They positioned themselves in front of the municipal hall. They sat behind a hand-lettered sign announcing to the logging trucks, "Loggers Stop: We Are on Picket." They called the sign a roadblock, and they referred to themselves as "the picketers."

Among them were the San Fernando residents with whom we are talking, including the young mother, then seven months pregnant. "We were very tense at first," she confesses. "We thought they would drive a truck through us . . . or someone would throw a grenade at us. But then, much to our surprise, the trucks stopped."

So began the first of many "citizens' arrests" of logging trucks descending from the mountains, the arresters claiming they were simply exercising their constitutional rights. For eleven days and nights, in staggered shifts of about fifty per day (so they could tend their fields), they slept, ate, and held mass on that road—until there stood thirteen fully loaded (or, more accurately, overloaded) 10-ton-capacity trucks coming down from the mountains on one side of the makeshift blockade. On the other side were eighteen empty trucks trying to climb back up the mountains for the next load.

Then, on the twelfth day, a military detachment appeared. The picketers "held mass . . . and sang the national anthem. There were 35–40 soldiers and 80–90 people. The people were crying, but wouldn't move," recollects Father Pat Kelly, a Canadian missionary in San Fernando who offered his support to the picketers. One of PSK's leaders recalls for us what happened next: "We locked arms and blocked the road. . . . They used rattan sticks and rattan shields and twenty-four of us were so badly beaten we had big welts afterwards."

The attack seems only to have convinced the people of the importance of their actions. To begin with, the military claimed it was simply enforcing a court restraining order the logging company was able to get against the picketers. Rather than scare the people, the injunction incensed them, for in it the Almendras family claimed losses of the peso-equivalent of more than $15,000 per day, "the gross value of logs which are transported . . . every day." [10] As a PSK leader later explains to us, "But this backfired, because the people said, Aha, now we know what you're making from our mountains." The old man with whom we are speaking purses his lips at the thought of this profit: "Others get rich on nature, while we get nature's revenge."

In addition to the physical harassment, the picketers tell us, they suffered verbal attacks on their motives. "The military said, When you join the picketers, you are already in grade 5 in communism. If you are in grade 6, you don't believe in God anymore," a farmer recounts. "But people who know better know we are doing this for the next generation." (Later, when we interview DENR Secretary

Fulgencio "Jun" Factoran, Jr., his discussion of San Fernando makes it clear that he too harbors suspicions that the peasants' action was somehow Communist-inspired—a sad throwback to the mentality of the Marcos days.)

Other issues besides trees were clearly on the minds of some local and national officials. The local mayor, we are told, beseeched the people to act more rationally, since 30 percent of the municipal government's revenues came from logging companies and it was the logging companies that maintained the lone unpaved road from the province's main "highway" to San Fernando. In addition, one picketer tells us, "[Secretary] Factoran [during a later meeting] said that logging could be good to help [against] the economic recession, could earn foreign exchange to reduce the debt. But I told him, logging was big during Marcos's time but still our foreign debt got bigger." Similarly, claims another longtime San Fernando resident, Secretary Factoran explained to him, "You know we have big debts; the logs are a big [foreign-exchange] earner."

Although the action by the military ended the picket, very soon thereafter it offered a small victory for the farmers. The brutality of the military attack against the picketers was reported in national newspapers—and the coverage embarrassed the government into action. Less than a month after the picket line was so brutally broken, DENR announced the temporary suspension of Almendras's logging concession in San Fernando.

"We were so happy," laughs the young mother, cradling her toddler son. "We had won. But then, even after the license of Almendras was suspended, we would still hear the sound of chain saws." In addition, explains another picketer, some people went into the forest and saw "yarders there—which is not the machine of poor *kaingineros* [farmers who practice shifting agriculture]." It was clearly not just a matter of suspending Almendras. All logging in Bukidnon, the people came to believe, had to be stopped.

And so, in November of 1988, after many more meetings and discussions with government officials, the people decided it was time for another people-power action. This time more than two hundred people from San Fernando traveled to the provincial capital, fifty-three kilometers away. Their ranks swelled with residents from six other municipalities, until over three hundred of them had pitched their tents in front of the provincial office of the Department of Environment and Natural Resources.[11] The women who were pregnant in the first blockade brought their babies to the second.

After five days, frustrated by the lack of government response, they moved to the one main road—this time the paved, two-lane highway that our bus had traveled down and that is the only supply route from Bukidnon to the port city to the north. Again, for five more days, they halted logging trucks headed to and from the city. However, the blockaders understood what it means to be poor and understood who their opponents were and who they were not. Therefore, they shared their food with the truck drivers during the first picket and, during the second, sent sacks of rice to the drivers' families.

The picketers' demands were simple: they wanted Secretary Factoran to come to Bukidnon to meet with them, and they wanted all concession licenses for Bukidnon canceled.[12] National media interest in the blockade grew.

The people got their Christmas gift late that year. On December 28, Secretary Factoran not only came to Bukidnon, where nearly 2,000 Bukidnon residents awaited him, he used the occasion to cancel (not merely suspend) the license of Almendras as well as to order the other big logging firm in San Fernando, El Labrador Lumber Company, to cease logging in a critical watershed area.[13] An observer to these events sums up the picketers' reactions: "Despite the fact that the people's major demand [for banning logging in all Bukidnon] was not granted, nonetheless the people were empowered by their partial victory."[14]

As the San Fernando picketers recall for us, they believed that Secretary Factoran's actions had made logging illegal in San Fernando. But still it continued. The young mother shakes her head: "We had won again. But we still heard chain saws and we saw trucks from another logging company that had been logging on the other side of the mountain but now seemed to be moving into San Fernando." According to one estimate at this time, loggers in nine concessions on mountains encircling Bukidnon continued to cut one million cubic meters of timber a month.[15]

What allowed the logging to continue, the picketers came to believe, was the acquiescence of the military and some local officials. Local DENR personnel, earning only the equivalent of $150 per month, seemed prime candidates for bribery. "Those [DENR] check points are supposed to stop the illegal loggers," one San Fernando resident explains to us. "But those are not check points; they are 'cash points.' And the military also are known to get a percentage of the sales from illegal loggers." (Secretary Factoran himself later admits to us that, although he feels he has been successful at cleaning up the top levels of what was once a very corrupt DENR, there are "still problems at lower levels; still people [at lower levels] making money.")

The people wrote to Secretary Factoran to voice their frustrations: "We, as Filipino citizens, we asked this question: 'Who is governing our country, is it the government or the loggers?'"[16]

And then the picketers decided to act again. This time, they decided, Manila would be the venue. Thirteen of them were chosen for the third stage of San Fernando people-power, seven women and six men, ranging from a fifty-three-year-old mother of eleven to a nineteen-year-old student.[17] For almost all, it was their first trip to the big city, their first time to leave Mindanao; for some, it was their first trip outside Bukidnon. For all except Father Pat Kelly, the Canadian priest who accompanied them, it was their first airplane ride.

Corazon "Dinky" Soliman, a community organizer who had years earlier worked with citizens' movements in Bukidnon and who now lives in Manila, was asked to serve as interpreter for the thirteen.[18] She smiles as she recalls for us their first days in the capital city: "They were really shocked at Manila. The pollution made them sick. And when we went to the zoo, they said they never dreamed they would see such animals. They were marveling at how long the neck of the giraffe is. . . . And they went to the exhibits of the Marcoses' possessions, the famous 1,200 pairs of shoes, and they looked at clothes and asked: 'Why are there so many clothes? Are there no *labanderas* [women who wash clothes] in Manila?' They looked at the Marcoses' belongings and said, 'Now we know why we have no good roads in Bukidnon.'"

In late September of 1989, in Manila's stifling tropical heat, the thirteen began what they called their "fast for trees." Living in tents and hastily constructed sheds just outside the main office of DENR, they drank only sparing amounts of milk and honey. They vowed to break their fast only if the government met all their demands. And their demands had expanded; among other requests, they asked the government to declare a total logging ban for all of Bukidnon and to provide money to train and employ forest guards. They took one further significant step. They demonstrated their understanding that some of the reasons for Bukidnon's deforestation lay outside the Philippines' national borders; they sent letters to the governments of Japan and South Korea, whose countries are the main importers of timber from the Philippines, and asked for aid for reforestation.

"The picketers were so impressive," says one observer. "They held a press conference and one-by-one they stood before microphones and cameras to introduce themselves and their mission: 'I am Clarita. I am a mother of two. And I left my family, not knowing what would happen to me here in Manila.' . . . 'I am an old woman and I think that the last legacy I can give my children is this.' . . . 'I am young but I think for my future I have to do this.'" Wearing papier-mâché masks depicting people in agony, the fasters explained that logging had led to increased hunger in Bukidnon: "We fast in union with those who are forced to fast because of destitution."[19]

U.S. vice-president Dan Quayle was in Manila that week; Ferdinand Marcos died that week: competition for media attention was tight. Yet, word of the Bukidnon 13, as the former picketers came to be known, spread. Secretary Factoran had actually asked to talk with them from the start, indicating agreement to some of their points. But they refused to talk until he had promised to meet their demands in full. It took eight days of fasting before Secretary Factoran agreed: the government would acquiesce to all. The people of San Fernando would get their twenty forest guards and their total logging ban for Bukidnon, and DENR would close illegal lumber yards.[20] As for the 167 logs, it was agreed they could be used for people's timber needs, to replace burnt houses and such.[21]

But still the Bukidnon 13 fasted, for they wanted to deliver an even broader message directly to President Aquino. They wanted her personal commitment, one participant tells us, "to support a total log ban in Bukidnon and to encourage all provinces to do the same." As Clarita Escoto, the group's spokesperson, explained, "It is not only the protection of the forest of Bukidnon that we want but also that of the entire nation."[22]

Ten days after the fast began, very early in the morning, the fasters went to the presidential palace to meet with Aquino. It was a
meeting that almost did not happen. The fasters were wearing rubber thongs, the only footwear most poor Filipinos own. Aquino's
palace guards at first refused to let them enter; it is expected that
formal shoes will be worn to a meeting with the Philippine president. Finally ushered inside, the thirteen waited for the president
in wonderment. Dinky Soliman, their translator, recalls their reactions: "'How do they wash this floor?' one asked, looking at carpet-
ing. Another eyed a fountain outside the window: 'What is it for?'
And they shivered from the air conditioning."

When President Aquino arrived, six of the Bukidnon 13 spoke in
turn. They spoke respectfully but forthrightly, complaining that
some local officials and military were either protecting illegal loggers or involved in the activity themselves. In a feudal society like
the Philippines, for a poor peasant to say such things to a rich city
person, let alone to the country's president, is a difficult task—but
they did it. Then Clarita, who had been four months pregnant
when beaten by the military during the first picket and whose
daughter (jokingly nicknamed "Picket")[23] celebrated her first birthday at the second, explained their demands.

When they had finished, President Aquino spoke, voicing her
support of the agreement they had signed. She then gave them
T-shirts with her picture from *Time Magazine*'s person-of-the-year
cover and stood up to leave. But the people asked her first to join
them in prayer: "With the grace of God, all things that have been
promised should happen." Then, on their tenth day without food,
in the guesthouse of the presidential palace, they broke their fast.

We ask Dinky Soliman, who was there with these "first environmentalists," what it all means. Have they won? Is their fight to save
the forests over? "Yes, they feel like they've won. But they know
this is simply the start of a lot of work. Yes, they now have gotten the mandate from the president. But they have to be strong
and they have to monitor," she says. "The people know they still
have to make the promises happen."

A headline in a national newspaper captured the moment: "The
work begins for Bukidnon 13."[24]

As we hike through the corn fields and rice paddies of San Fernando and listen to the wisdom of its farmers, we begin to grasp

several lessons that their experience offers to the environmental movement globally.

One is a lesson about poor people and the environment. Individually, poor people are under enormous economic pressure to exploit natural resources (albeit on a small scale) in order to survive in the short term. Yet, when working together, the poor themselves are likely to become not only the catalysts for halting the plunder but also the initiators of sustainable alternatives.

The people of San Fernando also defy a position at times advanced by poorer-country governments: that protection of forests and other natural resources is a concern being forced upon them by rich-country governments and environmentalists—and that it will keep them from developing. (We do agree that it is hypocritical for governments of richer countries that "developed" by stripping off their own and other countries' natural resources to argue that poorer countries should not do the same.) The actions of the peasants of San Fernando demonstrate that environment may or may not be their government's concern; it may or may not be a concern of richer governments and groups; but it is their own concern. For them, there is no trade-off between genuine development and environmental sustainability. Rather, genuine development cannot be rooted in plunder; it must be based on community management of those natural resources upon which they depend for their existence.

Finally, San Fernando provides a lesson about the role of civil society and the role of governments. The Philippine government, like most governments, is a mixed bag. Some officials are corrupt and beholden to the plunderers of land and natural resources. Others—particularly local officials—are often simply poor and hence easily susceptible to bribery. Still other government employees are genuinely honest and sincerely strive to do their bureaucratic job as best they can.

Given that mix, governments face severe limits on their ability to halt resource destruction. They can pass laws, revoke timber licenses, even ban commercial logging. But it will take a permanently mobilized citizenry to ensure that the resource plunderers in places like the Philippines do not flaunt the laws, ignore the limits, and circumvent the bans.

This last lesson is one with far-reaching implications. It is important not only for the resolution of the problems in the Philippines, but also for such ambitious undertakings as global environmental conventions and treaties to reduce the emission of greenhouse gases. Citizens' groups around the world can learn much from what the peasants of San Fernando did: they, too, must demand a place at the negotiating table. Like these first environmentalists, citizens' groups must force governments to acknowledge that organizations of civil society have the power to make the promises of environmental conventions happen.

Chapter Five

Life Along the Death March

States have the right and the duty to formulate appropriate national development policies that aim at the constant improvement of the well-being of the entire population and of all individuals, on the basis of their active, free and meaningful participation in development and in the fair distribution of the benefits resulting therefrom.

> "Declaration on the Right to Development," adopted by the United Nations General Assembly, Resolution 41/128, December 4, 1986

Half a century ago, Philippine and U.S. soldiers fought side by side in some of the bloodiest and most valiant battles of World War II, episodes that climaxed in what the world now knows as the Fall of Bataan and the infamous Bataan Death March. During that campaign, tens of thousands were killed in the Philippine province of Bataan. Most of Bataan's buildings were burned to the ground.

To discover what has happened in the fifty years since then to the survivors of the Death March and to Bataan's forested mountains, where many of those battles occurred, we take the two-and-a-half-hour (120-kilometer) bus ride northwest from Manila to this small peninsular province. We are curious as well to retrace the route of one of John's grandfathers, who survived the Death March (and subsequent years in a concentration camp north of Bataan), only to be machine-gunned by his captors during the final months of the war.

Half the size and population of Rhode Island, Bataan juts down like a giant breakwater to separate Manila Bay from the South China Sea, and eleven of the province's twelve towns ring the coast. Traversing the province over several months in 1989 and again in 1991, we interview dozens of people, from the governor to town mayors, from the military commanders of today to World War II veterans, from business leaders to fishers, farmers, workers.

What we discover is that, on the surface, Bataan has been rebuilt and modernized. Forests have given way to roads. Fishing and farming have now been joined by industrial establishments that assemble goods for the export market. Millions of dollars of U.S. aid, investment, and loans have poured into the province. As a leading Bataan business executive phrases it, "Bataan has risen." Yet, the vast majority of the province's fishers, farmers, and factory workers remain desperately poor. Insurgency and counter-insurgency rage throughout the province.

But the story of what has happened to Bataan over these five decades is not simply the tale of a single province. In the history of this province reside the clashes of colonial versus Filipino aspirations, clashes which continue well into the postcolonial period. In addition, Bataan's "modernization" is a revealing example of a kind of debt-driven, resource-plundering, export-oriented development that has been tried across the developing world—but has largely failed to make life better for the majority of the population. And Bataan's deforested mountains and depleted fishing grounds form a telling backdrop to a wide range of citizens' organizations clamoring for another kind of development. As such, Bataan offers powerful insights into the most pressing problems and challenges that face those fighting to assert more democratic control over that country's natural resources.

Row after row of man-made fishponds stretch like large, murky swimming pools across the several hundred yards between Manila Bay and Bataan's rice fields. Then, three or four miles inland, the rice fields give way to mountains sculpted by centuries of volcanic activity.

The first of Bataan's fishponds were meticulously engineered as early as the 1920s, out of swamps and mangrove forests near the bay, Mayor Godofredo Galicia tells us over lunch at his Fredelie's People's Resort on the outskirts of the town of Orani. As we dine on prawns from his family's nearly 50 hectares of fishponds, Mayor Galicia entertains us with vivid memories of the ponds during World War II.

He begins with events that many older residents of Bataan recount as if they had happened just the other month, remembering exact dates, days of the week, and sometimes even specific hours.

The day after Pearl Harbor, the Japanese launched their invasion of the Philippine Islands, then a U.S. colony. Following an old plan for the defense of the Philippines, U.S. and Philippine soldiers retreated into the mountainous jungle of the Bataan peninsula, with the Japanese in hot pursuit.

As the mayor explains, "Many of the civilians here fled to the mountains, where there was lots of malaria and where the fighting was. But we were among the more fortunate. We evacuated to the fishponds and built our shanty there [on the earthen dikes that separate the fishponds]. Almost all the dikes were full of shanties. I was seven years old at the time. We survived by harvesting the *bangus* [milkfish] and bartering some of it with farmers for rice."

The mayor is proud of his province's role in World War II. Japan had initially planned to take over the entire Philippines within seven weeks. But it turned out not to be quite that easy. Through the determined efforts of U.S. and Philippine forces, the Japanese were stalled for over three months in Bataan—a defense that, many argue, critically set back the Japanese war effort. Following the surrender of U.S. and Philippine forces on April 9, 1942, a grueling 83-kilometer death march of 75,000–80,000 Philippine and U.S. soldiers ensued. As many as 10,000 died along the way: some executed by the Japanese, others succumbing to a combination of intense tropical heat, disease, dehydration, and starvation.

Although World War II destroyed all but a few dozen buildings in the province, most of the fishponds survived. Beginning in the late 1970s, many were upgraded into today's high-tech, rectangular prawn ponds, like those of our current host.

As we eat the seafood feast with the mayor, a blind, middle-aged singer strums his guitar beside our outdoor dining table, serenading us with a medley of English and Filipino songs. The musician sings Imelda Marcos's favorite, *"Dahil sa Iyo"* ("Because of You"). The mayor looks a bit nervous, but the song fades quickly into "To Dream the Impossible Dream." This was the theme song of Benigno "Ninoy" Aquino, whose assassination on the Manila International Airport tarmac in 1983 eventually led to his widow Corazon's presidency.

Our host grins at the musician's political acumen and beckons an aide to bring over his briefcase. The mayor opens the briefcase and takes out two photos. He first shows us one that was snapped in

1972, when he originally became mayor—a photo of himself with Ninoy Aquino at his side. Before we have a chance to comment on the photo, we are handed its companion, a photo of a somewhat older and heavier Mayor Galicia taking the oath of Ferdinand Marcos's New Society Party. This time, it is Marcos at his side. The mayor laughs at the insight he is giving us into elite Philippine politics: "We dance to whatever music is playing."

And he sings too, a local newspaper man sitting with us whispers loudly enough for the mayor to hear. "He's the singing mayor of Bataan." The mayor chuckles again and, just before obliging us and launching into song, provides us with yet another piece of the Philippine political puzzle: "I won because in each speech I rendered a song. This is the favorite song of my wife. My wife loves me because of this song." And also for his prawns, whispers the newspaper man.

We find ourselves talking about the ponds again in the neighboring town of Samal, but this time with a poor fisherman. Prawns are the new craze among fishpond owners, Arnel (not his real name) tells us. But not just any prawn: most of these ponds are filled with giant black-tiger prawns, the majority of which will end up in the refined gullets of Japan's urban population. Arnel launches into a quick lesson in "prawnomics" to explain why it is that, all along the Philippine coast, coastal mangrove forests are being chopped down and old milkfish ponds are being transformed into prawn ponds. It is apparently quite simple: whereas milkfish earn the fishpond owner some $3.00 a kilogram, prawns bring in about $10.00 (although, as we later witness, prices swing widely according to the vagaries of the world market).

There is at least one hitch, however. Prawn ponds require a substantial initial investment, a minimum of $25,000 and up to $50,000 per hectare to cement the embankments and further renovate the former *bangus* ponds. In addition, input costs—for fertilizer, "prawn fry" or baby prawns, and the "pellets" or prawn food—are high. Over lunch, Mayor Galicia had told us that for each hectare of prawn pond, input costs of $5,000 yielded him a harvest of $30,000 three times a year.[1]

That is a considerable profit. But, Arnel asks, who has those initial thousands of dollars? Indeed, in Bataan, prawn cultivation is limited to the wealthiest thirty or forty families who, as a provincial agriculture official explains, have understandably "become crazy on prawns" since the mid–1980s. These include the vice-governor (whom we hear referred to as the "prawn king"), the ex-governor, and several mayors.

We pursue the subject further with Lydia David, the head of the provincial bureau of fishery and aquatic resources. We ask her about the consequences of the shift from milkfish ponds to prawn ponds. Fish, she answers, is the main source of protein for the 425,000 inhabitants of Bataan (as it is throughout the Philippines). Most people in Bataan simply "cannot afford prawns." And, as prawn cultivation displaces milkfish, the price of milkfish rises. According to David's figures, milkfish prices jumped from $2 per kilo in 1988 to $3 per kilo in 1989. "Malnutrition is going up as fish prices go up," she tells us. "In recent years, *bangus* has become almost a luxury. The time will come when we can no longer afford to buy fish."

One Bataan government agriculture official sums it up well: prawn farming, he confides, is an example of "a kind of development that's very good for the people who are producing but not so good for the people who are consuming."

The prawn craze is not unique to Bataan. In coastal areas all over the Philippines, people with access to the requisite amount of capital have, over the course of the 1980s, become "crazy" about prawns. How crazy is clear from Philippine export statistics: from 1980 to 1987, the value of prawn exports increased nearly eightfold; by 1988, prawns had become the country's fifth largest export earner.[2]

Residents of other Philippine provinces have begun to discover a pressing ecological problem associated with prawn farming in addition to the destruction of mangroves: water. These new, intensive methods of prawn cultivation require a careful mix of fresh and salt water, which is why the ponds are located on the coast. Vast quantities of fresh water are pumped from underground aquifers into the ponds and mixed with salt water drawn from the sea.

In 1986 Negros, in the central Philippines, became the first Philippine island to enter into the prawn age in a big way. There, in the province of Negros Occidental, prawns soon became the number two export (after sugar). Huge turbines can pump 25,000 gallons of potable water into the ponds each minute. Coastal farmers and fishers who live near the ponds now complain that their own water wells are drying up as the prawn owners draw down the water table. In one town in the heart of the Negros prawn-farm region, the water supply has already been reduced 30 percent; potable water is being rationed.[3]

After several years of prawn farming, the parched underground aquifer begins to suck in water from the sea, raising salinity levels. This inland saltwater migration has already started in parts of Negros. Left unchecked, it will eventually ruin the land for agriculture—and, ironically, for aquaculture too. Experts claim that it would take a generation after the prawn farms stopped operating to flush out the salinity. In Taiwan, excessive pumping of water has even led to land cave-ins. Yet, the prawn craze is still going strong in Negros.

Another risk lies in the narrow market, since over 80 percent of Philippine prawn exports go to Japan.[4] The dangers of such overdependence on a single market came home to roost in late 1989, when Japanese consumers cut back sharply on purchases of luxury foods such as prawns as they mourned their dying emperor Hirohito. And the Philippines was not the only country with prawns to unload: Taiwan, Thailand, Indonesia, Sri Lanka, Bangladesh, China, and other countries were simultaneously rushing into the prawn business. As the competitors battled for a suddenly glutted Japanese market, prices plunged 50 percent.

Yet, the Philippines' surge into prawns was supported by the World Bank and the United Nations Development Program. It has also been promoted and subsidized by the Philippine government. Indeed, the Department of Trade and Industry, seemingly immune to concerns about ecological or market sustainability, targeted eleven provinces to be transformed into prawn centers. Part of the promotion involves such incentives as granting Dole Philippines, a leader in banana and pineapple exports, a four-year tax holiday to set up a huge new prawn operation in Mindanao.[5] As for Bataan, according to a briefing we are given at the Bataan branch of the government's Department of Trade and Investment, aquaculture (that is, prawn- and fish-farming) is one of the five priority investment areas for the province. Later, back in Manila, one of that department's national under-secretaries speaks glowingly about the prospects for this latest "miracle export." We ask about the wisdom of pushing prawns in such a big way throughout the country, considering the inherent adverse ecological costs. He looks at us with surprise; no one, he says, has briefed him on this.

Arnel, the fisherman, tells us of yet one more problem presented by the prawn ponds. The fishing area itself has been reduced as the prawn ponds of the vice-governor and others expand along the shore and into Manila Bay. With the ponds encroaching onto the shallow coastal areas, the small-scale fishers find themselves having to go further and further out into the bay to fish.

Arnel suggests we see this for ourselves, and he offers to serve as our guide. So, early one morning, we follow him as he briskly makes his way over a maze of fishpond partitions, the approximately four-foot-wide dirt and cement embankments that separate one man-made prawn pond from another. Each prawn pond is the size of one to two football fields; the partitions that form the embankments are waist-high. We walk on the dikes alongside the ponds for perhaps half a mile until we reach a river where Arnel keeps his *banca*. The *banca* resembles a large wooden canoe, except that four curved bamboo poles are tied across the top, reaching out into the water on both sides like a spider's eight legs. To provide balance, bamboo poles connect the ends of the four legs on each side, skimming across the water as the boat glides forward.

Joining us on board are two other fisher *nakikisama* (shareworkers) who, not possessing or being able to borrow the peso-equivalent of $500 and up to buy their own *banca* and a used motor, regularly accompany Arnel. Arnel's *banca* is powered by a small, single-cylinder engine: the motor and the fact that others fish with him indicate that Arnel is not the poorest of fishers, though he is still poor. As we head down the river, skirting the prawn farms of the wealthy to head out onto Manila Bay, we pass an old man paddling a one-person, motorless *banca*. Arnel points to him and sighs: "How will the poorest fisherfolk like him who don't have motors be able to fish if more fishponds are built and we have to go even further out to find fish?"

The water of the bay is a murky brown, but the view is stunning, with a panorama spanning six provinces and two mountain ranges. On a clear day like today, you can see all the way across the bay to Manila itself. Most of the east coast of Bataan is visible from the bay, a reminder of how small is this province that managed to stall the Japanese for so long. Hidden from view are the province's four

largest enterprises, which dot the southern and western shores of
the peninsula: a special industrial zone housing some two dozen
factories, a $2.2 billion Westinghouse nuclear power plant built
during Marcos's reign and mothballed by President Aquino in
1986, a processing center for Vietnamese refugees most of whom
are bound for the United States, and nearly two-thirds of the giant
U.S. Subic Naval Base.

Back on shore, Arnel and his family share with us a lunch of rice
and some oysters that were part of the morning catch. As is common in the rural Philippines ("in the provinces," as it is said), we eat
with our hands. "It tastes better," explains Arnel as he reaches for
a handful of steaming rice. We notice that his palms are cut, his
fingernails split. To gather oysters and clams, he explains, hands
are the main instrument.

Arnel's wife cradles their sickly two-year-old daughter and apol-
ogizes for the lack of utensils and for the simple surroundings and
meal, not realizing that raw oysters are a delicacy for us. A single
high school diploma hangs on one wall. But the prime spot is given
to a poster of a chubby, blonde, Caucasian baby who wears oversized, adult-like spectacles. The small house has no running water
or electricity. Luckily for Arnel and his family, the public water
pump is located nearby, making the hauling relatively easy.

Like most of the other fishers we visit in Bataan, Arnel and his
family are squatters on public land. And, like the majority of fishers
and farmers we interview, Arnel has no savings. At best, when
times are very good, he has no debts. Today, for example, all eight
buckets of Arnel's catch, minus his gasoline costs, net him the peso-
equivalent of $4.50, a couple of dollars better than usual. It was a
good day; "Jackpot," grins Arnel. But most of this "jackpot" has already been consumed in purchasing medicine for his daughter's
asthma. The big killers of Bataan's children include pneumonia and
diarrhea.[6] To combat these and other ailments, Arnel explains,
many parents go deeply into debt, borrowing from family members
if that is possible and, if it is not, from informal credit sources at
outrageous interest rates.[7] A survey in another very poor fishing
village in the Philippines found that three out of ten died as infants,
and that all the children were malnourished.[8]

After lunch, Arnel and a small group of neighbors put their lives,
and those of the nearly 10,000 in Bataan who fish along Manila Bay,

in broader perspective. Some, like Arnel, were born into Bataan's fishing industry; his father and grandfather were fishers here too. Enticed by stories of rich fishing grounds in Manila Bay, since the 1950s numerous other fishers have been migrating to Bataan from poorer provinces of the Philippines. When the migration began, the waters here were among the richest in the Philippines; the men recall their fathers returning home after a day on the bay with boats piled high with fish. But in recent years, many of them complain, the average catch in the bay has dwindled.

In Bataan, the enemies of the fish, shrimp, clams, and oysters are many. Besides the loss of the mangroves and the incursion of the fishponds, Manila Bay is subject to the waste-disposal practices of perhaps 12 million Filipinos. Hundreds of industries also line its shores, discharging such heavy metals as mercury, cadmium, and lead. Silt from Bataan's overlogged mountains and phosphate and nitrate residues from chemical fertilizers and pesticides flow down the rivers and into the bay, burying coral reefs that serve as feeding grounds for the fish. High levels of phosphate have been confirmed along Bataan's eastern coastline. The pesticides used in prawn ponds add to this damage. In addition, large foreign-owned trawlers overfished the bay for decades, and local fishers, in ignorance and desperation, have dynamited many of the coral reefs. The dynamite kills a large number of fish in one swift blow, but it greatly reduces further catches by destroying the coral as well.[9]

One final woman-made creation contributes to the fishers' woes. Under the direction of Imelda Marcos in the late 1960s, close to ten acres of the bay off Manila were transformed into land to house a lavish cultural center, folk arts center, and five-star hotel, as well as the famed Coconut Palace, where you can still get a tour of the rooms in which Brooke Shields and George Hamilton graced the sheets as Imelda's guests. Since ecology was undoubtedly far from the First Lady's mind, she failed to note that the landfill area would block the circulation of water in the bay, inhibiting the natural flushing of its wastes into the South China Sea.[10]

Efren Pascual, who was the governor of Bataan from 1971 to 1987 and, some claim, is still the "king-maker" in provincial and local politics, estimates that, because of all this, Manila Bay will be biologically dead in ten years. Arnel thinks that twenty years is a more accurate guess. Be it ten or twenty, no one we interview contests

that the children of the thousands who depend on the bay for their
survival will have to find alternate employment.

As a harbinger of this uncertain future, red-tide microorganisms
(*Pyrodinium*, marine algae that bloom when fed with the nitrates,
phosphates, and other chemicals and garbage on the seabed)
reached critical levels in Manila Bay during the final months of
1988. Since eating certain red-tide–infected fish and shellfish can
be deadly, the fishers of Bataan were unable to sell their catch; incomes plummeted. Therefore, shrugs Arnel, he and his family, like
their neighbors, had no choice but to ignore the government warn-
ings and live on the potentially toxic red-tide–infested catch themselves—"and pray."

A year later, in January of 1990, the waters surrounding Bataan
again turn color but this time it is along the southern coast of Bataan
and the sea becomes, not red with pollution-fed microorganisms,
but black with bunker oil. Since Bataan houses the country's largest
oil facility, small oil spills are a regular occurrence—and a problem
for the local fishers. But this time a tanker containing a shipment of
Caltex oil actually sinks and discharges half a million liters of oil. It
is the biggest oil spill ever recorded here. And it spells disaster for
the affected 6,000 fisher-families in the towns of Limay, Pilar, Mariveles, Orion, and Balanga. According to a report by the Center
for Environmental Concerns, "The bunker oil . . . was floating 10
inches deep on top of the waters. . . . Dead fish and other sea animals and plants were found on the shore. . . . Nets and boats . . .
became black because of the oil. . . . Fish and other marine animals, which usually existed in the waters near the shoreline, have
completely disappeared."[11]

The development workers at the Bataan branch of the Philippine
Rural Reconstruction Movement (PRRM), one of the Philippines'
largest and oldest nongovernmental organizations, share statistics
with us that put the plight of the fishers into the larger picture of
poverty in the province. Before World War II, perhaps 60 percent
of the people of Bataan depended on fish for their livelihood; 40
percent, on farming. Today, fishers, farmers, and factory workers
together make up well over half of the province's population, but
the majority are still fishers and farmers. On average, the fishers,
earning the peso-equivalent of $0.75 to $1.50 each day, are slightly
poorer than the farmers. But the farmers make only $1.00 to $2.00

per day. And industrial workers earn a daily wage of anywhere from $2.50 to $3.75. The average incomes for all three groups compare poorly to national estimates that a daily wage of the peso-equivalent of approximately $6.00 to $9.00 is necessary to meet the minimum basic daily needs of a family of six and hence keep them above the poverty line.

Across the Philippines, both fishing and farming sectors are characterized by gross inequities. Fishing is a major earner of foreign exchange and provides livelihood for as many as 6–7 million Filipinos (a tenth of the population). Benefits are highly unequal.[12]

The fastest-growing segment of the fishing industry is aquaculture. Several thousand owners of aquaculture ponds along coastal areas and fish pens in lakes produce a third of the nation's catch. Employing about 250,000 workers, these owners harvest shrimp, prawns, seaweed, oysters, *bangus*, and a few other varieties of fish. As in Bataan, they represent the wealthiest Filipinos in the fishing industry, particularly those who own the high-tech, man-made ponds for the so-called intensive cultivation of prawns. Until the mid-1970s, it was relatively easy for mayors, governors, military officers, and other members of the elite to gain title to coastal swamplands, cut down the mangrove forests, and build fishponds. Nationwide, as in Bataan, this conversion has destroyed breeding grounds for fish and has infringed on fishing areas of smaller fishers. Despite government restrictions on the destruction of mangroves, by the late 1980s almost all had been cut. But still, as we see for ourselves, the expansion of prawn ponds along the Philippine coastal area continues.[13]

Another segment of the fishing industry consists of the approximately 50,000 larger, so-called commercial fishers, who pull in around a quarter of the catch.[14] Like most of the aquaculture sector, commercial fishing is capital-intensive, requiring substantial financial outlays. It is this segment that has proven highly lucrative for foreign interests, especially in tuna, the Philippines' "miracle" fish export of the 1970s. Indeed, most of the biggest commercial fishing corporations are foreign, largely either Japanese or joint ventures with Japanese. Not only are many of the larger fishing vessels— trawlers and purse seiners, with their enormous drift nets—from Japan, so too is much of the gear, technical expertise, and invested capital. This rapid entry of Japanese money and technology into the industry was greatly facilitated by a 1973 Philippine-Japan Treaty of Amity, Commerce, and Navigation, a treaty that numerous smaller fishers blame for many of their ills. Large Japanese vessels, they claim, have fished many formerly abundant fishing grounds clean.

Arnel and his friends are of the final, "municipal"-fisher class, the over 770,000 small-scale fishers (or, with their families, about 5,000,000) who fish within municipal waters and sell most of their catch locally. They provide the remaining two-fifths of Philippine fish production. Using only hook and line, fish traps, or simple nets, they are among the poorest of Philippine laborers.

And, they are getting poorer. Indeed, what we hear of in Bataan is a national trend: as a result of the spread of fishponds, the Japanese trawlers and other unsustainable fishing practices, silt from denuded mountains, and increasingly polluted waters, these small fishers have watched their annual catch dwindle nationwide from an average of 4.2 tons in 1905 to 1.6 tons by the late 1980s.

The skewed distribution found in Philippine fishing has analogies in farming. Concentration of land began in earnest during the Spanish colonial period (1565–1898). The Spanish system awarded large grants of land to Spanish colonizers and the emerging Philippine elite, who in turn leased small parcels of land to tenant rice-cultivators. A share of the produce was paid as tribute to the Spanish. In the seventeenth and eighteenth centuries, the religious orders acquired most of this land. In the nineteenth century, as trade with the West grew, the Catholic church shifted large portions of these "friar estates" to sugar, coconuts, and other cash crops.

The passing of the colonial mantle to the United States at the turn of this century changed little for the agricultural tenants. The United States purchased some of the friar estates and announced its intention of selling them to so-called owner-occupants. But the asking price was out of the reach of most tenant-cultivators. As a result, wealthy Filipino landlords were able to acquire sizable new holdings and continue tenancy relationships with the cultivators. Not surprisingly, over the decades the situation gave birth to peasant uprisings. Desire to quell the peasant unrest motivated numerous land-reform laws, from the U.S. colonial period through Marcos to the present administration, none of which ever scratched the surface of these inequalities.[15]

Unequal access to land was exacerbated by Marcos's adherence to advice from the World Bank and other international development agencies that cash crops bound for export markets could be the engine of economic development.[16] Marcos's courting of foreign investment for this purpose, coupled with sharp increases in the price of most primary commodities in 1973–1974, stimulated an expansion of foreign agribusiness concerns across the fertile lowlands of Mindanao.

This expansion, along with that of sugar and coconut lands in other parts of the country, pushed millions of Filipinos into the uplands in search of a livelihood. By the late 1980s, over 18 million poor Filipinos (between a fourth and a third of the population) were eking out an existence in the uplands. This migration hastened the destruction of the forests and infringed upon the ancestral domains of the indigenous peoples.

Conservative estimates of land ownership by the Department of Agrarian Reform soon after Marcos was removed from office suggested that 20 percent of the population owned 80 percent of the land.[17] At the other end of the scale, as many as seven out of ten Filipinos in the agricultural sector do not own the land they till.[18]

Corazon Aquino's presidential campaign against Marcos pinpointed land reform as vital to a new order, and a land-reform bill was one of the first measures to come out of the new Congress. But that success is only paper deep. Ironically, this issue bids fair to go down in history as one of her administration's greatest failures. The Aquino government's land reform has had, at best, minimal impact. U.S. academic Roy Prosterman, often a U.S. government consultant on land-reform issues, argued in late 1988 that "without strong executive action, the program is likely to redistribute barely 1 percent of the Philippines' cultivated land, with benefits to fewer than 4 percent of the landless."[19]

Within just a few months of this assessment, the Philippine Department of Agrarian Reform was mired in a series of scandals. The scandals grew from the land-reform law itself. During this initial period of reform, landlords in essence were able to name their own price for their land, then "voluntarily" sell it at that price to the government. The government would then sell it to the former tenants, who were obligated to repay the government for the land over the next thirty years. Compounding this chicanery were numerous loopholes and ambiguities—including long implementation periods and high land-retention limits per landlord-family—that offered openings for graft and corruption and for minimizing the reform's actual redistribution.[20]

Against this national panorama, it should come as little surprise that nearly 70 percent of Bataan's fishers are "municipal" and that a majority of its farmers are landless tenants; to make ends meet, many of these tenant farmers and farmworkers slip in and out of such service-sector jobs as driving passenger tricycles. Nor is it surprising that about half of Bataan's adult population are either unemployed or underemployed (according to calculations provided to us by the provincial office of the government's Department of Social Welfare). Or that almost 60 percent of Bataan's infants are underweight, suffering from some degree of malnutrition.[21]

Provincial and local governments, as Bataan's public officials readily admit, lack the resources to make much of a dent in Bataan's poverty. Outside the government, such development organizations as PRRM are trying to fill the void by working together with groups of the poorer fishers and farmers. One such group is LAMBAT, an organization of Bataan's fishers formed in 1986 by Arnel and others. Like almost all Filipino acronyms, LAMBAT is a clever play on words: the initials stand for the first letters in the Tagalog words for "united Bataan fisherfolk," but *lambat* is also the Tagalog word for fishnet.

LAMBAT's goals are ambitious, ranging from rehabilitation of Manila Bay and Bataan's rivers, to stronger sanctions against factories dumping wastes in the bay, to providing members with social services and livelihood programs, to striving for a more equal distribution of fishing resources. Whereas PRRM is a nongovernmental organization (NGO), whose staff works in partnership with peasant and fisher groups, LAMBAT is one of what are referred to as people's organizations (POs), which are made up of members of a particular grass-roots constituency: fishers, farmers, laborers, indigenous peoples, and so on. Like many Philippine people's organizations, LAMBAT has individual chapters of fishers in the province's towns, which are affiliated with a provincial chapter that is, in turn, affiliated with a national umbrella group of fishers.

Through education and training sessions in various locations across Bataan, PRRM development workers are helping to strengthen the community-organizing work of groups such as LAMBAT and to start livelihood, credit, and health programs. A PRRM worker explains to us the philosophy behind the multi-tiered approach: "The main goal is empowerment of the poorest of the poor—people's empowerment. This is different from the people-power that brought Cory Aquino into office, which turned out to be mainly for the rich. This is for the poor, their own power."

To see what these words mean in practice, we accompany two PRRM workers and a LAMBAT leader, himself a poor fisher, to the tiny neighborhood or *sitio* of Agwawan on the southern coast of Bataan. Agwawan, we are told, consists of thirty-eight households or about 140 persons, almost all of whom make their living from fishing. The morning's plan is to show a slide show about the problems of Filipino fishers and then to let the people discuss whether forming a local LAMBAT affiliate might help them begin collectively to address some of their problems.

Agwawan is, as they say, off the beaten track. Indeed, the final 2 kilometers of our journey test the skills of our driver and the endurance of our jeep. The dirt road has given way to a path of stones that borders the sea; on occasion, we must cross streams of water. As we near Agwawan, we see that the shore is lined with small wooden *bancas*, mostly motorless, of the sort that is paddled by one person who then fishes with a handmade handnet—in other words, a municipal fisher even poorer than Arnel.

We turn onto a dirt way that seems to be Agwawan's main street. Small wooden, cement, and bamboo homes line the sides. Revealing a favorite Philippine pastime that transcends classes, two basketball nets—a court of sorts—occupy a prime position. We stop at what appears to mark Agwawan's central plaza: a simple one-room church and, across the street, a sparsely stocked *sari-sari* store. We are at least a couple of hours late—more the norm than the exception in the rural Philippines, given the lack of transportation and communication and the constant stream of emergencies that accompanies life at the subsistence level. To our surprise, fishers have packed themselves onto the two wooden planks that serve as benches in front of the tiny store. Dangerously rough seas, we discover, have grounded them for the day and they are eagerly awaiting the activity we bring.

After introductions, we move across the street to the church. On the way, an old woman points to the almost bald hills that surround the community to indicate the patches of bananas and *camote* (a root crop similar to a sweet potato) that supplement their meager diets. Inside the church are half a dozen wooden benches and an ample cement floor, enabling the building to double as an all-purpose meeting room.

Word of our arrival has spread quickly, and the church is soon filled with nearly one hundred men, women, and children. Their tattered T-shirts offer glimpses of U.S. culture—"Spring Break Daytona," "Alf"—that seem incongruous in the present setting. Many wear rubber thongs; some are barefoot. (Like fishing boats, footwear—or the lack thereof—is quite revealing of income bracket.)

Since there is no electricity in Agwawan, PRRM has brought a gas-powered generator to run the projector and tape recorder. To turn the church into a projection room, a white sheet is hung over the simple altar, covering the four well-dressed saints who adorn it but leaving visible Christ on the crucifix. Large wooden boards are placed over the windows to block out the light. The people wait patiently as extension cords are arranged and rearranged. Some sit on their rubber sandals; others squat. A young mother breast-feeds her diaperless baby. There is excited chatter and laughter as the Agwawan locals look from us to the slide equipment.

Near us are a couple and a small child who seem typical of the crowd. The man is shoeless, with brown polyester pants that have been torn, mended by hand, retorn, and restitched. His wife wears a mismatched pair of rubber sandals, one held together by string. This is a special day. You can see it in the toothless smiles they flash us and you can hear it in the answers they give to their young daughter's persistent questions about what is going on. For them and for quite a few in the patient audience, this clearly will be their first glimpse of slides.

The slides begin. In photos, graphs, and figures, they describe the Philippine fishing industry, from the huge Japanese trawlers that have depleted fishing banks down to the poorest municipal fishers. At several points during the half-hour show—for example, when the destructive effects of the big trawlers are detailed—several in the crowd react. *"Tama* [correct]," they say aloud to no one in particular, as if completely engrossed in seeing their lives re-flected on the screen.

After the slides have been shown, the boards are taken down from the windows. The stifling heat subsides a bit. Now it is time for the open forum. To lead off, the LAMBAT and PRRM representatives ask for reactions to the slides: "Do the slides tell a story similar to the experience here in Agwawan?" Discussion begins. Later, the LAMBAT organizer describes LAMBAT's experience with fishers elsewhere in Bataan; a young woman from PRRM explains what her NGO is doing as it works with a PO like LAMBAT. Discussion continues.

After many questions and much free-flowing talk, the LAMBAT organizer interjects a pointed question: "*Ano ang dapat gawin?* [What should be done?]" The response comes from a older man: "*Magkaisa tayo.* [Let us unite.]" Another repeats this call. Others nod and, as the nodding spreads, the audience breaks into a chorus of applause.

Yet, as we discovered in San Fernando and Palawan, this is only the beginning. In each of these provinces, citizen action takes on different forms, yet exhibits certain similarities. In Palawan, a national environmental group has joined with local activists to set up a chapter. In San Fernando, people come together in a new, rather spontaneous formation to address a pressing environmental concern. Here in Bataan, well-established NGOs and POs expand their development agendas to include environmental concerns. However different their ancestry, all three sets of citizens' groups are heading in the same direction: toward a new conception of development that has democratic control of natural resources at its core.

1. Northern Palawan. Debbie Hird. As recently as World War II, the more than 7,000 Philippine islands were lavishly endowed with rainforests, coral reefs, fertile lowlands, and extensive mineral deposits. Today, these ecosystems remain intact only in pockets such as the island of Palawan, the country's final frontier.

2. Logging concession, northern Palawan. Debbie Hird. Since World War II, the plunder of Philippine natural resources has been taking place at a rate that is among the fastest in the world. At the current rate of deforestation, the Philippines will enter the twenty-first century a barren landscape, with nearly all its rainforests destroyed. In Palawan, one powerful logger uses connections to local and national politicians to earn millions from his forest concessions.

3. Protesters, Bukidnon, Mindanao. Scarboro Missions. Poor people in the Philippines depend heavily upon forests, fish, minerals, and fertile lands for their livelihood. As the destruction of those resources accelerates, farmers, fishers, and other ordinary Filipinos are becoming environmental activists, acting together to stop the plunder. These peasants from the municipality of San Fernando blockaded logging trucks to protest the adverse environmental impact of commercial logging on their farms and community.

4. Logging trucks stopped by San Fernando picketers, Bukidnon. Scarboro Missions. These logging trucks, loaded with hardwood from Mindanao's vanishing rainforests, were stopped for days by the blockade of the San Fernando protesters. The protesters were demanding the termination of commercial logging in the area; they continue to fight for community control and management of the forest.

5. Street children, Manila. Paul Tañedo. The Philippines is a land of poverty and youth. As many as 7 out of 10 Filipinos live in poverty. Estimates of the number of street children such as these vary widely. A conservative figure for Manila is 75,000; nationwide, there may be as many as 1.2 million.

6. "Smokey Mountain," Manila. Debbie Hird. Thousands of Manila's poor live in a squatter settlement on the edge of the city's largest garbage dump. Most of the residents make their living as scavengers on the trash heap, called "Smokey Mountain" because it smolders in the dry season. Rag-clad children and adults dart in front of bulldozers, grabbing bottles, plastic scraps, pieces of metal, and anything else that can be resold.

7. Garbage dump, Baguio City. Chip Fay. Whether or not they live on the streets, the majority of Filipino children find no recourse but to enter the labor market, despite an official ban on child labor. In urban areas, some beg. Some, such as this boy, are scavengers. Others are self-proclaimed car watchers, who guard your parked car for a peso or so. Still others stitch and embroider fabric.

8. Squatter settlement, Manila. Debbie Hird. Millions in Manila live in make-shift homes that lack both running water and sewers. In this squatter settlement on the edge of one of Manila's rivers, raw waste runs into a biologically dead river and eventually ends up in Manila Bay.

10. Jeepneys, Mindanao. Chip Fay. In the provinces outside Manila, jeepneys such as these are the main form of transport from town to town. Poor roads and inadequate transport and communication facilities make both travel and move-ment of goods and produce extremely difficult in much of the country.

9. Cubao, Manila. Debbie Hird. Manila is among the most polluted and congested cities in the world, bursting at its seams with people who struggle daily with an urban infrastructure in decay. Thousands of buses, tens of thousands of jeepneys, numerous taxis, and an ever-increasing number of private cars spew noxious fumes at commuters and the people who live and work on the streets.

11. Peasant family, Bataan. Paul Tañedo. Most rural families live in simple huts constructed from local materials: wood, bamboo, palm, and *cogon*-grass. These homes offer little protection against the heavy rains and winds of tropical storms.

12. Peasant and *carabao* in rice paddy, northern Luzon. Chip Fay. Rural poverty in the Philippines is largely explained by the unequal distribution of land: less than 20 percent of the population owns 80 percent of the land. This farmer is among the vast majority of Filipinos in the agricultural sector who are not owners of the land they till.

13. Peasants threshing rice, Bataan. Robin Broad. Hope from landless peasants for meaningful agrarian reform met disappointment during the presidency of Corazon Aquino. Early in her administration, 13 peasants were killed when government forces fired upon a land-reform demonstration. Soon thereafter, the government passed a loophole-ridden land-reform bill. In the assessment of one land-reform expert, "the program is likely to redistribute barely 1 percent of the Philippines' cultivated land, with benefits to fewer than 4 percent of the landless."

14. Worker spraying pesticide on cabbage crop, northern Luzon. Debbie Hird. The shift from indigenous rice and corn to cash crops such as cabbage, bananas, and pineapples has led to an explosion in the use of chemical fertilizers and pesticides. This has taken a heavy toll on the land and adjacent rivers, and agricultural workers complain of skin rashes, respiratory disease, pregnancy complications, and sterility.

15. Children fetching water, Puerto Galera, Mindoro. Debbie Hird. Across the Philippines, migration flows, settlements, and people's lives are built around water. As watersheds dry up from overlogging and as sewage and pollutants are dumped into rivers, the search for clean, potable water often requires long daily treks by family members.

16. Fishing village, Palawan. Debbie Hird. After farming, fishing is the second largest source of livelihood in the country, providing a living for as much as one-tenth of the population. Palawan is encircled by the nation's richest fishing grounds; approximately two out of three fish sold in Manila come from its waters.

18. Fishing village, Manila Bay, Bataan. Paul Tañedo. Nationwide, small fishers have watched their annual catch diminished by over 50 percent during this century. In Manila Bay, this shrinkage is a result of such practices as fishpond expansion, unsustainable fishing by large trawlers, and increasing pollution. In many parts of the country, silt from denuded mountains flows down rivers into the seas, smothering coral reefs and thus depleting fish resources.

17. Making fishing nets, near Manila Bay. Debbie Hird. As with farming, benefits from fishing are highly unequal, with the lion's share going to large commercial fishers (many of them foreign) and fishpond owners. Most small-scale fishers, such as this couple, use only hook and line, fish traps, or simple nets, and are among the poorest of Filipinos.

19. Itogon pocket-miner, Benguet. Debbie Hird. For centuries, indigenous pocket-miners have worked mineral veins in small-scale operations that offered a livelihood without threatening the environment. Using technology that has not changed much over the generations, these pocket-miners chisel rocks from mountainsides and transport them to locally owned mills, where minuscule grains of gold are removed.

20. Benguet Corporation's Grand Antamok open-pit mine, Benguet. Chip Fay. Over this last century, giant mining firms, many with significant foreign owner-ship, have received government concessions and begun large-scale operations, with much of the output destined for export. During the past decade, these firms have increasingly shifted from underground to open-pit mines such as this Ben-guet Corporation project, which has threatened the livelihood of the pocket-miners and wreaked environmental havoc. Today in the Grand Antamok area there is crisis, confrontation, and a growing movement challenging the right of the few to mine in a fashion so detrimental to the many.

21. Children from indigenous community, northern Luzon. Debbie Hird. Through the centuries, lowlander migrants—first commercial loggers and big corporations and then, in their wake, subsistence farmers—have pushed many of the indigenous occupants onto marginal lands in more and more fragile ecosystems. But it is these indigenous Filipinos who have traditionally lived sustainably in the forests.

22. Indigenous peoples' protest, central Luzon. Chip Fay. Despite having long been forest occupants, millions of indigenous people in the uplands are technically squatters on public land. Many indigenous communities are today struggling for survival, demanding recognition of their ancestral domain, including rights to lands lost

23. Mount Apo, Mindanao. Chip Fay. A dramatic instance of indigenous peoples'
resistance to encroachment on age-old forests is the struggle against a government
geothermal energy project on Mount Apo, the site of the last major forest cover
in south-central Mindanao. This Bagobo mother and child stand in front of a
geothermal test-well that has been dug on their ancestral land. The Bagobo and
others of Mindanao's indigenous peoples have signed an intertribal compact to
defend Mount Apo against the project.

24. Monument to Ferdinand Marcos on the road to Baguio. Chip Fay. As monuments such as this remind Filipinos, much of the plunder of Philippine resources occurred during the two-decade reign of Ferdinand Marcos. But the early exuberance that ushered in Corazon Aquino's administration has given way to a conviction that little will change until a government comes to power that is willing to challenge the control of the few over the country's land, forest, and marine resources.

25. Central plaza, Balanga, Bataan. John Cavanagh. Fifty years ago, Philippine and U.S. troops fought side by side in this Bataan town and across the province to stall the Japanese conquest of the archipelago. Today, Filipinos and Americans in new citizens' organizations are again working together in Bataan and elsewhere, this time to advance equitable, participatory, and environmentally sustainable development.

26. Protest rally, Manila. Debbie Hird. As Corazon Aquino's presidency neared its end, the Philippine Senate voted to expel two large U.S. military bases, for almost one hundred years the centerpiece of U.S. interests there. Large demonstrations such as this one by citizens' organizations helped build pressure for removal of the bases. Several of these groups are now demanding that the United States government clean up vast quantities of toxic wastes dumped and buried at the bases.

27. Children, Bataan. Paul Tañedo. "There is one dream that all Filipinos share: that our children may have a better life than we have had. So there is one vision that is distinctly Filipino: the vision to make this country, our country, a nation for our children" (the late human-rights advocate, Senator Jose W. Diokno, speech delivered October 12, 1984).

Chapter Six

The Wall

Free trade zones are like Hilton Hotels. When you're inside one, you don't know what country you're in, and the hassles of the country don't touch you. It's the businessman's dream. And the workers are polite and obedient and almost look alike—sometimes you wonder if they're Mexicans, Filipinos, Malays or Arabs.

American businessman in Seoul, South Korea, quoted in Australia Asia Worker Links, "Denzil Don in the Philippines: Dunlop Moves to Asia," Case Study No. 1, Fitzroy, Australia, 1981

If developing nations focus their efforts upon eliminating poverty and satisfying essential human needs, then domestic demand will increase for both agricultural products and manufactured goods and some services. Hence, the very logic of sustainable development implies an internal stimulus to Third World growth.

World Commission on Environment and Development, *Our Common Future* (New York: Oxford University Press, 1987), pp. 51–52

From the hill high above Bataan's southernmost town of Mariveles, the 1,209-hectare Bataan Export Processing Zone (BEPZ) appears like an oasis in the distance: a miniature modern industrial park. Rectangular buildings dot what seems to be a neatly laid out grid of streets, dwarfing the small, crowded fishing village beyond. Less than a mile offshore stands the tadpole-shaped island fortress of Corregidor, or the Rock, as it is called fondly by World War II veterans.

It was Corregidor that withstood another month of constant Japanese bombardment after Bataan fell on April 9, 1942. And it was from the Rock that General Jonathan Wainwright (left in command when General Douglas MacArthur was submarined to safety) signed the total surrender of the Philippines on May 6, 1942. The industrial zone itself occupies the spot where the Bataan surrender took place and from which, in the broiling tropical summertime sun, tens of thousands of U.S. and Philippine soldiers began their nightmarish march of death.

We descend the zigzag road to the zone in a rickety old wooden mini-bus carrying many more passengers than there are seats. Above the dashboard is a square compartment, draped with dried yellow chrysanthemum-like flowers and housing a plastic figurine of a white-skinned saint. Pasted on either side of the altar is a colorful sticker, some variation of which adorns almost every mode of public transport in this country. Beseeches the sticker on the left, "Bless our trip, O Lord, we pray. Make it safe by night and day." Its companion sticker on the right: "Driver Is Good Lover." Not unlike Mexico, from whence the Spanish administered their Philippine colony for several centuries, the Philippines is an intricate blend of Catholicism and machismo.

Most of the passengers on the early morning bus are women in their twenties on their way to work in the factories below. When the Marcos government launched the industrial zones in the early 1970s, it claimed they would attract foreign investors to Philippine shores and thereby provide employment and skills for a new generation of workers.

BEPZ was the first of these special zones. And building it was no minor effort, as the government itself boasted in an advertisement in *Fortune* magazine in 1975: "To attract companies like yours, we have felled mountains, razed jungles, filled swamps, moved rivers, relocated towns, and in their place built power plants, dams, roads."[1] The price tag just to build the zone in 1973 came to nearly $200 million.[2]

But what BEPZ promises investors is more than just "felled mountains" and "razed jungles." Tax breaks and an array of incentives are offered by the Philippine government to U.S., Japanese, and other firms that import such semi-processed materials as cloth and semiconductor chips into the zone and use cheap, Philippine labor to sew shirts, wire semiconductors, assemble cabin cruisers, and carry out other such labor-intensive assembly activities. The processed goods, too expensive for the majority of Filipinos, are then exported back to foreign markets. Most of the new generation of workers were young women like those on our bus—advertised to the foreign firms as more meticulous in tedious assembly work, more docile, and less likely to organize unions.

Former president Ferdinand Marcos pinned his hopes for the industrialization of the Philippines on these zones, particularly on Bataan, the largest. By 1980, over fifty foreign and Philippine-owned firms had set up shop in the Bataan zone, churning out millions of dollars' worth of doors for Ford vehicles, clothes for Barbie dolls, Dunlop tennis balls, Nike sneakers, and other famous brand-name products. On a hill not far from the zone, Marcos built one of his most luxurious vacation homes; his wife, Imelda, is reported to have imported white sand from Australia to beautify the nearby beach. The Aquino government has likewise continued to favor the zones, embarking on an expansion drive that originally aimed to increase the number of firms in the zones to 150 by 1992.[3]

Although, across Asia and Latin America, the export processing zone was predominantly a 1970s phenomenon, the development vision it encompasses is in many ways nothing new. Indeed, government acquiescence in integrating the Philippines as a junior partner into the world economy dates back to the 1640s, when the Spanish forced each Filipino in certain areas of the country to plant 100–200 coconut trees to provide caulking and rigging for the galleon trade.[4] In succeeding centuries, fertile lands were shifted from food crops to tobacco, hemp, sugar, and other cash crops for export.[5] The process has continued to be repeated over the decades up to the present, with the banana and pineapple "booms" in Mindanao in the 1970s, and with prawns in the 1980s.

But not only Philippine agriculture was affected. The world economy brought similarly momentous changes to industry as early as the late 1800s. Just as the British were destroying the textile industries of India, Persia, and elsewhere with imported fabrics, so they were undermining what were then surprisingly advanced handwoven textile industries in such urban centers as Iloilo in the central Philippine island of Panay. In Iloilo, as described by historian Alfred McCoy, the textile merchants were encouraged to shift their capital to sugarcane plantations in Negros.[6] In other words, in Philippine agriculture, economic activity was reoriented to serve the world market; where industry existed, it was eliminated to make way for industrial goods from the West.

U.S. and Philippine trade legislation in 1909 helped to solidify this outward orientation of the Philippine economy: that is, industrial goods were to be imported and, to earn foreign exchange to pay for those goods, agricultural products had to be exported. The trade acts allowed United States manufactures into the Philippines duty free and permitted Philippine sugar, coconut products, hemp, and tobacco almost totally unrestricted entry into the U.S. market.[7]

Today, the tragic consequences of unintegrated development are overpowering. Take the state of the fiber, textile, and apparel sector, for example. Instead of spinning Philippine cotton on Philippine spinning machines, weaving the yarn on Philippine looms, and sewing the cut cloth into shirts and dresses in Philippine factories to produce affordable clothing for Filipinos, the Philippine sector looks something like the following: the Philippines produces small amounts of cotton and synthetic fibers (a large share of which is exported), but not enough to service the underdeveloped spinning, weaving, and knitting industries that make up the textile industry. These industries must spend scarce foreign exchange on imports of these fibers, despite the fact that several areas of the Philippines could readily produce more cotton.

In turn, the small textile industry can service only a third of the cloth needs of the garment industry, which is geared primarily toward exports. The garment industry itself is large and growing, but consists mainly of sweatshops, where laborers who are denied basic worker rights produce for foreign buyers. It is an industry that blatantly serves foreign over local interests. But it is not unique in this country; a similar story can be told for the other main industrial export sector, semiconductors.[8]

In this approach to development, the emphasis has been on exporting products at minimum cost to the rich markets of the West and, more recently, Japan. Unlike the philosophy of Henry Ford, who believed the ability of Ford workers to buy the cars they built was key to the company's long-term viability, that of the crafters of the Philippine development plan does not view the majority of Filipinos as potential consumers of these products. The lack of an agricultural or industrial policy that serves domestic needs, let alone a policy that integrates agriculture with industry, leaves the majority of Filipinos unable to buy the most basic industrial products. Meanwhile, the ample fertile lands of the Philippines are feeding the consumers of the West and Japan while Filipinos starve.

The integration of only certain segments of the economy into the

world economy results in the three-tiered society so insightfully
described by Philippine economist Sixto K. Roxas. As he eluci-
dates, 30 percent of the population, in the cities and the export
enclaves, are linked to the world economy, while the remaining 55
percent in rural areas and 15 percent of indigenous peoples slide
backward:

The first tier is often described as if it were the entire country when it is a
minority. This is a dangerous error. Because of the lack of integration, it is
possible for the first tier to show great progress while the conditions in
the other two tiers continue to deteriorate. . . .

It is a dangerous duality. The prosperity in the first tier exacerbates the
misery in the other two. The first tier produces delusions of national prosperity. The other two breed migrations into the cities and towns, formation of squatter colonies, insurgency in the hills and mountains, destruction of the environment.[9]

Furthermore, Roxas and others argue, the enclave economy has
not worked particularly well even in the enclaves. The only real
dynamism in them since the mid–1980s has been in a real estate,
construction, and retail boom, much of the benefit of which has
gone to investors from Taiwan and elsewhere in Asia.[10]

As our overcrowded mini-bus completes its slow descent to the Bataan export zone, we get a much better look at this enclave.
Up close, it presents a startling contrast to the view from the hill
above. We pass two large factory buildings, seemingly abandoned,
windows smashed, paint peeling, and surrounded by overgrown
grass and weeds. The first, we are later told, was a Singaporean-
Indonesian-Filipino cocoa-processing factory; the second, the
sprawling Ford stamping plant that had been the flagship factory in
the zone before Ford transferred operations to even lower-wage
China.

Finally, we drive by an operational factory, Dunlop Slazenger,
which produces 25,000 tennis balls a day for Australia, for the elite
of Southeast Asia and for Boris Becker and Steffi Graf to blast across
the nets at Wimbledon.[11] But even this building looks run down, in
need of a new paint job.

By knocking on the bus ceiling, we signal the driver to stop at
the administration building, the most luxurious and modern of the
structures we have seen. Outside the building, beyond a large and

almost empty parking lot, is a grassy knoll that serves as a helicopter pad for potential investors who prefer not to spend three hours driving here from Manila. At the building's entrance, an armed security guard stands beside a plaque dedicating the building to then-president Marcos "and the First Lady in recognition of their sincere desire to improve the economic condition and quality of life of the Filipino and in creating [*sic*] a New Society, where labor and dignity can stand side by side."

The guard greets us as would-be investors and points beyond the spacious, empty foyer toward the second-floor office of the zone administrator. Administrator Raphael Miñoza is expecting us, his secretary informs us, but he is not yet in. She suggests we spend some time at a large wood-paneled display just outside the office that advertises the merits of investing in the zone: "Strategic location . . . competitive wage rates . . . low cost of living . . . full government support . . . sophisticated managerial and technical personnel . . . direct telephone, telegraph and telex lines to major cities of the world."

Nearby, glass-topped display cases show off some of the current products of the zone: yellow-green Dunlop tennis balls, Reebok sneakers with their British-flag logo (produced here, we later discover, by a Korean-Filipino-U.S. company that also makes Adidas, which are then exported to compete with one another in retail stores throughout the United States and Europe), Flint disposable lighters, many varieties of industrial gloves made by the U.S.-owned Manila Glove, and so on.

We have absorbed all the display has to offer, but the zone administrator still has not arrived. We are escorted into the Information Promotion Division and offered the first of three Coca-Colas we will be given this morning. (The alternative is a cup of lukewarm instant Nescafé, which, as the standard morning fare of most Third World coffee drinkers, has helped propel Nestlé to a position among the world's largest multinational corporations.) We are clearly presumed *not* to be able to understand as, addressing the secretary in Tagalog, the information officer politely protests the unscheduled meeting. A potential Japanese investor will be arriving by helicopter within the hour and there are still preparations to be made.

To the relief of all, the administrator (officially the "officer-in-charge" or acting administrator) arrives soon after the information officer has begun to entertain us by reading aloud from a prepared text. Her few minutes of recitation reveal that 23 firms, employing 15,800 workers, are currently operating in the zone, down from more than 50 firms and close to 27,000 workers less than a decade ago.

The young officer-in-charge greets us from behind a large, semi-circular, glass-topped desk on which rest four telephones and an intercom. Raphael Miñoza must be used to visitors commenting on the phones: as he reaches across the desk to shake hands, he quickly tells us that one phone does not work and another is a direct line to Manila. He must also be accustomed to foreign visitors' difficulties with his first name, for it is shortened to Ralph on the calling card he hands us.

Mr. Miñoza explains the reduction in the number of firms in the zone by ticking off a grocery list of problems that he says have now largely been solved. Telephone lines were hard to get. Power outages were frequent. Although a special labor code had been crafted for the zone to guarantee a no-strike labor force, during the course of the 1980s, organized labor launched a series of crippling strikes that culminated in zonewide general strikes in 1982 and 1987. It was this last strike (during which one worker and one child were killed when government troops fired on the strikers) that led to the dismissal of Mr. Miñoza's predecessor.[12]

Not all the problems have been resolved, he admits: "Because of the 'peace-and-order' situation, there are a number of military checkpoints along the way here that aren't really good for our promotion. They [the potential investors] feel that it must be a war zone."

Visibly uncomfortable talking about negatives, Miñoza leads us to a miniature model of the zone that hangs on the far wall of his vast office. "You know, this zone is a mini-city in itself," he begins as he points to the various structures. "We have to provide our own housing, commercial and recreational facilities, power, sewage and garbage disposal. . . . Really this is a very expensive zone. We've had to construct a small city to attract foreign investors. That's a very ambitious thing." He points out a hundred-bed hospital, a cinema, a bowling alley, schools. There is even a half-finished airport runway that the zone authority was building for Mattel—until the company decided to pack up its Barbie-doll machines and move on to Thailand.

We ask Miñoza what the "mini-city" has meant for the rest of Bataan. What have been the benefits? He tells us that some of the workers are from the province, that "our [zone] fire trucks were there when several fires erupted" outside the zone and that, because of the zone, a concrete road links Bataan to the next province.

Overall, however, the picture that emerges is of an enclave largely removed from the economy of Bataan and with only minimal connections to the larger Philippine economy. As Miñoza himself explains, firms in the zone import almost all the machinery and materials used in production, export almost all their final product, and, if you subtract the import costs from the export revenue, do not leave much "value-added" in the Philippines. Miñoza does not specify, but other studies have calculated value-added to be as little as 40 percent in the Philippine garment industry and even less in electronics. In 1989, the Bataan zone overall actually spent more foreign exchange on imports than it earned through its exports.[13]

Property tax on the firms is minimal and is split three ways: half to the zone, one-quarter to the town of Mariveles, in which the zone is officially located, and one-quarter to the province. Nor is the zone a source of much corporate income-tax revenue. This is partially due to generous tax breaks, which the Philippine government claims helped attract the firms in the first place. In addition, the companies appear adept at making these already liberal concessions even more beneficent. As World Bank consultant Peter Warr discovered, "Many firms [in the Philippine zones] have declared losses every year for over a decade while still producing and, in some cases, expanding operations considerably. It is well understood that vertically integrated firms utilize transfer pricing to relocate their profits internationally."[14]

Provincial authorities later tell us that the zone's impact on Bataan's estimated 50 percent combined unemployment and underemployment rate is less than might be expected. Fewer than 30 percent of the zone's workers, they estimate, are from Bataan.[15] Why, then, we ask, did Bataan officials want to turn the fishing village of Mariveles into the export processing zone, if its employment and tax benefits were only marginal? Efren Pascual, governor of Bataan when the zone was created, tosses aside our question with a wave of his hand. He had no role in setting up the zone, he explains. "In projects like this, the provincial government isn't even consulted."

We walk out of the administration building, past what must be the Japanese visitor's helicopter, and head toward a wall that was built to separate the zone from the town of Mariveles. Such a wall is an integral feature of the zone concept, as Warr's study for the World Bank explains: "An EPZ consists of a heavily fenced area with a perimeter and gates. . . . Policing is necessary to prevent duty-free materials from being smuggled into the domestic economy."[16] The fence protecting BEPZ from the outside world is a long, concrete wall, ten to twelve feet in height, with a metal gate leading to the town of Mariveles. To reach the town from the north, vehicles must pass through the zone, with guarded gates at each end. The guards carefully inspect the identification cards workers must display to walk inside the zone.

Just outside the gate stands the "zero-kilometer marker," a monument to the spot where the Death March began. An old man is bent over, tediously clipping the grass by hand. He wears a baseball cap with the slogan "I ♥ BEPZ." (Many of the caps and T-shirts one sees in the provinces carry the emblem of a soft drink, tobacco, fertilizer, or other company, passed out free or at reduced prices as part of countryside advertising campaigns.) Clearly pleased to see visitors, the old man accompanies us to the monument, which consists of a commemorative plaque and a simple metal sculpture of a soldier's helmet resting atop a bayonet.

The old man, it turns out, is the monument's caretaker, a job that, he tells us, earns him the equivalent of $1.50 a day. On the other side of the wall, the average laborer in the zone pulls in over double this but still earns under half the poverty level for a family of six.

For most of the 1980s, Philippine real wages declined.[17] As the World Bank admitted toward the end of that decade, the combination of "declining real wages and labor earnings" with high levels of underemployment and unemployment "resulted in an increase in poverty in terms of labor income." As a result, by 1985 the Philippines had one of the most unequal income distributions in the

Third World: the top 10 percent of the population earned more than 15 times the income of the poorest 10 percent.[18]

From the zero-kilometer marker at the wall, we flag down a tricycle and negotiate the price of a ride to the Mariveles mayor's office in the center of the town proper. In places like Bataan, jeepneys provide transportation from town to town, but tricycles—motorbikes with a sidecar—are the main form of transport within rural towns and villages. The going rate is the equivalent of a nickel per person, but foreigners typically have to make it clear that they know this or the price can shoot up tenfold. Each tricycle can accommodate two people relatively comfortably but at times as many as eight passengers cram onto the tricycle: four inside the sidecar, two standing behind or on top of the sidecar, and two more sitting sidesaddle behind the driver on his motorcycle.

Mayor Oscar delos Reyes's office, like the other six mayors' offices we visit in Bataan, is located on the second floor of a small, overcrowded town hall. As we sip our first Coke of the afternoon, the mayor gives us some background about himself. He is just over forty, a former seventh-grade teacher who decided to run for mayor in 1988 (in the first post-Marcos local elections) without the backing of any national party. "So I was elected against all odds," he chuckles. "The only party I had was my birthday party."

Mayor delos Reyes becomes serious upon hearing that our previous meetings were with zone officials. Relations with the zone are an obvious sore point in his reign as mayor. "The officer-in-charge [of the zone] is a mayor in another republic," delos Reyes fumes. "We are second-class citizens in the zone. We, the city managers, are powerless in the zone."

He briefs us on the intricacies of Marcos's Presidential Decree 66, which set up the Export Processing Zone Authority soon after Marcos declared martial law in September of 1972. The decree (amended on numerous occasions) not only provided special rules for the export processing zones on issues that ranged from labor laws to taxes but also set up a structure so that zone officials would report to national government authorities in Manila rather than to local officials.

The mayor ticks off the number of times he has lobbied officials in Manila to give him more authority inside the zone, since it lies within the municipal boundaries of Mariveles. "At the very least," he says, "the mayor should have a representative on the board of administrators. Right now, when we talk to zone authorities, we talk to the wilderness, to the fish and to the dogs, who cannot really respond properly."

It is not fair to his relatively poor constituents, he continues, to have in the zone such facilities as a modern hospital "with very sophisticated equipment" but with medical services priced beyond the reach of most of his people. Even emergency cases from Mariveles, he laments, are often brought to the public hospital one hour away. "All the best and good things are inside the zone and only a few ever come out," he tells us. "I want to tear down that wall."

Just a short walk down the main street from the mayor's office is the headquarters of the zone's strongest labor union, affiliated nationally with the Kilusang Mayo Uno (May First Movement). Beneath banners proclaiming greetings from workers in Japan, we talk first with a male labor leader who helped organize a successful general strike in the Bataan zone in 1982, and then with several other union members.

Most of the union members are young women, wearing makeup, jeans, and T-shirts proclaiming the name of the factory in which they are employed. Like many Filipinas, they are soft-spoken, modest, and reluctant to talk about themselves. But when prodded, they speak forcefully of the low wages, lack of job security, and what they describe as persistent efforts by management to bust their unions. They describe with alarm a new phenomenon becoming commonplace in the zone: management fires some regular workers, who earn about $3.70 per day plus benefits, and instead farms out that work to smaller factories near the zone where non-unionized women earn just $2.50 a day with no benefits. Sometimes the work is subcontracted to individual women working out of their homes. This tactic, the union members explain, is particularly prevalent among the apparel firms, which account for half of the zone's exports in 1988.

One twenty-five-year-old woman is encouraged by the labor leader to tell us her story. Four months before, her company, claiming a slowdown in orders from overseas, laid off nearly a hundred workers, including many union members. A month later, new orders came in, but rather than rehire the workers, the company "farmed them out instead" as homework to nonregular, nonunion workers in Mountain View, a nearby village. To protest, the regular workers decided to block the vehicles that transported the fabric to the village. "We formed a human barricade against two six-wheel vans," she recounts. "There were military, zone police with truncheons and guns. We were crying already. Many were hurt. But they were able to get the vans out. We were so very disappointed. Then, escorted by some military, management carried out some important papers, then padlocked the factory, and then announced that the plant is shut down."

According to the Manila-based economic research group Ibon Databank, such U.S. retailers as J.C. Penney procure increasing amounts of their clothing from the Philippines through such subcontracting arrangements. The system allows maximum flexibility for the retailer, since orders can quickly be increased or decreased without any need to worry about the demands of organized labor.

But from the standpoint of the full-time workers to whom we talk in Mariveles, the system is a direct assault on workers' rights. "We're not against the workers at Mountain View," the young woman adds quickly. "They need work too. We talked to the management and we said, 'If you need the workers at Mountain View, you just hire them' [as regular workers]."

Hearing these complaints, we ask if the workers share the mayor's dream of tearing down the cement wall that separates the zone from the town. "He can tear down the physical wall," a union official responds, "but the wall of Presidential Decree 66 remains. The place is not the problem. The strategy is. We are asking the government to produce goods that Filipinos need. What does the Philippines get from sewing a sleeve on a jacket, from assembling a two-way radio or cassette? We can't even make a nail, although iron ore is mined here to be transported to Japan."

In the provincial capital of Balanga, Governor Leonardo "Ding" Roman is proud to talk about the Bataan Export Processing Zone. He turns around to face the wall behind him and points to a portrait of his late father, who represented Bataan in the pre–martial-law Philippine Congress. "My father visited Taiwan in the 1960s," the governor tells us. "He was very impressed with the special industrial zone he saw there." Upon his return home, he became a vocal proponent of similar zones in the Philippines. Marcos abolished the Congress when he declared martial law in 1972, but his presidential decree setting up the zones began the implementation of ideas similar to those advanced by the governor's father.

The governor's conversation shifts from the topic of the zone to another Taiwan-related issue: a proposed petrochemical plant that, at the time of our visit, Taiwanese investors are considering building in Bataan. It would be the first petrochemical complex in the Philippines. Whereas his father had traveled to Taiwan to see industrial zones, the governor recently flew to Taiwan to investigate petrochemical plants similar to the one being considered by the Taiwanese for the Philippines.

When we ask provincial and local officials about Bataan's future, the petrochemical plant and prawns are the favored topics of almost all. The petrochemical plant, Ding Roman and the others claim, would be the biggest industrial investment ever made in the country and would provide a new engine of growth. According to the governor's figures, the plant itself would create 1,000 new jobs, with as many as 25,000 more in downstream plants where the petrochemicals would be shaped into synthetic fibers and plastics. Despite the fact that, at the time of our visit, the Taiwanese investors have yet to make a decision about whether to build their plant here or in the nearby province of Batangas, most officials in Bataan are pinning their hopes on it. Typical is one mayor who tells us dejectedly of his town's unemployment problem and confides, "I'm praying that this petrochemical plant will come."[19]

Only one official with whom we meet indicates mixed feelings about the desirability of the venture. This is Ditas Consunji, a dynamic young mother of six and a provincial board member (a position roughly equivalent to that of a state legislator). Consunji tells us that she joined the governor's delegation to Taiwan and made a point of talking to people other than the potential investors. She was told that Taiwan had four plants similar to the proposed Philippine plant and that the Taiwanese government would allow no more such plants to be built there. The problem, one Taiwanese official reportedly informed her, was that Taiwan had spent up to $300 million cleaning up pollution from the plants.

Consunji admits to being torn between the petrochemical plant's promise of jobs and what she fears will be a similar detrimental impact on Bataan's environment. "For me, it's so difficult to make an assessment at this point. Right now the plant is only an idea. What kind of employment will it bring? Will there also be down-stream jobs? How do we know all this in advance? . . . The employment aspect is very tempting. But how come no one is discussing the problems?"

We ask the governor and other officials about the potential environmental problems of the petrochemical plant, but no one else considers them a worry. A local official in Balanga acknowledges that there may be reason for misgivings. But, he concludes, "First things first. We need jobs. We'll worry about pollution later. If we could worry about the two at once, we would. But we can't afford to."

It is precisely this sort of short-sighted reasoning against which many Filipinos are arguing and organizing. In an article entitled "Blueprint for a Banana Republic," economist Sixto Roxas writes:

By following a strategy of creating enclave industrial estates and export processing zones, the country is marginalizing whole rural populations. . . . The displacement creates colonies of miserable, impoverished populations. . . .

The growing pool of misery [breeds] dissatisfaction, unrest and revolution. The countervailing answer of the government and the elite is to expand the Armed Forces, and militarize the civilian population.[20]

This militarization has transformed the struggle for development in the Philippines quite literally into a struggle of life and death.

Chapter Seven

Hearts and Minds

The government is winning the hearts and minds of the people. We see the light at the end of the tunnel. We can see victory ahead.

> Philippine Defense Secretary Fidel Ramos, quoted in Red Batario and Girlie Alvarez, "1M Have Fled Homes to Escape Fighting," *Philippine Daily Inquirer*, August 8, 1990

To the soldiers, we would like to sound this appeal: if you sincerely take the interests of the ordinary people [to] heart, we would like to see you defending the small farmers, fishers and workers instead of the landlords, the big fishpond owners, the big loggers, the big businessmen and the big gambling lords. We look forward to that day when you shall be one with us in fighting the common enemy of peace and just development.

> Attorney Dante Ilaya, chairperson, BAYAN–Bataan Chapter, quoted in *National Midweek* 5 (June 6, 1990), p. 36

Our original schedule called for a courtesy call and interview with Bataan's governor on our first day in the province. Upon our arrival at the provincial capitol building for that midafternoon meeting, however, we are informed that Governor Leonardo "Ding" Roman has made other plans. He has been called to witness an historic event: the first professional basketball game in the history of the province is about to begin. As foreign visitors, we are asked to be special guests at the event. The interview will have to wait.

Teenage girls in their school uniforms—some in green and white outfits with green neckties, others in dark blue skirts with white blouses—line the main street of the provincial capital, Balanga, a town of about 50,000. An air-conditioned bus drives slowly down the street. The windows are tinted against the tropical sun so that only the outlines of the passengers are visible. Nonetheless, the girls scream wildly. "It's one of the teams," a mother explains. Military escorts surround the bus, keeping the streets cleared of the jubilant fans. The screams reach a crescendo as the second darkened bus—the other team—crawls by.

As the mother, who is giggling as excitedly as her daughters, tells us, basketball stars in this country are on a par with movie stars. And though Bataan is less than three hours by bus from Manila, visitors like this are few and far between. Indeed, this is the first time either she or her daughters have seen professional basketball players up close.

Accompanied by provincial government officials, we make our way through the fans to the town's youth center. There we are greeted by Lt. Col. Arsenio Tecson, who stands out in front in full uniform, pistol bulging at his hip. "Just call me Tec," he says. He points to the nickname blazoned across his cap and then holds out his hand to us. As Tec is happy to explain, he is the commander of an army battalion of six hundred men sent to Bataan just over a month earlier to help "clean up" the insurgency.

We are not the only ones who get a warm greeting from Tec. In a gesture common among Filipino men who are good friends or long-time drinking buddies, Tec slaps a town mayor on the rear end. He greets other mayors, provincial board members, and distinguished citizens in general by first names and easily slips into animated and friendly chitchat. It strikes us as a marked contrast to the reputation of many of Marcos's military officers, who were seen as aloof and abusive.

Inside the youth center, a prominently displayed banner announces the event: "The Bataan Tourism Council and the Provincial Government Proudly Present a Dream Match of the Year." The governor's young wife, who is dressed entirely in white for today's event, heads the private-sector Bataan Tourism Council. She tosses up the ceremonial opening tip-off and the game is under way.

The contending teams are Purefoods Hotdogs and Presto Ice Cream. Filipinos' love for basketball is but one of the many vestiges of a half-century of American colonial rule. In the Philippines, however, the teams are named for the big corporations that own them: Añejo rum, Shell oil, San Miguel beer, and so on. The games, generally played in Manila, come to the provinces on television and radio. In addition, video stores throughout the country contain a relatively well-stocked basketball section where major matches from the U.S. National Basketball Association can be rented. Still a luxury, video machines are beginning to spread even to rural areas—often purchased in duty-free shops by returning overseas workers. The Los Angeles Lakers' Magic Johnson was long the local favorite, with the Celtics' Larry Bird a close second.

But for the teenagers of Balanga, the clear favorite of the moment is young Purefoods star Alvin Patrimonio, who is widely reported in the gossip pages of Manila's twenty-odd newspapers to have had a brief fling with Cory Aquino's youngest daughter, Kris. Whenever Patrimonio gets the ball, the small hall shakes with screams: "Alvin! Alvin!"

We are seated at mid-court, between Colonel Tecson and the mayor of Pilar, a nearby municipality where some of the fiercest battles in World War II's Bataan campaign were waged. Another mayor shares Colonel Tecson's chair. As the game progresses, Tec keeps up a stream of commentary to us about his work, past and present. He is quite at home in the United States, he brags, since he was based there for a time in the 1970s, first in charge of security at the Philippines' New York properties (including, presumably, the infamous ones whose ownership was contested in U.S. courts) and then as a military bodyguard of presidential daughter Imee Marcos while she studied at Princeton. Discovering that we too are Princeton alumni, Tec remembers with fondness his favorite Princeton pancake house on Nassau Street and recounts with some pride how he researched a few of Imee's papers at the university's Firestone Library. We subsequently ascertain that Tec was once so close to Marcos's righthand man General Fabian Ver that he remained a Marcos loyalist up to the moment when the former president was helicoptered out of Malacañang Palace in February of 1986. (Later, in 1990, we learn that Tec has been jailed as one of the participants in the December, 1989, military coup against Aquino, the sixth attempted coup and the one that some say would have succeeded had not the United States come to Aquino's assistance.)

But today Tec has other concerns. He talks with conviction about his counter-insurgency assignment in Bataan. "Winning this war is not just a matter of killing," he says before stating the cliché that will be repeated by two of the three other colonels we interview. "You have to win the hearts and minds." At halftime, he elaborates: "We have to convince people that we are just like them. . . . That's our job. I might be talking to [a member of the insurgent New People's Army] and I wouldn't know it. So I always have to assume I am talking to an NPA. But by how I act, by what I say, I may be able to convince him that I am just like him."

By now it is getting dark outside and several bats have entered the hall, which is open at the sides, and are swirling above the basketball court. As we look around the packed hall, we realize that we could be sitting in a high school gymnasium in small-town U.S.A., were it not for the bats—and for a number of young, well-muscled men leaning on high-powered rifles which they nonchalantly point upward toward the crowd (an unnerving and inexplicable position assumed also by armed security guards at banks and other establishments throughout the Philippines).

The heavy military presence in Bataan exists in response to the largest and longest-standing revolutionary movement in Asia. Organized resistance to ruling authorities has a long history in the Philippines and in this province. As the "Brief History" section of a provincial government report on Bataan puts it: "Bataan was among the first provinces to rise in revolt against Spanish tyranny."[1] One Bataan resident recounts with pride an incident that occurred in his town in 1787. In protest against the Spanish monopoly of tobacco-growing, Bataan tobacco farmers attacked a Spanish military force. The Spaniards retaliated brutally: they hanged and quartered the rebellion's leaders and displayed their heads on stakes.[2]

A century later, Bataeños (people of the province) joined tens of thousands of Filipinos to fight off Spanish colonial rule. After the United States grabbed the colonial mantle from Spain at the turn of the century, somewhere between a quarter- and a half-million Filipinos were killed while resisting the new invaders. From the 1930s to the early 1950s, a peasant-based movement known as the Huks rose in the central rice-plains of the main Philippine island of Luzon to fight for the overthrow of the largely feudal agrarian structure. Substantial U.S. assistance, under the leadership of Col. Edward Landsdale, helped defeat the Huks. Indeed, the CIA looks back upon the anti-Huk campaign as its first major Third World counter-insurgency success and as a model for its strategy in Vietnam.[3]

The current wave of revolution began in 1968, when student activist Jose Maria Sison and a small group of colleagues launched the

Communist Party of the Philippines, followed quickly by the establishment of an armed wing, the New People's Army (NPA). Fueled
by high poverty rates and gross inequality, the insurgency grew
rapidly across the archipelago. The movement received some material aid from the People's Republic of China until the mid–1970s,
but since then has developed largely free of foreign influence. According to various estimates, by the late 1980s the Communist
Party had somewhere between 20,000 and 35,000 members; it is
said to have "influence" in one out of every four or five villages in
the country.[4] This influence is obvious in rural areas, where Filipinos often refer to the NPA as the "*Nice People Around*"—only half-
kiddingly.

The Communist Party and the NPA are members of a broader
left coalition called the National Democratic Front (NDF), which
includes a number of activist organizations: of peasants, workers,
the church, students, teachers, and women. The NDF and its com-
posite organizations have been declared illegal by the government
and so, like the Communist Party itself, they function underground.[5]

In addition to this illegal or underground left, there is what Filipinos refer to as "the legal left," a wide variety of progressive organizations not affiliated with the NDF. Most of these share some of
the NDF's goals for "genuine" land reform, industrialization by and
for Filipinos, a nonaligned foreign policy, and a "democratic coalition government" wherein workers and peasants are represented.
Unlike the NDF, these legal groups organize and operate in the
open.

Having spread steadily under the repression of Marcos, the illegal left mistakenly threw its weight behind a boycott of the 1986
"snap elections" that they believed Marcos would steal as he had
done in the past. As millions of people took to the streets to bring
Corazon Aquino to power, the illegal left was relegated to the side-
lines. This error was followed by a honeymoon period during which
Aquino released Sison and other movement leaders from Marcos's
prisons. Then, in late 1986, to the enormous discontent of her military, Aquino opened a short-lived ceasefire with the NDF. It was
in this context that we first heard of the town of Samal, Bataan: one
day during the ceasefire, large numbers of armed NPA soldiers pa-

raded through the streets of Samal, to the obvious glee of local inhabitants and foreign photojournalists, the latter snapping photos that appeared in newspapers and magazines throughout the world. However, the display and the camaraderie infuriated the military and, as the officers we interview explain to us, were seen as a symbol of what had to be crushed in Bataan.

By late 1987, after the ceasefire broke down and five military coups were attempted against her government, the president decided to let the military run the counter-insurgency as its generals saw fit. For Bataan, this translated into the current "hearts and minds" campaign. By the end of the 1980s, the province had more soldiers per inhabitant than any of the country's other seventy-two provinces—a distinction it had not enjoyed since the fierce battle for Bataan in 1942. Says one Bataan resident with a chuckle, "How many military are there in Bataan? Well, I don't know. But there are so many that if you smoke a cigarette in Bataan and throw away your butt, it is likely to land on the shoulders of a [government] military."

Our formal briefing on the strategy the military has adopted takes place in the austere and hastily built headquarters of the 702d Infantry Brigade of the Philippine Army the morning after the basketball game. (Purefoods won, 136–128.) The deputy brigade commander is a last-minute substitute for his boss, who has been called out to battle. A young soldier wearing regulation khaki pants and a T-shirt with "Born to Kill" on the front and "Philippine Army" on the back serves us frozen beers, which erupt when opened, like seventh-grade science-fair volcanoes fueled by vinegar and baking soda. Whatever the intent, the result is a liberal soaking of our notes from the previous day.

According to the deputy commander, "the enemy has a hold on" at least 25 percent of Bataan's *barangays*, neighborhoods typically made up of 1,000 to 2,000 people. Then, with evident pride, he describes the new instrument developed by the armed forces to counter the enemy's success: the Special Operations Team, or SOT. As the deputy commander explains, the modus operandi of the SOT is borrowed from the insurgents' tactic of winning people over by living among them. He adds that the SOT model was developed a few years back in the southern Philippines, "in Mindanao, where we discovered we were much more successful if we weren't destroying things by raiding a *barangay*, but instead by knowing the people."

In an interview two weeks later at the same camp, the commander of the battalion (promoted to general soon after our visit) describes a thirty- to forty-man SOT in action: "We go to the *barangay*. We live with them. Initially, they despise us. They look at us with dagger eyes. But we keep on. Eventually they look on us as brother Filipinos. We protect them from the Communists." In Bataan in particular, the commander tells us, the biggest enemy of the military is not the NPA. Armed encounters are relatively infrequent; indeed, by some estimates, the NPA of Bataan number fewer than a couple of hundred. Rather, the SOTs are here primarily to fight the broader NDF, which, as the military sees it, has "infiltrated" the legal organizations of teachers, students, workers, peasants, and women. Peasants seeking land reform; workers and teachers calling for higher salaries and better working conditions; students protesting tuition increases: all these are the work of the NDF, we are told.

The SOT's job is to "clear, hold, consolidate, and develop." Both the commander and his deputy tell us that their timetable for "cleaning up" Bataan is six months and that they are a third of the way through. "Communism per se thrives on the protracted-struggle concept wherein you bleed the government," the commander argues. "My concept is to finish the problem as soon as possible." When we leave the post on our first visit, we are presented with a gift from the deputy commander: a poster-size "Season's Greetings" calendar emblazoned with the red, white, gold, and green triangular SOT logo.

As the U.S. military discovered in Vietnam, winning hearts and minds is a tricky proposition. Residents of the Bataan *barangays* already visited by SOTs give a different version of their experience. After the military settles in, the villagers recount, they gather the inhabitants together to watch movies. The first movie is typically "Killing Fields," depicting the atrocities of the Khmer Rouge in Cambodia. Next they show a video, purportedly captured during a raid, of what is said to be an NPA graduation ceremony in Bataan. Do you recognize anyone? the viewers are asked. Then, in some instances, an SOT member has crumpled a Communist party flag, thrown it to the ground, stomped on it, and invited the villagers to join in the stomping. Finally, the SOTs pass around blank pieces of paper and request that the residents write down the names of any NPAs they know. In subsequent days, the SOTs make "visits" to individual homes to try to piece together the leadership of the organizations they claim may be affiliated with the Communist party.

The residents we speak with from four different *barangays* were surprisingly defiant toward the SOTs. "When they told us to stomp on the flag," recounts one peasant, "a man in the back shouted, 'If you want to crush them, you crush them. It's your job as military. But we don't want to get involved. We're civilians.'" As for the blank pieces of paper, comments another, people write things like "Yesterday I knew an NPA, but today I forgot his name." A fisherman admits to some deception in the answers he gave when the SOT came to his *barangay*. "They ask, 'Are the NPA here?' 'No,' we say. And that's true. They're only around at night."

A World War II veteran, soft-spoken and solemn in his responses to our queries, tries to explain this defiant attitude by putting the people's sympathies in historical context: "We had a dialogue with Colonel Tecson. I told him, you can expect the people of San Juan [this *barangay* in Samal] to sympathize with the NPA, because we were the first *barangay* to suffer military abuses in 1972. My son was killed [by the military] in 1972. . . . I [still] do not know why. . . . Not less than fifteen teenagers, male and female, of San Juan [were] killed by the military. . . . The casualties we have suffered from the military, the suffering, the lives lost . . . how can we forget this?"[6]

We talk to one tenant farmer just hours after he received a surprise visit from eleven members of an SOT detachment: "'You are a leader of ALMA-BA [Alyansa ng Magbubukid sa Bataan, the Bataan-wide peasants' organization]?' they asked. . . . 'Yes,' I replied. . . . 'Did you know that ALMA-BA is a Communist organization?' they asked. . . . 'No,' I replied. 'It's a legal organization. We are fighting for the rights of the peasants. Surely, you would support these,' I told them. . . . Then they asked for beer. I told them I was a poor farmer, that I had no money. Then they told me to come visit them later at their military camp and to prepare myself, meaning I should get money for beer. I told them I would come this evening but that I have no money." He is angry, probably scared, but tries to make light of the visit; his wife, standing at his side and bearing witness to his testimony with nods of her head, is clearly worried.

Officers of legal provincewide teachers' and women's organizations claim that military harassment and abuse, rampant in the Marcos military, continue. They recount stories of a drunken SOT soldier shooting his gun into the air and then threatening bystanders with it, of an irritated SOT member pulling out a grenade and playing with it in front of a terrified woman, and of others from SOT detachments taking items from vendors in the marketplace and refusing to pay for them.

One elementary school teacher, active in the legal teachers' group, recounts how his house was recently strafed. He, his wife, and their five kids were inside. "Our eldest son was grazed several times at the back by bullets. The pants near the baby were full of holes. But luckily no one was [seriously] hurt. . . . Months later, the military came back to my house, took a pair of sunglasses and 3,000 pesos [about $150] they found. But it's very hard to find a witness against the military."

A young woman, an insurance agent who is a member of another legal citizens' group, recounts her shock upon hearing her name announced over a loudspeaker in the *barangay* plaza during an SOT visit: "'Miss [name deleted], you surrender,' the military said, and then they referred to me as the 'amazon' head of the NPA of that place."

Such SOT tactics do have some impact. "I'm afraid," admits one woman who works with a local nongovernmental organization. "The harassment of the military is subtle, but it's there. They 'invite' you [to come to their camp] for questioning. They let you know they're watching you. Other people might not even be able to tell it's harassment. It can seem very friendly. But you feel it. Or it can be more direct, like the military going around telling people that you're a Communist."

A well-known lawyer, a provincial leader of a coalition of citizens' organizations, agrees. "For a period, SOTs were effective. Not effective in the long-term sense of winning hearts and minds, but people were afraid. But now, for some, that fear has changed to anger."

The anger is reflected in the strategy of the various citizens' organizations. A minister who also serves as a provincial leader of this citizens' coalition explains, "We project our legality by going on with our programs. We have no plans of lying low. If the military thinks they have evidence that we are Communist fronts, we dare them to file cases against us—if they still believe in the courts. Because we do believe in the courts."

In Bataan, it is common to see uniformed, armed military wandering around the public markets, standing on street corners, and traveling in large groups in trucks and jeeps down the town streets. In March of 1989, we count five military checkpoints along the ten-mile stretch that bisects the Bataan peninsula from east to west. At one point, when we are making a purchase in a small store in the center of Balanga, a soldier whom we do not recall ever having seen before approaches us, calls us by our first names, and informs us that his commanding officer (whom we had been trying to interview for several days) is free that afternoon.

Bataan's enormous military presence and the freedom with which the troops move trouble some of the province's civilian politicians. The mayors with whom we speak readily admit that they have no influence over military operations within their municipalities. In the words of one mayor, "There are many military here in Bataan. . . . We have no control over the police and the military. They usually inform me when they are carrying out an activity, but I can do nothing [about it]."

Discussion about the current military presence in Bataan almost inevitably leads to comparisons between Marcos and Aquino, and assessments of what brand of democracy Aquino's ascension to power has delivered to the Philippines. Most public officials we interview find it hard to discuss in specific terms what changes democracy has brought to Bataan or how their constituents' lives have improved as a result of that democracy. The provincial budget, Governor Roman reminds us in response to this question one morning over breakfast at his home, is the equivalent of only about $800,000 for one year. "We have more freedom now. But the people easily forget that." He stops to think for a moment and then chuckles, "Democracy means that the government will listen to people's problems, but [given the limited resources] not necessarily solve them."

On a municipal level, many top officials or their close relatives had been in office during the Marcos years. The wall behind one mayor's desk is adorned with photos of his grandfather, father, and mother, all of whom had warmed the mayor's chair before he arrived there. As he explains to us, his mother was the mayor in 1986 and was "kicked out of office by people's power" when the Aquino government appointed interim mayors. His younger brother and chief aide, who had also been their mother's chief aide, finishes the thought: "But then [in 1988] the people voted us back in. When we came back to the mayor's office, I said to my brother the mayor, it's still the same [now as when our mother was mayor under Marcos]. You just sit there and sign the papers."

From many of the farmers, fishers, and workers, we hear disappointment that, after the exuberance that ushered in Cory Aquino, her administration has changed so little. The farmer who had been visited by the eleven military men is angry: "Cory came here in 1985 during her campaign. I was there in the plaza in Balanga when she spoke. She promised to solve the problems of the peasants and of the fisherfolk. She promised us real land reform. Instead, after how many years, instead of real land reform we have gotten bullets."

A young student leader shares his witty definition of democracy in the Philippines: "Here, democracy means off the people, buy the people, and poor the people."

Less than half a year after our 1989 visit to the Philippines, we receive painful news from a friend in Bataan. A man who had accompanied us on our Manila Bay boating excursion and had generously shared his experiences and wisdom with us was murdered on a public jeepney on January 22, 1990.

Eliodoro "Ely" de la Rosa, a forty-three-year-old father of five, had been a fisherman and a leader of the fishers' group LAMBAT. The last time we saw Ely was during the fiesta of barrio San Juan in Samal, Bataan. Amid the playful water-throwing and other revelries that mark the fiesta day of all places in the Philippines named after St. John the Baptist, we discussed the tragic annihilation of the province's coastal ecosystem. Ely was deeply concerned that Manila Bay was dying, that there would be no fish for his children and grandchildren. He talked of his organization's efforts to halt the destruction of coastal mangroves. He spoke eloquently of the dangers of prawn-pond expansion, of the need to stand up to the prawn-pond owners and other mangrove destroyers, and of his plans to start a mangrove replanting program. For his visions and for his ability to inspire others to take action against the impediments to these visions, he was murdered.

Ely's assassination, according to the Philippine human-rights monitoring group Task Force Detainees, was part of a step-up in the SOT counter-insurgency campaign in Bataan. Several days before his murder, Ely had noticed that he was being followed; the military had visited his home. During a four-week period that included Ely's murder, the Bataan chapter of the Task Force Detainees reported one other extra-judicial killing (a form of murder to which Filipinos have given the eerie name *salvaging*), assaults on forty-eight civilians, and thirteen individuals illegally arrested and detained. And in the period from January through July of 1990, there were a total of seven salvagings in Bataan. Many others suffered assaults, but fear convinced them not to file reports. Like Ely, most of these victims were poor fishers, farmers, and workers whose common crime seems to have been affiliation with a legal organization that the military decided to deem subversive.[7]

One target of a terrifying 4:00 A.M. illegal search was a leader of the local farmers' group, the one whose house had earlier been encircled by the eleven military men. This man too had patiently tried to share the details of his life with us during our research trips to Bataan. He brought us to his small house in the middle of the hectare of land he tilled but did not own. He showed us the *carabao* that he fed early each morning but likewise did not own. He talked to us about the lives of Bataan's tenant farmers such as himself. He was poor. His family was poor. His five children and his grandchildren needed more food, clothes, the possibility of education. His life was hard.

Still, his eyes lit up when he described the peasant organization to which he belonged, its meetings, its marches, its goals. That organization has given our friend an opportunity to participate in a grass-roots democratic process through which he and others like him strive to define a better life for their children and then work, against overpowering obstacles, to make that vision a reality.

This peasant leader, along with Ely de la Rosa and dozens of other Bataan farmers and fishers we came to know, understands the correlation between ecological destruction and human suffering better than most of the rest of us. These people are the ones who suffer the consequences of Bataan's deteriorating environment every day. As a result, the organizations they and people not unlike them have created—from LAMBAT and ALMA-BA to newer environmental groups and even the National Democratic Front—focus on resolving both the human suffering and the ecological degradation by transferring control of natural resources from the few to the many.

The Philippine military officers we interview perceive the connections—the definition of the problem, the causes, and the solution—differently. They tend to lump all these citizens' organizations into one convenient category, under the label *subversive*, and then to focus on eliminating them through either savage force or other hardly less subtle means of "winning their hearts and minds." We are struck by how decades of U.S. military aid, promoted as "professionalizing" the Philippine military, have instead contributed to these brutal and misplaced efforts.

By the early 1990s, the military sees fit to declare that the hearts and minds of Bataeños have been won and that, after two years of strong SOT presence and military action, Bataan has been transformed into "a peaceful and beautiful place ripe for big investments," as a lieutenant colonel triumphantly and publicly declared.[8] The small NPA contingent has shifted most of its operations to provinces to the north. But local citizens, whose hearts and minds were supposedly the ones up for grabs, tell us that they have borne the heaviest cost. News clips, such as this one reporting on a December, 1990, event, only begin to suggest the continuing horror: "Two civilians were killed . . . by government militiamen in the town of Samal. . . . The militia thought the two were members of the insurgent New People's Army, but they turned out to be workers from a local paper mill."[9] Some people we interviewed, members of legal groups, have been charged with subversion. Others are in jail although, as their relatives explain to us in the summer of 1991, they have never discovered why. Among these are a thirteen-year-old boy who has been tortured brutally and a twenty-one-year-old woman who has been raped.[10]

Where do the hearts and minds of such people dwell? How are they "won"? At what cost? As we are reminded by conversations during our 1991 trip to the province, those working for more equitable and sustainable development in Bataan and elsewhere in the Philippines continue to organize and build in the face of the twin obstacles of powerful resource plunderers and a bloated military.

And, in a province littered with ugly reminders that the United States has too often contributed its share to the obstacles—from a mothballed nuclear power plant to the U.S. naval base to the factories inside the export processing zone—we are constantly surprised at how eager Bataeños are to work in partnership with people from the United States.

Chapter Eight

"The Bastards of Bataan"

What does it mean to be a friend to [the Philippines]? First, I think, to respect its national, cultural and ecological integrity. To recognize what you [Filipinos] have to teach us. To sit with a Bagobo healer for an evening and redefine the world. To sit with [the late human rights lawyer and former senator Jose] Diokno and understand human dignity.

Patricia Wagner, U.S. development worker in the
Philippines, "Companions on a Common Journey,"
Sunday [Philippine] Inquirer Magazine, July 20, 1990

On April 9, 1942, as U.S. and Philippine forces surrendered Bataan to the Japanese, U.S. Armed Forces radio in the Philippines broadcast the following promise: "The world will long remember the epic struggle that Filipino and American soldiers put up in these jungle fastnesses and along the rugged coast of Bataan."[1]

Half a century later, Philippine veterans of World War II do still remember. They vividly recollect the weeks of relentless fighting that preceded the surrender. They can retell their stories for hours at a time, recalling the most intricate details without reference to notes. And if their tales contain a common thread beyond the fighting itself, it is this: almost without exception, they include at least one soldier from the United States with whom the Filipino soldier fought or marched or simply talked, a soldier who typically is described as "very handsome and very tall." Although the interactions were sometimes as short as a week or a day, the Filipino veterans invariably refer to U.S. soldiers whose paths crossed theirs not as acquaintances but as "good friends."

And they mean it.

Jacinto Cruz of Bataan, some fifty years ago a teenage sergeant in a U.S. Armed Forces in the Far East (USAFFE) guerrilla unit after the fall of Bataan, wants us to know how he met his "best friend," Sgt. John Case of Kentucky. "He was with the first American unit to liberate Bataan in January, 1945. . . . Well, I think he was hungry. I was the mess sergeant. So I asked him, 'Do you eat this kind of food—*camote* [a root crop] and *carabao* meat?' . . . He gave me his spare fatigue uniform, although it was very big. . . . That was the first time I'd seen a fatigue uniform and I didn't know what it was. . . . Later, when I was hospitalized with malaria and chicken pox, he got a pass to come visit me. He was really my best friend."

"I was born a farmer," says Maximo Capili, also from Bataan. But soon after the Japanese invasion, he pretended he was one year older than his real age of twenty and volunteered to "stand and fight" as a private in the Philippine Scouts. With emotion in his voice, Capili recounts in elaborate and, at times, painful detail another common theme of the stories we are told by Filipino veterans: the horrors of the Death March, and especially the abominations suffered by U.S. soldiers. "The Japanese ordered us to fall in line single file, segregating Americans in their West Point khaki, Philippine Scouts in light-brown shirts, and Philippine Army who wore plain *maong* [denim]. The Japanese told us, 'Americans will not come home. [And neither will] the Philippine Scouts, because the Philippine Scouts are . . . American soldiers.' . . . On the Death March . . . the [U.S.] soldiers were forbidden to find some water to drink; they were also forbidden to eat. When a Filipino soldier dares to give him something to eat, the order is [that] both will be killed."

Yet, Capili continues, he and many other Filipinos in the Death March, as well as citizens along the route, could not bear to see their U.S. "friends" suffer so. Even as Capili witnessed the threatened punishment being meted out to others, he decided to take the risk and give rice, quinine, and canned goods to six emaciated U.S. soldiers trudging near him in the Death March. The grateful U.S. soldiers offered him money in return, "but I did not accept it. . . . One of the six cried . . . [and] they gave me six packs of Pall Mall cigarettes." To this day, Capili has but one lingering regret from his courageous act of friendship: "I didn't take note of their names." But perhaps, he says, some of his "friends" are still alive today and will read his words on these pages and contact him.

This friendship between Philippine and U.S. soldiers is commemorated in plaques, monuments, statues, and markers from one end of the province to the other. A steel and concrete cross, taller than a thirty-story building and visible all the way across the bay in Manila, rises on top of Mount Samat, the site of the fiercest fighting of the Bataan campaign. (Mount Samat, then thickly forested, was also where the mother and father of Environment and Natural Resources Secretary Factoran, like many other Bataeños, hid during the war.) Below the cross on Mount Samat is the memorial Dambana ng Kagitingan, the Altar of Valor. Halfway down the length of the peninsula in Pilar, a giant cement rendition of a "flaming sword" marks the second line of defense, which Philippine and U.S. troops held for two grueling months. In a nearby town a statue of a U.S. soldier stands at attention, rifle in hand, atop a globe symbolizing the world. In another monument, two soldiers, seemingly about to collapse, are depicted as they stagger along the Death March route. And Imelda Marcos turned the Death March route into a tree-lined memorial, with a marker at each kilometer of the coastal road to tick off the distance trudged.[2]

If relations between the people of Bataan and the soldiers of the United States are remembered with great fondness, almost the opposite can be said of interactions with the U.S. government. "I don't know if you will forgive us," admits one of Bataan's veterans, "but I don't like what your government did to us." Indeed, each of the dozen or so Bataan veterans with whom we speak lashes out at a series of broken or unfulfilled promises of the U.S. government that have haunted these men throughout their adult lives.

At the onset of the Bataan campaign, the Philippines was a commonwealth of the United States, and Philippine soldiers were made part of the U.S. Armed Forces in the Far East. Of the 82,000 USAFFE forces in Bataan, 70,000 were young Filipinos.[3] And, as we are told over and over, they were promised not only the same benefits as their U.S.-born comrades but also that they would be granted U.S. citizenship through naturalization.

Soon into the battle, they were led to believe that reinforcements—a "mile-long convoy"—would be arriving.[4] None came; only three years later did MacArthur stage his announced return. In the meantime, as the Bataan surrenderees plodded either to their deaths or to concentration camps north of Bataan, some turned their abandonment into a sorrowful chant: "We are the bastards of Bataan. No mama, no papa, no Uncle Sam."[5]

But MacArthur did at last return, and when U.S. soldiers came back to Bataan, recalls Bataan campaign and Death March veteran Diony Blas, "we were hugging and kissing. And the civilians here were crying. . . . Victory Joe, we called the Americans." However, as the war ended the second deception began. Blas speaks with bitterness of how the U.S. government "promised that we'd receive equal pay with Americans. Instead, a U.S. private received [much more than] a Filipino private. . . . That promise was not kept." Adds another Filipino veteran, "We believe there is discrimination with regard to the payment." In general, we are told, U.S. soldiers received at least double what the Filipinos fighting alongside them got.

But the real slap in the face came in 1946, when a U.S. congressional act, the Rescission Act, broke the Roosevelt administration's promise of naturalized citizenship and veterans' benefits for all Filipino members of USAFFE. Only Filipino soldiers wounded or killed during the war were to be recognized as U.S. war veterans; all others were ineligible for most benefits under the G.I. Bill of Rights of 1944.

Today, the Veterans Federation of the Philippines is seeking claims from the tens of thousands of living Filipino veterans, for a total of $3 billion in unmet pledges by the U.S. government. But the average age of the Filipino veteran is over seventy and, as one wrote in the late 1980s, "In a few more years they will be gone without ever having tasted the rewards for their sacrifices . . . with hate in their hearts for having been double-crossed by those who mandated them to fight in a war in the front lines, extolled their gallantry . . . but pulled the rug from under their feet."[6]

Veteran after veteran in Bataan brings us yellowing papers—and decorations and ribbons and "medals made in Missouri"—to prove that he was a member of USAFFE. They ask us, as citizens of the United States, for help. "It's for my children," beseeches one. "I have spent nearly fifty years of my life asking for what was promised to me. Do it for my children."

Other Filipinos, too young to fight in the war, share this sense of outrage at the U.S. government's broken promises. Senator Joseph Estrada, a popular action-film movie star who returned to the screen in 1989 to star in an anti-bases movie titled "Sa Kuko ng Agila" ("In the Claws of the Eagle"), was a young boy during World War II. But he sums up for us the anger many Filipinos feel:

I can't forget. As a seven-year-old kid, I saw thousands of my countrymen killed by the Japanese. Our country was virtually destroyed by the Japanese in that war. The Americans, who fought alongside us, promised us war reparations and veterans' benefits. Then, right after liberation, the Americans left us and instead went to help Japan become one of the richest nations on earth. Why? Why? Many Philippine veterans died without ever receiving a cent of the promised benefits. Instead, the Americans occupy choice Philippine land for their military bases, making us a target in any nuclear war. I cannot ever forget what I saw as a seven-year-old boy.

Since the pitched battles of Bataan in World War II, there is arguably no other province in the country where U.S. influence has been stronger. At the level of appearances, we see many of the same manifestations of U.S. culture that are visible throughout the archipelago. Brooke Shields' face graces the windows of numerous beauty parlors. In a simple eatery near the Bataan Export Processing Zone, we drink beer under posters of Tom Cruise, U.S. fighter planes, and the latest U.S. car models. No matter how small and remote the barrio, favorite T-shirt emblems are Garfield, Felix the Cat, and famous U.S. universities (sometimes misspelled).

In Bataan as elsewhere in the Philippines, the juxtaposition of U.S. culture and Philippine reality is at times jarring. Resting inside a four-hundred-year-old church in the town that is honored as the first major line of defense in the Bataan campaign, we watch five-year-olds practice dance routines for their kindergarten graduation to "Come On Baby, Do the Locomotion" and "I Know You Don't Love Me No More." Inside the bamboo hut of an obviously poor fishing family in a nearby barrio, two prized possessions are proudly displayed on a simple shelf: an airmail envelope with U.S. stamps, and a Barbie doll ("Magical Barbie—She Moves"), perhaps partially made in the zone, never unwrapped from its box. And for a dollar and a half in a small store in the provincial capital, we buy a package of toy soldiers, World War II–style U.S. troops: plastic, made in Hong Kong.

Beneath the intense U.S. cultural presence in Bataan stand decades of economic and military ties and the legacies of a half-century of colonial rule. For nearly one hundred years, the centerpiece of U.S. interests was Clark Air Base and Subic Naval Base, deemed by the U.S. military vital to its projection from northeast

Asia to the Middle East. Two-thirds of the giant Subic Base occupied prime coastal and forest lands of northwestern Bataan, accounting for over 7 percent of the province's land area.

During the Vietnam War, the United States staged many operations from Subic. Now, just a few miles south of Subic stands a facility that exists because of that war: the Philippine Refugee Processing Center. This center, one of its directors explains, receives a substantial number of the Indochinese refugees. At the time of our visit, 16,500 refugees prepare for departure to the United States: they are being given six months of language and vocational training and acculturation programs (about customs, U.S. currency, behavior in supermarkets, how to take a U.S.-style shower, and so on).

Another few miles to the south stands the tomb of some of the largest U.S. bank loans to the Philippines: the $2.2 billion Bataan nuclear power plant. Commissioned by Marcos, funded by major international banks (with help in the form of both loans and guarantees from the U.S. government's Export-Import Bank), and built near an earthquake fault not far from Mount Pinatubo and other volcanoes, the Westinghouse plant was finished just as Marcos fell. The timing was fortuitous. Aquino had made a campaign promise that the controversial and unsafe plant would not be operated. And, just days after the 1986 Chernobyl accident, she carried out her promise and mothballed the plant. As a result, the plant has stood idle since completion. The huge concrete structure is still tightly guarded. Nuclear engineers maintain and exercise the plant daily. They are supposedly keeping it ready to be operated, in case the government changes its mind. Still, the power plant is said to be beginning to deteriorate. The Philippine government seems unsure of what to do about it, except to keep repaying the quarter of a million dollars in daily debt service on the international loans that financed it as, in the U.S. courts, they pursue Westinghouse for fraud.[7]

U.S. firms, from Mattel to Ford, were also an important presence in the early days of the Bataan Export Processing Zone. Other U.S. multinationals helped set up Bataan's two largest industries outside the zone: Caltex invested in the Bataan Refining Company, the country's largest oil refinery, and Boise Cascade invested in the Bataan Pulp and Paper Mill.[8]

Since we two visitors are from the United States, many of Ba-

taan's public officials and business executives make a point of stress-
ing to us how instrumental U.S. banks, corporations, and the government were in setting up these factories, the nuclear power
plant, the refugee center, the base—into which much of Bataan's
economic energy has been poured for half a century. We try, politely, to push further: what, we ask time and time again, has been
their impact on the province and its people?

Many speak first about the Subic Naval Base. For decades, base
officials spent time and resources trying to win important friends in
Bataan. The widespread poverty and general lack of resources in
the province meant that a little extra money went a long way. With
an annual provincial budget equivalent to somewhere in the vicin-
ity of $800,000 and town budgets that average around $250,000,
government resources can do little more than pay the salaries of the
bureaucracy. As many local officials admit to us, they have been
able to tap U.S. resources to enhance their ability to provide some
services.

The Philippines has historically been one of the largest recipients of U.S. aid; in 1991 the country was fourth on the list, following only Israel, Egypt, and Turkey. Over the years, one of the most
abundant sources of U.S. assistance was aid specifically earmarked
by the United States to help communities near the bases. Through
this Economic Support Fund (ESF) assistance, millions of dollars
flowed into Bataan to build schools, roads, and bridges. Former
governor Efren Pascual is very grateful: "Most of the bridges in this
province were constructed through ESF. . . . All the big schools,
even in the barrios, were built through ESF."

Some Bataan officials appear to have received other perks from
this official aid. Elsewhere in the Philippines, we are told by a former government contractor that, in most provinces, the "standard
operating procedure, or SOP," is for local and provincial officials to
skim off 30 percent of any government foreign-aid contract. Such a
practice is hard to prove, but signs of the perks of being a province
with a U.S. base are everywhere.

For example, after particularly destructive natural calamities the
base offers aid in the form of food and medicine. One mayor confides that, after a typhoon strikes, he does not even bother to ask
the Philippine government for assistance: "Too much red tape." He
goes to Subic, he explains, and tells them what he needs; they

quickly deliver the supplies. To emphasize his connections, he pulls out of his wallet the calling cards of base officials, at least one of whom is, the card says, attached to naval intelligence. A particularly helpful base official, the mayor continues, was thanked by being made an honorary citizen of the town. And to show his appreciation in general, the mayor used paint donated by the base to write on the roof of the town hall: "GO NAVY." The huge letters, the mayor tells us, are clearly visible to U.S. Navy helicopters flying to and from Subic Base. However, the words cannot be seen from the ground, where they might offend many of the mayor's anti-bases constituents.

Another mayor tells us that, even though Bataan is at that moment off-limits to base personnel (as a result of the province's "peace-and-order" situation and the perceived risk to U.S. military personnel), he was recently able to convince base officials to send a two-person medical mission to his town. The two distributed medicine for half a day—rather nervously and hurriedly, according to some. And when they departed, they left behind several large cardboard boxes of Anacin tablets for the mayor to distribute himself.

Such a windfall fits the pattern of Philippine local politics, where constituents routinely line up to ask their mayor's help in a wide range of affairs, from a loan for a funeral to a recommendation for a job. During the course of our interview with the Anacin-rich mayor in his office, he constantly excuses himself to see to a visiting constituent. Whatever the problem, each seems to leave with a pat on the back and a few bottles of Anacin—but no mention that the expiration date on the medicine is only weeks away.

The bounty has sometimes been even better. A provincial government employee describes three U.S. officials who visited Bataan regularly—"intelligence, I presume," he says. One brought fruit and chocolates for the provincial Christmas party. The governor and vice-governor received turkeys, canned hams, and other delicacies.

Such largess, both official and unofficial, wins a certain kind of loyalty. The attitude of the majority of Bataan's top provincial and local government officials toward the United States is summed up for us by one vice-mayor: "The United States has been playing a great role in the development of this country. . . . So I would say, God bless America."

From other people, however, we hear a very different percep-
tion of the relationship and even of that phrase. "God Bless America?" queries an older tenant farmer as he describes to us his ele-
mentary-school education under the U.S. colonial administration.
"We were taught to sing 'God Bless America' in grade school." He
pauses to sing us the first verse, which he still remembers in full.
"It made me so angry. Excuse me for saying this. You are an American couple and you are our friends. But why not 'God Bless the
Philippines'? Are we to believe that God only blesses America?"

In 1988, Governor Roman prepared a report for the U.S. State
Department on the impact of Subic Naval Base on Bataan. To the
surprise of many who view the governor as a cautious politician, the
report concluded that the base, with its vast land area off-limits to
the local people, had economically isolated the two towns on the
western coast of Bataan from the next province to the north. The
result, according to the governor's report, was "a paralysis of economic growth" there. A briefing paper also prepared by Governor
Roman on Bataan's "problems and issues" termed Subic "one of the
biggest stumbling blocks . . . [to] continued progress in Bataan."
By Roman's "conservative estimate," the lost "opportunity costs" of
the base land since World War II had reached $500 million.[9]

As the leases on Subic and the other U.S. military facilities in the
country were renewed periodically, extension of the bases agreement was almost always a subject of intense national debate. Some
supported the bases because of the jobs and the U.S. aid they have
brought to the country. But, over the course of the Aquino administration, a number of Philippine politicians and citizens argued
that the bases violated a nuclear-free provision of the 1987 Philippine constitution (since the U.S. government maintained its right
to bring nuclear weapons in and out of the bases—or, at least, neither to confirm nor to deny doing so).[10]

We are in the Philippines in June of 1991, when these issues
reach a heated climax. During a stalemate in the bases negotiations, the supposedly dormant Mount Pinatubo ends its six-
hundred-year slumber—and begins a series of events that change
the course of those negotiations. Over a foot of ash is deposited on
Subic and the other large U.S. facility, Clark Air Base. At the height
of the volcano's activity, the U.S. government evacuates all Americans from Clark, leaving Filipinos to guard the facility. A London

newspaper reports that the bases are placed on nuclear alert. Much to many Filipinos' distress, the U.S. government sticks to its position of neither confirming nor denying either this rumor or the mere presence of nuclear weapons. Around the same time, the mayor of Olongapo, the city that serves as Subic's rest-and-recreation area, seeks permission from the U.S. base officials to quicken the evacuation from Olongapo by allowing residents to pass through Subic. Even as most of Olongapo's buildings collapse, however, the U.S. military refuses to open the gates.

We interview a number of Filipinos who tell us that they had previously supported the bases but that their outrage over these callous U.S. actions and reactions has moved them into the opposition camp. Emboldened by shifting public opinion, the Philippine Senate in September, 1991, votes down a multi-year extension of Subic Naval Base. The United States abandons the more heavily damaged Clark and begins to wind down operations at Subic.

Although many rejoice at this outcome, there are lingering concerns. Some in Bataan worry about the condition in which the U.S. forces are leaving the former base lands. We talk to poor farmers growing bananas and other fruits at the foot of a mountain; the Subic Base is just on the other side, they tell us. They worry about the vast quantities of toxic wastes said to be buried there.[11] "What's dumped on the bases?" one asks us. "Can the land still be farmed and the water used? Do their wastes affect our land and water? Why isn't the U.S. government responsible for cleaning it up?"

We encounter similar skepticism concerning U.S. corporate and bank incursions into Bataan. From the governor to tenant farmers, we find no Filipino who has anything positive to say about the Westinghouse nuclear power plant. Provincial officers complain that they were not consulted about its construction. Fishers in the nearest town, pointing to the huge structure, swear at it and recall how tens of thousands of citizens protested against its construction. Years earlier, they tell us, large numbers also successfully demonstrated against extensive pollution coming from the Bataan Pulp and Paper Mill.

The highly unequal, if not negative, impacts of so many of the U.S. ventures in Bataan have led some to conclude that a better future for U.S.-Philippine collaboration lies along another path.

But this new direction, Philippine Rural Reconstruction Movement vice-president Isagani Serrano argues, must grow from a critical reassessment of U.S. aid and must center on the fostering of people-to-people relations. On aid, Serrano claims, "the crucial question that should be addressed, but which is carefully avoided, is 'Who benefits?' Structural guarantees must be in place to ensure that development aid reaches the people—fisherfolk, farmers, workers, women—most in need. Beyond that, these groups of people must have a strong say in the planning, implementation, and evaluation of any development program."

One of the most ardent advocates of people-to-people linkages is Provincial Board member Ditas Consunji, head of the board's tourism committee. She details with enthusiasm successful precedents in people-to-people ventures with Japanese organizations: since the early 1970s, groups of Japanese Buddhists have come to visit the province. "They come," another official tells us, and "they pray and they cry" about their country's role here in World War II. And, says Consunji, they spend time trying to learn about the local people's lives and problems. From these visits many friendships have developed, as have some concrete projects. Indeed, we conduct several interviews in a beautiful library constructed through aid given by an organization of Japanese Buddhists and administered by a local Bataan youth organization. Schoolchildren are brought to the library to learn more about the province, and the library is sponsoring a project to research and write the province's history. Japanese groups are also talking with local people's organizations about setting up a demonstration farm to train peasants in ecologically sound regenerative agriculture.

Consunji has one people-to-people dream that grows out of Bataan's history. She wants to build an alternative tourism industry that would bring more U.S. World War II veterans and their families back to Bataan. She shows us a project proposal to reforest the base of Mount Samat and transform it into a Friendship Park and museum of the war. She speaks of including visits to fishing villages and farms in the tours of Bataan. This is the only way, says Consunji, that people from the United States can learn more about the lives of Filipinos today. Consunji has discussed her dream with tourist agents—who have told her that U.S. travelers do not typically go for such a brand of tourism, that you need hot water and air conditioning and five-star hotel accommodations to attract tourists. But Consunji's enthusiasm has not yet been dampened.

The United Church of Christ in the Philippines and other religious and citizens' groups have been organizing a variation on Consunji's dream. Beginning in 1990, the organizations have orchestrated an annual March for Life in which people from Bataan and other Philippine provinces and from Japan, Australia, the United States, and other countries join to retrace the route of the original Death Marchers. But this time they march, in the words of one of the organizers of the event, to call "attention to the need to protect life and protest ongoing threats to it." Some Filipino veterans of World War II have joined the march; others have talked with the marchers along the way. Douglas Cunningham, a U.S. minister who was one of the U.S. participants in the 1991 march, recounts to us his experience:

During the six-day journey, we got a feel for the Death March—both the sobering moment in history and the ongoing reality. We had numerous encounters with the [Philippine] military. One day they prohibited us from stopping for lunch in a fishing village they said was influenced by Communists. The next day they halted the march, brought several of us to the headquarters for questioning, then escorted us out of town. . . . Trekking across Bataan, we crossed mountains stripped bare of trees and rivers dead with pollution and met desperately underpaid workers at several factories along the way.

In 1991, we speak with religious activists who are planning a much larger march for April of 1992, to mark the Death March's fiftieth anniversary. They are working to contact U.S. veterans and their families. This might be the last chance for some of the surviving Philippine and U.S. veterans of that campaign to see one another and share stories. It could also be an opportunity to embody visions Consunji and others have of the veterans' children and grandchildren forming a new generation of friendship and collaboration.

Such friendship, collaboration, and partnership do already exist on a number of fronts. Delegations of U.S. workers, women, and religious activists regularly visit the Philippines and coordinate campaigns on everything from AIDS education to human-rights advocacy. And researchers and activists from the two countries have long worked together to expose the dangers of the U.S. bases.

One of the most exciting new forms of people-to-people collaboration was born in 1989 with the creation of the Philippine Development Forum, based in Washington, D.C. This organization serves as a clearinghouse for Philippine-U.S. ventures to promote sustainable development. The forum draws together U.S. environmental, development, religious, and grass-roots groups and links them with counterparts in the Philippines. Taking the lead from the views of the Filipino partners, the groups have developed common positions and campaigns to oppose environmentally destructive aid projects, highlight forest destruction in Palawan and on Mount Apo, and, in general, spread awareness about each other's work. The forum has even taken up the case of the Bataan Nuclear Power Plant by publicizing the fraudulent nature of the loans from U.S. creditors that helped fund the plant.

The Philippine Development Forum and similar citizens' groups in Canada, Australia, and Europe have also built positive economic ties that advance the sustainable-development agenda. This includes work to promote "green trade" in Philippine products produced under environmentally sustainable conditions, international safeguards for Philippine workers' rights, and new programs to channel portions of government aid to Philippine NGOs.

Such dynamism on the citizens' level has been matched by the U.S. government only on a symbolic level. In late 1990 the United States government passed legislation to address one of its broken promises. Within the 1990 U.S. Immigration Reform Act the U.S. Congress placed a Filipino Veterans Naturalization Bill, offering naturalization to Filipino veterans who served as active members of the Philippine Scouts, the Philippine Army, the U.S. Armed Forces of the Far East, and recognized guerrilla units.[12]

Yet, overall, the act is "too little, too late," as numerous Filipino veterans tell us. Says one, "There are times when we'd hear about the 'Ugly American' before. I'd say, no, not all Americans are ugly. We were always hopeful that the Americans would keep their promise. But it's a long time to wait for promises to be kept."

The nearly fifty-year gap is not the only problem with the bill. Other broken promises remain. The act contains no language to remedy the discriminatory pay and benefits. In addition, perhaps half of the Filipinos who fought in World War II were killed during the war; perhaps another half of the remainder have died since. For their descendants the act offers nothing.

And even for the aging surviving veterans, it is a bittersweet victory. Forms have to be filled out and sent to the United States. And, even if all goes well, the applicant then has to travel at his own expense to the United States for the exam and oath-taking. At best, it is a time-consuming enterprise, requiring money and strength. As one laments: "We veterans deem that the U.S. government cheated us of our rights and privileges due us. We call the U.S. government a cheater because of the stiff requirements. . . . With all these farcical requirements only millionaire veterans can qualify for U.S. citizenship. Nobody from the 90 percent majority composed of indigents and semi-illiterate veterans would qualify. The hundreds of forms sent to our headquarters by the U.S. embassy will just be wasted."[13]

This episode of unkept promises may appear to some as a minor historical anecdote with little relevance to any beyond a limited group of veterans. It is offered here in part because it so typifies the past century of U.S.-Philippine relations. Unequal alliances and unkept promises have been the rule, not the exception.

We find these stories important also because those older Filipinos with historical ties that bind them to U.S. veterans as best friends and brothers are dying. The young of the Philippines, even the young of Bataan, do not have the same emotional bond to the United States. As Governor Roman points out to us, "More of our students have seen the giant shopping malls of Manila than [have seen] the Mount Samat monument."

Fifty years after the Death March, there are Filipinos charting new partnerships with citizens' groups not only in the United States but across the world. These new partners can draw inspiration from the remarkable efforts and accomplishments of Philippine and U.S. soldiers two generations ago in slowing the advance of fascism. And, with the end of the Cold War, the dissolution of the Soviet Union, and the phasing out of U.S. bases, they stand at a propitious moment in history to begin to transform a Philippine-U.S. relationship long rooted in military interests to one that advances mutually beneficial development.

Chapter Nine

From Plunder to Sustainability

There is one dream that all Filipinos share: that our children
may have a better life than we have had. So there is one vision
that is distinctly Filipino: the vision to make this country, our
country, a nation for our children.

The late human-rights advocate Senator Jose W. Diokno,
speech delivered October 12, 1984

Development is a process by which the members of a society
increase their personal and institutional capacities to mobilize
and manage resources to produce sustainable and justly dis-
tributed improvements in their quality of life consistent with
their own aspirations.

David Korten, *Getting to the 21st Century: Voluntary Action*
and the Global Agenda (West Hartford, Conn.: Kumarian
Press, 1990), p. 67

On December 4, 1991, over five hundred representatives of citizens' groups from all around the Philippines gather in Manila to put the final touches on a document they call a "Covenant on Philippine Development." The date of the gathering marks the fifth anniversary of the passage of the most comprehensive United Nations resolution on development, the 1986 "Declaration on the Right to Development." The goal of the meeting, in the words of its organizers, is "to bring together nongovernmental organizations (NGOs) and people's organizations (POs) from a wide political spectrum in a common effort to accelerate Philippine socioeconomic development." At the core of the "Covenant on Philippine Development" is the affirmation of the fundamental right of the Filipino people "to actively participate in the process of development"—a right, the participants emphasize, recognized both by the United Nations Declaration and by the 1987 Philippine Constitution.[1]

The covenant represents yet one more instance of the innovative NGO initiatives we find throughout the Philippines. But gatherings such as this are impressive for more than the documents being finalized; the diversity and dynamism of the assembled groups are noteworthy in themselves. They are a mixture of new and old, of groups that call themselves environmental and others that call themselves development organizations, including in both sets a number of representatives of organizations that guided us through Palawan, Mindanao, northern Luzon, and Bataan. The mix reminds us of a favorite Philippine dessert, the *halo-halo* (literally, mix-mix), a combination of ice cream, ice, fruits, gelatin chunks, and a sprinkling of corn flakes, corn, and other unlikely ingredients—all of which taste fine on their own, but take on a new and surprisingly enticing flavor when combined. Like *halo-halo*, in union these groups become something more than the sum of their parts.

Some, particularly Western funding agencies, are known to despair at the constant flux in Philippine civil society attested to by this gathering: continuous creation of new organizations and realignments of old. But, as we have come to enjoy *halo-halo*, so too we have come to appreciate these changes as a strength of the country's civil society: it constantly attempts to evaluate past successes and failures, to learn its lessons, and to profit from them. Corazon "Dinky" Soliman, a veteran of these movements, terms the process "building on the mistakes and learning to avoid them. We keep changing so that we can add more: the politics of addition. By adding more and more people, we've got more articulators of the movement who are different."

Admittedly, one disadvantage of the constant change is that any overly specific characterization of the groups is destined to go out of date almost instantaneously. Still, although some of the groups' names may change and new permutations and alignments will undoubtedly appear, the broad outlines of the sustainable-development movement are beginning to be clear.

This *halo-halo*, this nascent movement, contains perhaps four main strands. The strand with the longest history is what the Philippines ought to consider a prized national treasure: large, mass-based people's organizations set up along what Filipinos refer to as sectoral lines. Like the women workers we meet in Bataan, well over a million Filipino workers belong to one of several large trade-union movements. Likewise, over a million Filipino peasants belong to some one of several major peasants' associations. Smaller but still significant people's organizations exist among women, fishers, urban poor, students, teachers, and indigenous Filipinos. As with the Bataan fishers' organization, individuals belong to local chapters that are affiliated with provincial chapters that in turn are affiliated with national organizations.

Growing out of different progressive political parties and groupings (or "tendencies," as they say in the Philippines),[2] most of these sectoral groups were born during the era of Marcos's martial law, and much of their energy was spent fighting that regime's often brutal repression of their memberships. Over the past half-dozen years the organizations have adopted some aspects of the sustainable-development agenda, giving their work a decidedly environmental flavor. The peasant alliance in Bataan with its concern for sustainable agriculture is a prominent example, as is the provincial fishers' group with its work to prolong the life of Manila Bay.

Often intertwined with these mass people's organizations is a second strand: thousands of NGOs, such as the Baguio-based Cordillera Resource Center and the Philippine Rural Reconstruction Movement, that seek to promote and work for the interests and demands of the people's organizations. Some focus on education, others conduct research and serve as advocates for policy and legal reform, and some channel funds from foreign donors into socioeconomic projects aimed at empowering the nation's poor majority.

As with the POs, in recent years these NGOs have expanded their understanding of development to place far greater emphasis on ecological sustainability. Since 1986, they have also begun to cross sectoral and political lines and work together in national coalitions or umbrella groups. The organization that planned the 1991 development covenant meeting, the Caucus of Development NGO Networks (CODE-NGO), is one example. It is a coalition of ten major national NGO networks (several defined by either political tendencies or religious denominations) consisting of over 1,300 development NGOs whose operations extend to every region of the country.

Similarly, many of the sectoral groups come together to form issue-based coalitions that focus on advocacy and education at the national level. These include several peasants' coalitions, including the Congress for a People's Agrarian Reform (CPAR), which has put together its own technically feasible agrarian-reform code based on the concept of land-to-the-tiller and has begun to experiment with regenerative agriculture.[3] Another, the Freedom from Debt Coalition, comprises several hundred organizations that are fighting to reduce Philippine debt payments and reorient the "saved" financial resources toward people-centered and environmentally sustainable ends.

Together, these formally organized POs and NGOs comprise some 5–6 million Filipinos, or around a tenth of the Philippine population—a highly organized base within civil society.

A third strand in the *halo-halo* that is the emerging Philippine sustainable-development movement is made up of the more spontaneous citizens' formations that organize around local environmental issues. These include the logging-truck blockaders of San Fernando and other anti-logging peasant crusaders in communities stretching from Gabaldon in central Luzon to Midsalip in Mindanao (the latter called the People Power Picket Movement of Midsalip). As in San Fernando, these more spontaneous environmental actions often are aided by innovative local church leaders, some of whom feel greater latitude to act since a 1988 Catholic Bishops' Conference of the Philippines pastoral letter encouraged the country's Catholic majority to take action against "what is happening to our beautiful land."[4]

The fourth and final strand is the relatively new phenomenon of environmental organizations, like Haribon with its ten chapters, that are building up their ranks not only from the POs and the NGOs but also from previously unorganized concerned citizens of the middle and even the upper classes. Most of these groups started with ecology and natural-resource issues as their foremost concerns and built from there to a more expansive understanding of sustainable and equitable development. Haribon, for instance, began in 1972 as a bird-watching group but a decade later had metamorphosed into a leading advocate of natural-resource conservation issues. In 1986–87, starting with its national campaign to "save Palawan" from loggers, the organization redefined its very conception of environmental work to revolve around even broader questions of sustainable and equitable development.

Parallel to the development NGOs' and POs' significant advance in coalition work, at the onset of the 1990s the environmental movement took a major step forward with the organization of two nationwide networks that have well-articulated environmental agendas. The Philippine Environmental Action Network (PEAN), launched on International Earth Day in April of 1990, is a coalition of nearly one hundred organizations centered on several major sectoral people's organizations. PEAN's chairperson, the Reverend Jose "Pepz" Cunanan, explains the rationale of this membership: "We are concerned not so much with the people who are on top but the people who are affected, the victims. For example, the fisherfolk who are affected by the kind of pollution in Manila Bay; or the farmers and the fishermen in Calaca [Batangas, who are hurt by the] coal-fired thermal power plants; or the fishermen who were affected by the oil spill in Bataan."[5]

PEAN's focus evolves from its membership: it calls itself a "people's movement" and defines its work as an effort "to synthesize the various environmental concerns of the different sectors and groups." In this vein, PEAN's secretary-general Noel Duhaylungsod, a soil scientist, describes to us a series of local environmental actions the network helped to advance and publicize, including investigation of mine tailings in Negros. The focus of PEAN's work for the next three years, Duhaylungsod emphasizes, will be to build a national "people-based environmental agenda" through education and action.[6]

Around the time that PEAN was formed, leaders of other dynamic citizens' groups—including Haribon's Kalaw, PRRM's Isagani Serrano, and economist Sixto Roxas—came together to organize the Green Forum–Philippines, a self-described "NGO–People's Organization–Church Forum on Social Equity, Sustainable Development and Environment." The forum has become a lightning rod for national policy advocacy on environmental issues and, in the words of its founders, works "to create and articulate our national vision for the Philippines through the forging and implementation of policies, strategies and action programs towards peace and sustainable development."[7] In this vein, the Green Forum's 1991 "Economic White Paper" lays out a bold set of proposals to shift "agricultural land, urban land, forest access, mineral access, fishing rights, etc.," to community control and delineates a new accounting system to assess the community costs and benefits of economic activities.[8]

Advancing the sustainable-development agenda, Haribon, the Green Forum, and others of the longer-established citizens' groups are deliberately trying to reach out beyond the 10 percent of the populace that is already organized, to create new alliances that can challenge traditional power centers more effectively. New ingredients are being mixed into the *halo-halo*, and the flavor is constantly being enhanced.

Some might argue that it is still premature to label this diverse collection of organizations that are embracing different pieces of a sustainable-development agenda as anything approaching a coherent movement for sustainable development. But PEAN's Cunanan sums up the moment: "Although it may not be a nationwide movement yet, you can say that there's a trend in these responses [of citizens' groups against environmental destruction]. Each response is like one stone rolling in its own particular situation and place. But now this one stone is being joined by other stones of different sizes. There's some sort of solidarity being developed among the people."[9]

True, no single unifying strategy connects all these organizations, and not all would define themselves as part of a Philippine environmental or sustainable-development movement. But, as we talk with various members of these groups all over the country, we find striking similarities in their analyses of the root causes of the problems, in their critiques of existing development strategies, and in the components of their alternative visions.

In dozens of interviews with leaders and members of these groups, we repeatedly hear variations on four connections which define the trajectory of the movement. Some groups come to these connections as they dig for the roots of the country's development problems; others uncover the connections by seeking the roots of the country's environmental problems. These connections are uniting individuals as diverse as the San Fernando peasant who put her body in front of logging trucks and the Bataan peasant whose house was surrounded by armed soldiers, are making them both part of a new movement for a very different kind of development.

The primary connection is seen in the very phrase used by these various groups when they discuss their vision: "equitable and sustainable development." That is, *the environmental movement is a struggle for equity in the control and management of natural re-*

sources. Wherever we go, we are told that environmental problems spring from a development model that is rooted in inequities and fosters greater inequities. In Palawan, an environmental NGO tells us that the income of the one big commercial logger is three times the size of the combined income of the other 500,000 inhabitants of the province. In the Cordillera Mountains in the north of the country, an indigenous peoples' NGO gives us photographs showing how a huge mining company is enriching its shareholders by dumping toxic mine tailings into the river that is the source of water for thousands of farmers downstream. In Bataan, a fisher explains that a few dozen elite families control the lucrative prawn ponds, which are threatening to dry up the province's coastal fresh-water sources. In each case, the political and military connections of the offending enterprises and individuals provide protection for the plundering.

Hence, the centerpiece of the environmental agendas of communities who depend on the natural resources for their very survival is what at first blush may not sound like a environmentalist's agenda: redistribution of the resources more evenly among the people so that they may use them sustainably—in other words, getting the resources out of the hands of the loggers, big mining companies, and other plunderers and into the communities, be they the Itogon pocket-miners, the San Fernando peasants, or Mount Apo's Lumad. Peasant groups fight for a thoroughgoing redistribution of land. Fishers advance a similarly redistributive "aquarian reform." Indigenous peoples' groups and others concerned with forest issues work for the recognition of ancestral domain and the end of the forest concession system that gives the government the power to concentrate commercial logging concessions in the hands of a few. Small-scale miners seek recognition of their right to continue their age-old pocket-mining against the encroachment of a handful of giant firms. In each case, in the words of one Philippine environmental leader, "Democratizing control of resources is the key to sustainable development."[10]

The "few" who are the objects of these citizens' campaigns include the enclaves of large foreign banks and other creditors who are squeezing far more financial resources out of the country than they are putting in. If you combine the outflow of debt service and people with the hemorrhage of agricultural and other natural resources, Philippine NGO leader Isagani Serrano tells us, "development is not trickling down to the people; it is trickling out." Building on Sixto Roxas's enclave analysis, Roxas, Serrano, and others argue that the dominant development model, with its lack of community-based logic, will by its nature always engender trickle-out economies for the few.

Redistribution, we learn, is a necessary but not sufficient step toward sustainability. Indeed, the environment-equity connection leads to another: *The struggle for the environment and for control of resources requires a far more participatory notion of development.* The Philippine elite and Philippine development planners, along with their foreign funders and advisors, have tended to view the broad mass of Filipinos as cheap productive forces who will contribute their sweat and muscle toward the economy's growth; the benefits of that growth are expected eventually to "trickle down" to those people. In contrast, the new agenda of democratizing control of resources pulls people from the margins to the center of the development process. Groups fighting for the forests are not waiting for trees to be replanted; they are working to achieve their new vision of indigenous upland communities sustainably managing ancestral domain as forest reserves. As part of CPAR's People's Agrarian Reform Code, peasants are occupying and planting idle lands, fighting for reduced land rents, and setting up their own research stations to experiment with traditional seed varieties and organic fertilizer.

Participation, these groups stress, is not just an integral part of the development process; it is a necessary component of environmental protection. As the picketers in San Fernando learn and as we are taught time and time again, even the best laws, treaties, and government decrees cannot alone stop environmental destruction in a country like the Philippines. Many wealthy Filipinos—including the resource destroyers—either ignore laws, have learned to work around them, or, at times, find it cheaper to pay the meager penalties than to comply with the laws.

Recall that struggle of the corn and rice farmers of San Fernando, Bukidnon. After two daring blockades of logging trucks by these peasants and their families in the late 1980s, the Philippine government canceled the timber license of the main firm that was overlogging the surrounding hills. Yet, with the clear complicity of the firm and some local military and government employees, "illegal log-

ging" continued. But the people persevered: they confiscated illegal logs; they launched a hunger strike in Manila. Without this kind
of active participation by citizens' groups, even the most genuine
attempts by governments to halt resource destruction will come to
naught. And, many Filipinos tell us, without democratic control of
resources and without participation, the formal democracy that exists in the Philippines and much of the rest of the world means very
little to the poor people who are in the majority in these countries.

As we have seen, the priority that Philippine groups accord to
democratizing resources and to participation often pits the Philippine environmental movement squarely against some of the most
powerful political and economic figures in the country. Of necessity, the struggle for the environment becomes a struggle for power.
As Serrano explains to us, "It is a cruel illusion to expect the marginalized majority to keep their peace while the rich continue to
enjoy the safety and comfort of their homes because of their monopoly of development benefits." From this comes a third connection: *The struggle for peace is a struggle for sustainable development*—and the struggle for sustainable development is a struggle
for true peace and justice.

In other words, in the analysis of the emerging environmental
and development movement, the absence of equity, participation,
and ecological sustainability has generated widespread social unrest, including the largest insurgency in Asia. As we saw in Bataan,
to combat this insurgency the Philippine government relies on military might. Yet, however many battalions occupy a place like Bataan, there will be no peace—no winning of hearts and minds—
until there is sustainable and equitable development. It therefore
does not surprise us that, increasingly, the growing peace movement in the Philippines (a movement advocating a negotiated
settlement between the government and the insurgency) is discussing development questions. As a priest active in the peace movement phrases it: "For peace to be sustainable in the Philippines,
there must be equitable development."

In turn, growing portions of the environmental movement are
working for the broader peace agenda. They realize that as long as
there is fighting in the countryside, it is nearly impossible for sustainable-development experiments to move forward. Environmen-

tal leader Maximo Kalaw, Jr., has captured it in a clever phrase, as he often does: "The Philippines must transform its notion of national security into natural security."

In this context of conflict, Philippine environmentalists stress yet one more connection vital in their work: *To work for environmentally sustainable development requires working for human rights.*[11] This connection is exemplified by a non-Filipino martyr of the Third World environmental movement, the Brazilian rubber-tapper Chico Mendes, assassinated because his vision of a sustainable future differed from the prevailing notions of nearby wealthy cattle-ranchers.[12] Filipinos working for environmentally sustainable development face similar threats as they challenge the most powerful elements of society: landlords, mining corporations, loggers, and large commercial fishing ventures, along with politicians who protect them. Our fisher friend in Bataan, Ely de la Rosa, was but one of many victims. In February of 1991, for instance, the Philippine military arrested—without warrant—fourteen members of the Haribon Palawan environmental chapter whose launching we witnessed. The arrests came just after the group exposed a military racket that was illegally exporting logs to Malaysia. The Haribon members were charged with "subversion."[13] Frightening and outrageous as these charges are, the fourteen are thus far still among the lucky ones: they are alive. Less fortunate were two young men working with farmers to save the forests in the central island of Samar. Just a week after Ely de la Rosa's murder in Bataan in January of 1990, the two were picked up by the military. A few days later a fisherman had a ghastly catch in his fishnet: the severed head of one of them, showing clear evidence of torture.

To become an active environmentalist in the Philippines is to risk one's life. Under these circumstances, those working in partnership with Philippine environmentalists are learning that part of their work is the struggle for the basic human rights of the Filipino people—and are coming to their support with international protests of outrage when necessary (as was done in the case of the Palawan 14).

Our constant exposure to these four connections that many in the emerging Philippine sustainable-development movement see at the root of both environmental degradation and development problems helps us understand why many conventional explanations regarding the causes of Third World environmental degradation, while not necessarily false, do not go deep enough.

Take perhaps the most commonly proffered conventional explanation of forest destruction, one we hear repeatedly in Palawan from big commercial loggers and from government officials. The main destroyers of the forest, they claim, are the millions of poor Filipinos crowding the uplands. Put simply: poverty causes environmental destruction. This is not totally false; some poor farmers do contribute to environmental degradation. But they are not the root cause. As Jorge Emmanuel of the California-based Philippine Environmental Support Network stresses in summarizing the Philippine environmental movement: "They do not say that the poor are the cause of environmental destruction. Rather, they look at poverty in the context of gross inequalities in the distribution of resources, income, economic and political power."[14]

Discussion about the millions of poor farmers pushing (and being pushed) further into the fragile ecosystem of the forested uplands inevitably leads to a second conventional argument, the demographic one that a high population growth rate is the root cause of natural resource degradation in this overwhelmingly Catholic country. The problem, some posit, is not just poor people; it is *too many* poor people. The Philippine population growth rate is indeed shockingly high: each year the Philippine population grows at a rate somewhere between 2.4 and 2.8 percent, among the highest of the rates in Southeast Asia. The rate means that the current population will double in around a quarter of a century. (The United States, with four times the population of the Philippines, has thirty-one times the land area—although intensity of resource use per person in the United States is much higher than in the Philippines.)[15]

Again, there is a grain of truth here: such rapid population growth does pose tremendous human and environmental challenges in a poor society; it is not a trivial problem. But we have come to appreciate in our extended visits with rural Filipinos why poor Filipino peasants deprived of power over economic assets are inclined to have as many children as possible. It is a rational response to grinding poverty. Children become not only additional hands to plant and harvest more crops but also the only savings account and financial safety net that most poor peasants will ever have. In addition, we often observe that for people who live lives of tedious work and sacrifice, children serve as a major source of joy and laughter.

Development economist James Boyce concisely sums up the root causes of population expansion in the Third World with arguments that bear special relevance to the Philippines:

Rapid population growth is a symptom of . . . unequal distribution of wealth and power. For the dispossessed, and for impoverished women in particular, children may not be the "ultimate resource," but they are one of the few resources at their command. At the same time, many women and men who want safe birth control and abortion cannot get it, just as they cannot get adequate food, health care, education, and other basic needs. The need for children and the lack of birth control both contribute to rapid population growth. This in turn can have a negative feedback effect, putting greater stress on environmental resources. But to identify population as the root of the problem is to mistake a symptom for the cause.[16]

Boyce's observations on the need for family planning programs and easily available, inexpensive contraceptives ring especially true in the Philippines, where neither is a reality. Indeed, many Filipinas indicate in surveys that they would like to stop having children.

In sum: current Philippine population growth rates are unsustainable. But rapid population growth is motivated primarily by widespread poverty; the root problem is inequity. A sustainable and equitable development path, in attacking the root causes of poverty, is likely to be the best population policy—and the best environmental policy as well.[17]

A more recent addition to these traditional arguments comes from economists: environmental destruction, it is said, is caused by wrong prices. By this, economists at places like the World Bank mean that, for instance, the prices Philippine commercial loggers pay for their concessions are far less than full social costs would dictate, are indeed so low that they encourage particularly destructive forms of cutting. As we discovered in Palawan and elsewhere, these charges clearly are too low; society overall is subsidizing the loggers and this underpricing undoubtedly contributes to the destruction.

But we also learn quickly that an increase in fees will not necessarily solve the problem. Follow what happened when Aquino's

DENR Secretary Factoran attempted to raise charges to loggers. The moment the government announced the fee increases, an association of logging concessionaires took the Department of Environment and Natural Resources to court, calling the new fees "excessive and arbitrary."[18] Whether or not DENR prevails in court, there is also Congress to contend with. Indeed, Congress refused to allow DENR to increase the logging fees as much as Factoran had originally announced. As this example illustrates, in a system where the powerful loggers control many of the politicians, getting the prices right is not a simple feat.

In other words, the identity of the resource plunderers in a country like the Philippines indicates a key fact: the prices are deliberately set too low. And, considering the economic and political power of the plunderers and the relative poverty of the government bureaucracy, "there is no reason to assume that the tax [or fees] can be more easily assessed and collected than quantitative rules [such as logging bans] enforced," as an Asian Development Bank paper on the subject concluded.[19] The only way out is to break the connection between the politicians and the few large resource controllers, a feat which—once again—requires democratizing control of resources.

From these root connections that link environmental issues inextricably to development issues, Philippine citizens' groups are led to an entirely new vision of development, one that stands in marked contrast to the traditional vision of the Philippine government and its main supporters in the business and donor communities. This new vision is part of what makes the direction of Philippine environmentalism so exciting.

Whereas the traditional focus looks to economic growth as the key indicator of development, the proponents of sustainable development tell us that the goals of development should be recentered on four principles: ecological sustainability, equity, participation, and improvement of the lives of the poor majority.

In addition, many citizens' groups are looking to the indigenous peoples of the Philippines for guidance on formulating an additional principle that stresses respect for cultural identity.[20] They point out that indigenous Filipinos still living on their ancestral lands, such as the Bagobo of Mindanao's Mount Apo, have sustainably managed mineral, land, and forest resources for thousands of years. From the dazzling centuries-old rice terraces in the northern Cordilleras to the simple techniques of the Itogon pocket-miners, the technologies and practices of these people are being restudied for their contribution to a more sustainable future for the whole country.

If these new criteria for measuring the development process are different from the traditional ones, so too are the principal agents of development. Proponents of the traditional approach view the market as the primary agent of development; state-socialism advocates assign the central role to the national government. The emerging sustainable-development movement in the Philippines rejects both of these approaches and instead places primacy on the institutions of civil society, and particularly on the mass-based organizations of peasants, workers, fishers, women, urban poor, and indigenous peoples.

Unfettered markets in highly unequal societies, the new movement argues, only exacerbate the inequalities. Governments, in turn, suffer from three weaknesses. First, in an increasingly globalized world economy where large corporations and banks are highly mobile, these firms can effectively play governments off against one another as they search for ideal investment sites. (Witness the courtship necessary to entice firms to the Bataan Export Processing Zone.) Second, the Philippine government, like many others, is so laden with debt and fiscal crises that its potential as a dynamic social and economic actor is severely curtailed. Third, in countries where natural resources have been the key to economic power, governments are easily molded to serve the needs of the resource exploiters.

This said, it is nonetheless true that most Filipino proponents of sustainable development do not entirely shun either markets or governments. On one hand, some tell us, the private sector remains the most efficient producer of most goods; with proper incentives, it could produce for the broader social good. On the other, the national government remains crucial to the equity equation; it is uniquely positioned to abrogate logging and mining concessions, implement land reform, and redistribute the rights to other resources.

In other words, governments and markets are important in the development process, although their precise roles are still the subject of enormous debate.[21] But the key agents, those who can engender participation and sustainably manage natural resources, are the rapidly growing citizens' organizations. Engaged at the local, regional, and national levels, these organizations can become—and, indeed, as we see throughout our travels, are already becoming—central actors in the Philippine development process.

Despite this growing unity among Philippine citizens' groups on the root connections, the vision, and the identities of the principal agents in development, no unified strategy on how to build a sustainable alternative has yet emerged. Why is this? We heard and saw at least three reasons. First, the groups spearheading the sustainable-development movement come from diverse political groupings; they are gaining experience in working together in coalitions, formal or informal, but they are still new at it. There remain understandable tensions and growing pains. Second, twenty years of repressive rule by the Marcos conjugal dictatorship drove many citizens' groups underground; a number of the most promising leaders were imprisoned or killed. Only since 1986 has there been opportunity for open organizing, and even so, military harassment—as in Bataan—is still all too common. Third, with the collapse of state socialism in Eastern Europe and the Soviet Union and the electoral defeat of the Sandinistas in Nicaragua, many political groups in the Philippines are reassessing both strategy and a number of major components of their worldview.

These reasons are particularly applicable to one of the largest and historically most dynamic centers of the Philippine citizens' movement, the broad left groupings associated with the underground National Democratic Front. For two decades, Filipinos inspired by the national democratic vision organized hundreds of thousands of workers, peasants, and others marginalized by the dominant development model. At the core of that movement has historically stood a well-organized, hierarchical Communist party that held the ultimate goal of seizing control of the national government, primarily through the armed resistance of a largely peasant-based New People's Army. Now, many within this movement are revising these precepts as they seek to draw insights from world events.[22] One loud lesson involves a greater awareness of environmental problems and the need for more sustainable alternatives.

Not only are the national democrats reassessing strategy; so too are other organizations that comprise the broader sustainable-development movement. Many are learning more about the nature of development, democracy, and participation from some of the newer, more spontaneous organizations within that larger movement, such as the peasants of San Fernando. Among the many lessons that San Fernando's peasants and their counterparts elsewhere are teaching is that development is not an absolute goal but, rather, a constant process in which there will be both gains and setbacks. Through active participation by the community, the people of San Fernando keep expanding their understanding of what is necessary for their community's ecological sustainability. Each victory they have won has provoked a counterattack by those who control the resources, and each has unearthed some further complicating factor. The point is not so much victory or defeat as it is that the residents of San Fernando remain mobilized in their own organizations. As such, they are participating in the development process.

Saying that a unified alternative-development strategy does not exist does not deny that many mutually reinforcing strategies are being launched. As development is redefined as a process involving participation, equity, ecological sustainability, and enhanced well-being for the poor majority, a period of active experimentation in reshaping old strategies and creating new ones is under way. Citizens' groups are *not* looking for a new universal strategy for development. Rather, they are engaged in a variety of struggles against the dominant model and in numerous experiments that attempt to construct viable alternatives. In a wide array of activities at the local, regional, national, and international levels, the building blocks of equitable and sustainable development in the Philippine context are being forged.

Citizens' movements in the Philippines have a long and illustrious history of campaigns and projects that advance the sustainable-development agenda at a *local* level. In the thousands of small-scale socioeconomic development projects created and implemented by the hundreds of development NGOs, the principles of sustainable development have gained importance. This book has chronicled many of these projects. Peasant groups are creating demonstration projects to retrieve and improve traditional rice varieties less dependent on chemical fertilizers. Fisher groups are replanting mangroves and rejuvenating coral-reef fishing areas. And so on.

As many leaders of the NGOs and POs stress to us, a long-term vision of a sustainable, equitable future is inadequate: the lives of the poor and oppressed demand immediate improvement, even if the gains are only marginal ones.[23] Organizer Dinky Soliman tells us:

There has to be a balance between the vision and the here and now. The push is: what can [be done] to make a difference in their lives now? . . . and to look at it as a building block to make the vision happen. If you want to maintain the [local] base and make the base vibrant, there have to be palpable gains now. . . . At the local level, organizations have actually made a difference in the economic situation of the people as well as in their political life.

Aware that dynamic local projects do not necessarily scale up to a comprehensive alternative, some creative citizens' groups have begun experimenting with *regional development* or what they call area development. Notable here is a coalition effort called the Convergence for Integrated Community-Based Development. For Convergence, the unit of analysis and action is not the traditional political boundaries of provinces or regions but ecological zones of several municipalities that share certain environmental, social, economic, and political characteristics. "Nature," explains economist Sixto Roxas to us, "gives you a lead on how to define community." Serrano, who is, along with Roxas, one of the movers of the Convergence group, elaborates:

The area is a grid constructed from an overlay of ecological, economic and political factors. The first refers to the 350 river systems which basically defined the pattern of human settlements [in the Philippines] through time. The second speaks of an equal number of market poles or wholesale towns linking these communities. The third has to do with the division of the territory from the perspective of government. The whole fragile archipelagic ecosystem may be cut up into some 220 such areas.[24]

As of mid–1991, organizations in several areas around the country are initiating dialogues with people's organizations and local NGOs to begin strategic alternative-development planning exercises along these lines.[25] We attend one such session in Bataan in

May, 1991. The session begins with the presentation of a detailed assessment of the economic system of the small province and its adverse ecological consequences. The assessment involves delineation of the enclave nature of Bataan's development, focusing on the extensive trickle-out of agricultural and industrial resources from the province as well as on the identities of the resource controllers. The participants build from this a list of the victims of development in Bataan and another list of the beneficiaries. Of particular interest to many participants is that beyond the primary victims (the poor peasants, workers, fishers, and indigenous peoples), a secondary rung of victims includes groups that few had previously considered to be potential allies: small entrepreneurs, small fishpond owners, small fertilizer dealers, and other segments of the middle class.

A second, political assessment of the province demonstrates how the resource controllers are connected to the political clans who dominate the province. But it also identifies a broad range of regional, civic, cultural, and other community groups that might serve as allies in alternative development. Future sessions are planned for people's organizations with the goal of moving from area assessment to articulation of the communities' vision of area development and, eventually, to short-, medium-, and long-term plans of how to reach that vision. The idea, overall, is to devise an area-development logic that reverses the resource leakage and shatters the enclave character of the current development path in a province like Bataan. Once again, the centerpiece of this alternative is a shift in control of local resources to community-based ventures that will manage resource use more sustainably.

Will it work? The participants readily admit that they do not know. But they are determined to try, to recover and learn from the inevitable mistakes, and constantly to reformulate their strategy. "Jump, jump, jump . . . gain experience," one of the participants emphasizes to us, explaining that this is the moment for the sustainable-development movement to experiment at all levels.

Area development presumes a step-by-step process of people taking control of local resources. Serrano tells us that "a community can come to power without actually taking power. Slowly you pulverize centralized power by breaking it up and taking control." Moreover, once a critical mass of areas is undergoing the process, the area developers argue, you should be able to transform the development paradigm of the whole country. In other words, the area-based strategy is at its core a *national* strategy, a plan for sustainable development for the whole country.

As some organizations experiment with local and regional development, others, and especially national coalitions, have taken advantage of Corazon Aquino's resumption of constitutional government to push the government to do its share as an agent of sustainable development. This *policy advocacy work on the national level* is not undertaken naively. Most recognize that the still relatively young Congress and executive branch are dominated by landlords and others whose very power and wealth came through the plunder of resources, but still they feel that openings for change exist. Organizers have focused advocacy work on chipping away at the power of the resource controllers (including, ironically, the state itself, which officially claims ownership of forest, mineral, and marine resources) while simultaneously enhancing the power of the people.

The campaigns chosen for the advocacy work reinforce the point that sound environmental policy is one and the same as sound development policy. Examples abound; some have been detailed in earlier chapters. Groups concerned with forest resources lobby for a nationwide ban on commercial logging and for new measures to empower communities to serve as forest protectors and as sustainable users of forest resources. Organizations in the Cordillera push for a ban on open-pit mining. In lowland agriculture, peasant groups fight for genuine land reform. Fisher groups demand aquarian reform and the closing of such overfished areas as Manila Bay to all but municipal fishers. Other NGOs, such as the broad-based Freedom from Debt Coalition, lobby to end the trickle-out of financial resources through a cap on debt-service payments and repudiation of several loans, including those for the Bataan nuclear power plant, that their research has demonstrated to be fraudulent.

Groups engaged in advocacy, from the Freedom from Debt Coalition to Green Forum–Philippines, have found exciting new allies in a small number of NGOs that have launched legal battles in the executive branch, Congress, and the courts. These NGOs, such as the Legal Rights and Natural Resources Center, formed in 1988, are staffed with some of the country's foremost young lawyers. World Resources Institute lawyer Owen Lynch, who, when he was based at the University of the Philippines, taught many of the lawyers now leading these groups, explains the rationale: "In the Philippines . . . there are some good laws. It is interesting how good laws that empower people are often the ones that no one ever pays much attention to." Lynch, along with Philippine lawyers, has zeroed in on a 1909 U.S. Supreme Court decision (by the great Oliver Wendell Holmes) that held that indigenous Filipinos in the then-U.S. colony who had occupied their land "since time immemorial" had rights to that so-called public land. Such groups as the Legal Rights and Natural Resources Center are using the 1909 case and other laws to strengthen fights for indigenous peoples' rights, from Mount Apo in the south to the Cordillera Mountains in the north.[26]

These battles are vital to the larger struggle of shifting forested areas into community control. Despite being long-term forest occupants who have engaged in sustainable practices for centuries, millions of indigenous peoples in the uplands technically remain squatters on public land. As Chip Fay, director of the Manila office of Friends of the Earth, explains to us, "The key is recognizing their ancestral rights to the land and other resources." Fay describes the ancestral-domain fight in the Philippines as "perhaps the most advanced in the world in understanding that recognition of ancestral-domain rights is a major environmental and development issue."

For shorter-term forest occupants, proposals have been put forward to offer twenty-five-year "stewardship contracts" contingent on occupants practicing sustainable natural-resource management. Related proposals advocate replacing the timber licensing system with community-based schemes of resource management. Indeed, the common thread behind the national advocacy work is, as Fay stresses, something that makes environmental and developmental sense: "The people who are most directly dependent on the natural resources . . . are the greatest stakeholders and must be recognized as full partners in the effort to protect and sustainably manage them."

This is not just a long-term vision. Victories have already been won. With prodding from the Freedom from Debt Coalition, for example, both houses of Congress passed debt-repayment caps. A small victory was won in 1991 when the government's Department of Environment and Natural Resources announced a logging ban (effective January, 1992) in virgin forests, which constitute approximately one-tenth of the forest that remains. A sizable portion of this primary growth is in Palawan. As for the fishers' advocacy work, eleven overfished bays have been closed to commercial fishing. And DENR has announced initial steps toward delineation and recognition of ancestral-domain rights.

The list sounds impressive but, as many at the forefront of this advocacy work stress to us, these are, at best, partial victories. Without broader structural changes in the political economy, many will be decidedly short-lived. For instance, President Aquino vetoed the debt-cap in mid–1991. And, as the implementation problems of the logging bans that exist in Bukidnon and elsewhere already illustrate, well-connected resource controllers will most likely use their connections to continue cutting, fishing, and plundering. Moreover, as Secretary Factoran admits to us, DENR is plagued with corruption at lower levels and "the government will never have the resources to attend to the environmental problems adequately." Even well-meaning government officials face limited resources and power.

But the citizens' groups recognize the importance of this level of work, however tarnished or short-lived the victories may be. Through such work the movement is gaining experience as it lays the foundation for what could be major changes in natural-resource management based on the principles of equity and participation. The defeats seem simply to reinforce the belief in the primacy of civil society as an agent of development.

In addition to this work on local, regional, and national levels, Philippine citizens' groups have been active on an *international level*, forming partnerships with environmental, development, religious, and other groups in Australia, Europe, Japan, and the United States. Part of the motivation for expanding international links has been Filipinos' growing realization that transnational connections are the only way to fight international impediments to sustainable development, from the debt crisis and the power of transnational banks, to environmentally destructive foreign-funded aid projects, to uncontrolled flows of foreign investment.[27]

But this international partnership does not have only a negative agenda. These links are also becoming positive bridges of assistance, expertise, and even trade in products produced under equitable and sustainable conditions. Institutionalized through such groups as the Philippine Development Forum in the United States, these new alliances are serving as international conduits for innovative ideas, curricula, and campaigns based on sustainable development. In some countries, citizens' groups have convinced their governments to channel increasing amounts of official development assistance to Philippine NGO networks. The most notable example can be found in Canada, where over a third of the government's development assistance to the Philippines now goes directly to the major development NGO networks. Explains Horacio Morales, Jr., president of the Philippine Rural Reconstruction Movement, "There's nothing wrong with official development aid per se. If it's a true partnership, then NGOs should be able to work with the government, while continuing to advocate democratic development strategies."[28]

We first left Washington during the long hot summer of 1988, when fears of global warming were spreading through the public consciousness and reinforcing a growing concern over global environmental issues. During that year, the wide dissemination of a 1987 report issued by a special United Nations commission that was chaired by Norway's prime minister, Gro Harlem Brundtland, contributed to the popularization of the term *sustainable development*.[29] In December of 1988, Chico Mendes was murdered and the destruction of tropical rainforests became a topic of conversation globally. And by 1991, preparations for the 1992 United Nations Conference on Environment and Development, the Earth Summit, sparked reports of environmental catastrophes in mass-circulation magazines and newspapers.

As a result, we discover on each return to Washington that talk of environmental issues is spreading. Indeed, Washington is abuzz with many of the same terms we hear throughout the Philippines—in particular, *sustainable development*. Yet, we soon learn, the phrase as used in Washington represents a profoundly different conception of development than the one emerging from citizens' groups in the Philippines. The "Washington consensus" about development is captured in words like *structural adjustment* and *free market* rather than *equity* and *participation*.[30]

Among donor agencies from the U.S. government's Agency for

International Development to the intergovernmental ("multilateral") development and financial institutions, the collapse of state socialism in Eastern Europe and the former Soviet Union is trumpeted as the ultimate victory of "free-market" development. And we discover beneath this triumphalism in official development circles that there is near-total agreement that the debate on development has all but ended. In other words, the virtual silence we find in official Washington on development alternatives is the silence of people who think they have won. The remark made to a Washington, D.C., gathering by a top official of a leading international financial institution in late 1991 sums up the smug spirit of triumphalism: "The world knows much better now what [economic development] policies work and what policies do not. . . . [Now] we almost [never] hear calls for alternative strategies based on harebrained schemes."

We are struck by the absence of the vibrant debate we heard in the Philippines. And we are shocked that the model being hailed as the victor is precisely the strategy whose colossal failure we just witnessed in the Philippines. In a very real sense, the Philippines, under Ferdinand Marcos and Corazon Aquino, had become a guinea pig of sorts of this model—proof enough that it leads not to sustainable development but to what citizens' groups there now call unsustainable development.[31]

Moreover, the Philippines was hardly the only test case. Since the onset of the 1980s, throughout the Third World aid agencies have promoted "structural adjustment" and "market-oriented" reform packages that mandate severely cutting government spending to balance budgets, eliminating trade barriers and social subsidies, encouraging exports, devaluing currencies, and dismantling barriers to foreign investment. Author Susan George sums up the prescription in four words: "Earn more, spend less."[32] The primary proponents of the free-market approach to development have been the World Bank and the International Monetary Fund (IMF), the two main multilateral economic agencies set up in the waning months of World War II. As severe debt crises emerged in many developing countries during the 1980s, the IMF and the World Bank gained great power to attach to desperately needed loans conditions based on this structural-adjustment model.[33]

The triumphalism of the "Washington consensus" astounds us also because of what we observe, read, and are told by practitioners and observers of the development process in other Third World areas where the model was, and is still being, promoted. There, as in the Philippines, nature is striking back in reaction to decades of unsustainable development. To varying degrees, natural-resource plunder has been integral to the history of most of Latin America, Africa, Asia, and the formerly socialist economies of Eastern Europe. The recent wave of structural adjustment, with its heavy emphasis on increasing exports, has exacerbated the problem, for the export gains have often been accomplished by shifting more land to cash crops, expanding mining concessions, and cutting down more forests.

But if nature is taking its revenge across the Third World, so too are people beginning to fight back in its—and their—defense. Throughout the Third World can be found growing citizens' movements of ordinary people who have been ill served by the structural-adjustment version of free-market economics. According to one estimate, more than 100 million people belong to hundreds of thousands of organizations across the developing world that are campaigning against timber companies, unsustainable agriculture, industrial pollution, nuclear power plants, and the giant projects that many governments equate with development.[34]

In Sarawak, Malaysia, indigenous peoples have blockaded timber destined for export markets in Japan and Europe. "Greenbelt movements," organized by women, are trying to reclaim parts of urban Kenya and Mozambique for vegetable gardens and are rediscovering traditional, sustainable agroforestry techniques. In India in 1989, 60,000 indigenous peoples, landless laborers, and peasants gathered in a small town to protest a series of dams (partially financed by the World Bank) in the Narmada Valley. On the other side of the world, Brazilian Indians from forty tribal nations came together that same year to oppose construction of several hydroelectric dams planned for the Xingu River. Soon thereafter, Indians, rubber-tappers, nut-gatherers, and river people formed the Alliance of the Peoples of the Forest to save the Amazon. Even South Korea and Taiwan, the "model" countries of the export-oriented structural-adjustment school, have entered difficult periods in which the delayed repercussions of repressing workers' and democratic rights and exploiting natural resources are surfacing in widespread social upheaval.[35]

Moreover, we see evidence that citizens' groups across Africa, Asia, and Latin America are reaching a consensus about development that bears striking similarities to the notion of equitable and sustainable development we found in the Philippines. Participants and leaders of various movements from different countries have begun meeting with one another to share experiences and strategies and to build a common vision. In the documents and testimony of these emerging movements lies a compelling critique of the dominant model that complements the one we heard in the Philippines. Both critiques center on key consequences of the structural-adjustment model: its emphasis on the plunder of natural resources; its promotion of enclave-based, trickle-out resource leakage and trickle-down development; and its top-down approach by and for the elite few. From Arusha to Australia, from Managua to Manila, and from the thousands at the 1992 Earth Summit in Brazil, international citizens' declarations are being hammered out that represent the beginnings of a global sustainable-development movement.[36]

In short, the "Washington consensus" on the free-market approach that is shared so widely by governments and donor agencies is being rejected by growing numbers of Third World citizens' groups. The ranks of the opposition grow as the degradation of resources and people reaches critical levels.

Yet, as we discover back in Washington, for the moment the official development establishment is largely unaware of the strength of this movement and the depth of its convictions. Their ignorance of the gathering opposition—their blinders—reminds us of the international officials who gathered by the thousands in Manila for the 1976 World Bank–IMF annual meeting. The Marcoses removed much of Philippine reality from the visitors' direct line of vision by erecting fences that placed the worst slum areas out of sight. And most visitors chose not to venture beyond the fence.

We have the feeling upon our return to the United States that, in the face of these growing citizens' movements around the world, the fences separating the movements from the traditional development establishment cannot long stand. As the Philippines so dramatically illustrates, new issues in the post–Cold War world are replacing the old ones—but are just as critical for the survival of the world. Whereas for the past three-quarters of a century the main development debate was between capitalist and socialist options, the central debate of the next period will be between the free-market school and the growing ranks promoting an alternative vision of sustainable and equitable development.

On one level, what we have offered in this book are stories: tales of brave people organizing to fight for a future to bequeath to their children. But we offer these impressions of the Philippines also as fuel to kindle the development debate. The rich Philippine experience and the ongoing experiments will substantially enhance the global struggle for sustainable, equitable, and participatory development. It may yet seem a whisper to ears outside the Philippines—but it is already loud enough for us to hear and learn from, if only we are ready to listen.

Some readers, we know, will close this book unconvinced that the new visions shared here offer a concrete alternative to contemporary development models. To them we suggest that they regard these chapters as an invitation to witness an exciting edge of the political future and that they withhold final judgment for at least a few years. This is a story well worth following.

In this decade and into the twenty-first century, old and new Philippine movements with novel ideas and a battery of strategies will be creating sustainable-development alternatives that are exciting and challenging not only for Filipinos but for all people seeking new ways to hold the earth together while making life better for its inhabitants. The catalyst: fragile ecological limits that have been passed. The actors: one of the most dynamic networks of citizens' groups in the world, building on decades of activity. Key ingredients: enormous amounts of vision, of hope, and of commitment. The result: one of the most fertile countries in the world for experiments based on a different kind of people's power.

For the millions of Filipino children, paths leading not to plunder but toward a more equitable, sustainable, and dignified future are beginning to emerge. And these paths are already transforming the Philippines into a nation with something to offer its children.

Notes

Chapter One: Generation Lost

1. In the late 1980s, the exchange rate was approximately 20 pesos to 1 dollar. By the early 1990s, the peso had been depreciated to approximately 27 pesos to 1 dollar.

2. See, for instance, Bill Hewitt with Richard Vokey et al., "Children of the Gutter," *Newsweek* (May 1, 1989); Depthnews, "Govt. Steps Up Drive to Help the Country's 86,000 Streetchildren," *Manila Chronicle*, June 4, 1989; and Nimfa Rueda, "DOLE: Number of Working Filipino Children Now 5M," *Philippine Daily Inquirer*, July 28, 1990.

3. *Philippine Daily Inquirer*, December 29, 1990, quoted in National Movement for Civil Liberties, "Bulletin Board," *National Midweek* 7, 2 (November 27, 1991): inside back cover.

4. Statistics in the above two paragraphs are from Miguel Suarez, "All Work and No Play for These Youngsters," *Manila Chronicle*, October 7, 1988; study presented at the First International Conference on Children in Asia, held at the Philippines International Convention Center, May, 1989, as reported in Nimfa Rueda, "Street Children Turn to Sex," *Manila Chronicle*, May 12, 1989; Bureau of Women and Young Workers, Department of Labor and Employment, Republic of the Philippines, *Philippines: National Monograph on Child Labor* (Manila: Bureau of Women and Young Workers, September 4, 1987), pp. 1–3; and Sheila S. Coronel, "Child Labor: A Necessary Evil," *Manila Chronicle*, October 23, 1988.

In the rural areas, according to the Philippine Department of Labor and Employment, an estimated 9.5 million Filipinos work without pay on farms; the majority of these workers are children. Wages as low as 1 peso a day were reported in Mary Ann L. Ruiz, Ruby L. Dimaano, and Carmelita C. Rayala, "Children in the Garment Industry," *Philippine Labor Review*, special issue on "The Young Workers: A Closer Look" 10, 1 (January–June, 1986): 29. See also *Philippine Journal of Industrial Relations* (Journal of the University of the Philippines Institute of Industrial Relations), special issue on "Child Labor and Philippine Industrial Relations" 8, 1 (1986).

5. National Literacy Study Committee of the Department of Education, Culture, and Sports, "Study of the Literacy Situation in the Philippines," cited in Antonio Rimando, "Efforts Launched to Combat Illiteracy," *Manila Chronicle*, November 27, 1988; and 1988 Updated Medium-Term Development Plan published by the National Economic and Development Authority (NEDA), cited in Roberto Yap, "Our Leaders Don't See the Big Picture," *Manila Chronicle*, January 19, 1989.

6. This sentence disappeared in the sanitized public version of the study: World Bank, *The Philippine Poor: What Is to Be Done?* (Washington, D.C.: World Bank, 1988), confidential version, p. 1 of Summary and Conclusions. The final version, dated October 17, 1988, was titled *The Philippines: The Challenge of Poverty.*

7. The World Bank calculated that 12 million Filipinos entered the ranks of the "absolute poor" between 1975 and 1985, pushing the percentage of families whose incomes could not meet basic needs up from 45 to 52 percent (World Bank, *The Philippine Poor*, p. 1 of Summary and Conclusions). In the Visayas region of the central Philippines, the poverty rate jumps to 70 percent (World Bank, *The Philippine Poor*, p. 1 of chapter 1). The Presidential Commission on Urban Poor cited estimates of families falling below the poverty threshold that range from 59 percent to 71 percent for the country as a whole (Presidential Commission on Urban Poor, "Situationer on the Urban Poverty Problem" [Manila: Presidential Commission on Urban Poor, October 1987], p. 8).

A Philippine government working group on poverty calculated a 10 percent decline from 1986 to 1988 in the percentage of Filipinos under the poverty line (from 59 percent to 49 percent). Yet, by the admission of the former chair of the group herself, the figure was merely an "estimate," based on potentially overly optimistic assumptions, and not to be taken as the "gospel truth" (quoted in Margot Cohen, "A Menu for Malnutrition," *Far Eastern Economic Review* [July 12, 1990]: 38–39).

8. Some 52.8 percent of Filipinos are under twenty years of age; 40 percent are under fourteen, and 19.9 percent are not yet seven years old: United Nations Children's Fund and Republic of the Philippines, *Situation of Children and Women in the Philippines* (Manila: UNICEF and Republic of the Philippines, 1987), p. 50.

9. Note that this trip was before the July, 1990, earthquake that devastated the city of Baguio.

10. Katherine Ellison, *Imelda: Steel Butterfly of the Philippines* (New York: McGraw-Hill, 1988), p. 42.

11. Estimate on child prostitutes from the National Conference of the Filipino Child, cited in Joseph Collins, "The Philippines: A Nation of Children Under the Gun," *Food First Action Alert* (San Francisco: Institute for Food and Development Policy, 1989), p. 3; Nimfa Rueda, "Street Children Turn to Sex," *Manila Chronicle*, May 12, 1989.

12. Buklod Center, "Hospitality—What Price? The U.S. Navy at Subic Bay . . . and the Women's Response," mimeographed publication of the Buklod Center, Olongapo City, Philippines, November, 1988, p. 4.

13. Roy Prosterman and Timothy Hanstad, University of Washington School of Law, "Whether Failure Is Inevitable Under the New Philippine Land Reform Law," unpublished memorandum dated November 3, 1988, pp. 1–2.

14. World Bank, *Philippines: Toward Sustaining the Economic Recovery—Country Economic Memorandum*, Main Report, Report No. 7438-PH (Washington, D.C.: World Bank, October 31, 1988), p. 55.

15. Jose F. Lacaba, "Eye of the Needle," Editorial, *National Midweek* 4, 25 (June 7, 1989): 1. On land reform, see James Putzel, *A Captive Land: The Politics of Agrarian Reform in the Philippines* (New York: Monthly Review Press, 1992).

16. Address of President Corazon Aquino, quoted in Collins, "The Philippines: A Nation of Children Under the Gun," p. 3.

17. Statement by Corazon Aquino at graduation ceremony for the Philippine Military Academy, Baguio, March 22, 1987, quoted in Seth Mydans, "Aquino Demands Military Victory over Insurgents," *New York Times*, March 23, 1987. See also Sheila Coronel, "Dateline Philippines: The Lost Revolution," *Foreign Policy*, no. 84 (Fall, 1991).

18. Sheila Coronel, "Poverty and War Still Stalk a Resurgent Negros," *Manila Chronicle*, November 25, 1988; Frank Fernandez, "The Travails of Negros Occidental," *National Midweek* 5 (December 6, 1989): 18; and Angelito Inocencio, "Hope for the Children," a report by *UNICEF News and Features*, reprinted in *National Midweek* 4 (February 8, 1989): 40.

19. Sheila Coronel, "Sudden Concern for Sipalay," *Manila Times*, May 29, 1989; Red Batario and Girlie Alvarez, "Conflict Takes Its Toll on Children," *Philippine Daily Inquirer*, August 9, 1990; and Dellia Leyva, "Peace: A Distant Dream," *UUSC Philippine Reports* (Unitarian Universalist Service Committee, Boston, Mass.), no. 1 (Fall, 1989): 1. Quote is from Malou Mangahas, "The Children of Negros," *Manila Times*, June 4, 1989.

20. Mangahas, "The Children of Negros."

21. Miguel Suarez, "Dollars from Workers Overseas Still a Major Prop for Economy," *Manila Chronicle*, September 25, 1988; "1.5M Filipinos Now Work Abroad," *Philippine Daily Inquirer*, June 17, 1989; Dennis M. Arroyo, "RP Owns Records in World Health Scene," *Sunday [Philippine] Inquirer Magazine*, October 2, 1988; and M. L. Tan and S. E. Claudio, "Filipino Nurses Get Raw Deal in U.S. Hospitals," *Manila Chronicle*, June 30, 1989. On access to health care, see United Nations Development Programme, *Human Development Report 1991* (New York: Oxford University Press, 1991), p. 142.

22. Jun Alano, "Not Enough Teachers, Rooms This Year," *Philippine Daily Inquirer*, June 3, 1989.

23. World Bank, *The Philippines: The Challenge of Poverty*, Report No. 7144-PH (Washington, D.C.: World Bank, October 17, 1988), p. i.

24. "1.5M Filipinos Now Work Abroad," *Philippine Daily Inquirer*, June 17, 1989; Eric S. Caruncho, "'Katas ng Saudi' and Other Fuel," *Sunday Times Magazine* of the *Manila Times*, April 30, 1989; Suarez, "Dollars from Workers Overseas Still a Major Prop for Economy"; Jenina Joy Chavez, "Filipino Contract Workers: Clipped Wings, Sore Feet," *Ibon Facts & Figures* 14, 10 (May 31, 1991): 3; John McBeth, "Gulf Strike at Economy," *Far Eastern Economic Review* (June 13, 1991): 42; and Gianni Agostinelli, *Migration-Development Interrelationships: The Case of the Philippines* (New York: Center for Migration Studies, 1991). President Aquino is quoted from the Caruncho article.

Note that these figures are from before the August, 1990, invasion of Kuwait by Iraq, which precipitated a temporary exodus of workers from the Gulf. According to the Philippine government, before August, 1990, 63,000 Filipinos were in Iraq and Kuwait: Salamat Ali et al., "Exodus from Araby," *Far Eastern Economic Review* (October 4, 1990): table, p. 23. The *Wall Street Journal* put the figure at 90,000: "Filipinos in the MidEast," *Wall Street Journal*, September 28, 1990.

25. Editorial, "More Jobs Will Halt Export of the Filipino," *Manila Chronicle*, June 22, 1989.

26. Catholic Institute for International Relations, *The Labour Trade: Filipino Migrant Workers Around the World* (London: Catholic Institute for International Relations, 1987), p. 6.

27. According to calculations, respectively, of the Philippine government's National Economic Development Authority and the University of the Philippines School of Labor and Industrial Relations.

28. James Fallows, "A Damaged Culture," *Atlantic Monthly* (November, 1987): 58.

29. The late Lino Brocka on "The United States and the Philippines: In Our Image," television documentary produced by Stanley Karnow and shown on Philippine television (ABS-CBN) on June 12, 1989.

Chapter Two: Nature's Revenge

1. See, for instance, John Maddox, "Environment and Foreign Aid," *Nature* 326 (April 9, 1987): 539.

2. Sources for facts and figures on the transport sector include Gene Orejana, "Metro Transport Woes Still Around," *Sunday [Manila] Times*, June 4, 1989; Beth Pango, "Half of Metro Cars Belch Smoke," *Philippine Daily Inquirer*, May 8, 1989; Belinda Olivares-Cunanan, "Declaring War on Smoke-Belching," *Philippine Daily Inquirer*, February 16, 1989; Dana Batnag, "Factoran Cites Dilemma in Drive Against Belchers," *Manila Chronicle*, February 5, 1989; Romina delos Reyes and Patrick Paez, "Demand Slash in Prices of Spare Parts, Commodities," *Manila Chronicle*, November 15, 1988; and Tita Giron, "75 Per Cent of Manila Vehicles Smoke-Belchers," *Manila Chronicle*, November 7, 1988.

3. Celso R. Roque, "The Decade that Was (or Wasn't) for Filipino Environmentalism," *Diliman Review* 34, 4 (1986): 7.

4. The Grand Antamok Project is also called the Antamok Gold Project.

5. See William Henry Scott, *The Discovery of the Igorots: Spanish Contacts with the Pagans of Northern Luzon*, rev. ed. (Quezon City: New Day Publishers, 1974), pp. 43–46.

6. Center for Alternative Media, *Facts About the Grand Antamok Project* (Baguio: Task Force Against Open Pit Mining, Cordillera Resource Center for Indigenous Peoples' Rights, [1990]), p. 6; and Lulu Gimenez, *Going Against the Giant: The Pocket Miners of Itogon and Benguet Corporation's Grand Antamok Project* (Baguio: Cordillera Resource Center for Indigenous Peoples' Rights, 1991), p. 2. These two superb publications are the best sources of information available on the Grand Antamok Project.

7. In addition to the two publications of the Cordillera Resource Center, information in the above two paragraphs comes from Agnes Fidelis Gloria and Pamela Asprer-Grafilo, "Next Stop Cordillera," *Ibon Facts & Figures* 14, 12 (June 30, 1991); and Ibon Databank, *Primer on Philippine Gold Mining Industry* (Metro-Manila: Ibon Databank, 1979).

In 1986, Benguet was the Philippines' nineteenth largest corporation in terms of sales: Ibon Databank, *Directory of TNCs in the Philippines* (Metro-Manila: Ibon Databank, 1988), p. 72.

8. Benguet Corporation–Benguet Gold Operations, "Environmental Impact Statement," quoted in Center for Alternative Media, *Facts About the Grand Antamok Project*, p. 9; and Gimenez, *Going Against the Giant*, pp. 3, 6.

9. National statistics from Center for Environmental Concerns, "A Glance at Philippine Environmental Data" (Manila: Center for Environ-

mental Concerns, 1990), p. 3; and Jorge Emmanuel, "Green Movement Responds to Environmental Crisis," *WForum* (Washington, D.C.–based Washington Forum on the Philippines) 2, 3 (October–November, 1990): 4. On the mine tailings, see also Edel Guiza, Master's thesis in Development Management, Asian Institute of Management, Manila, 1991.

10. See Gareth Porter with Delfin Ganapin, Jr., *Resources, Population, and the Philippines' Future: A Case Study*, WRI Paper No. 4 (Washington, D.C.: World Resources Institute, 1988); and Norman Myers, "Environmental Degradation and Some Economic Consequences in the Philippines," *Environmental Conservation* 15, 3 (Autumn, 1988).

11. David M. Kummer, "Deforestation in the Post-War Philippines," Ph.D. dissertation, Boston University, 1990, pp. 70, 88; Republic of the Philippines, Department of Environment and Natural Resources, "State of the Environment," draft report (Manila, June, 1989), p. 2. Note that even the figures for the current period are estimates. As geographer David Kummer has said, "No one has any good idea how much deforestation or reforestation is occurring in the Philippines today."

12. In 1988 Owen Lynch and Kirk Talbott estimated that the upland population would reach 18.6 million in 1990. They based their estimate on the thorough demographic survey conducted by Maria Concepcion Cruz that put the upland population in 1980 at 14.4 million. See Maria Concepcion Cruz, *Integrated Summary Report: Population Pressure and Migration—Implications for Upland Development*, CPDS Working Paper No. 86-07 (Los Baños, Laguna: Center for Policy and Development Studies of the University of the Philippines at Los Baños College, 1986); and Owen J. Lynch, Jr., and Kirk Talbott, "Legal Responses to the Philippine Deforestation Crises," *New York University Journal of International Law and Politics* 20, 3 (Spring, 1988).

The term "indigenous peoples" of the Philippines is used here to apply to the 3.5–4.5 million non-Muslim, non-Hispanicized indigenous people of the Philippines. Some refer to these people as ethnic minorities, cultural communities, or tribal Filipinos. The two largest groupings are the 1.5–2 million Lumad of Mindanao and the approximately 1 million indigenous people of the Cordilleras. Some also include the country's approximately 3.5 million Muslim (or Moro) people in this indigenous-peoples category, to reach a total of 7–8 million. The estimates used in this book are based on interviews with Paul "Chip" Fay, Owen Lynch, Jr., and the Legal Rights and Natural Resources Center. For more on the indigenous peoples, see William Henry Scott, *Cracks in the Parchment Curtain* (Quezon City: New Day Publishers, 1985).

13. According to the Legal Rights and Natural Resources Center, "the term ancestral domain refers to all land and natural resources which can

be proved to be, or to have been . . . in the actual possession of indigenous cultural community-members, and all adjacent areas necessary for the utilization, enjoyment and environmental protection of areas actually possessed, including water sources, grazing and pasture lands, timber and forest lands, fishing grounds and the like." For more on ancestral domain, see Antonio G. M. La Viña, "Recognition of Ancestral Domains: An Imperative for Democratic Upland Resource Management," in Chip Fay, ed., *Our Threatened Heritage: The Transcript, Recommendations, and Papers of the Solidarity Seminar on the Environment* (Manila: Solidaridad Publishing House, 1989), pp. 119–25.

14. The term Lumad applies to all the indigenous non-Muslim people in Mindanao.

15. *"D'yandi* Declaration of Principles," sealed in blood and wine by twenty-one *datus* representing nine southern Mindanao Lumad tribes, Kidapawan, North Cotabato, April 13, 1989.

16. "Apo Sandawa *D'yandi* Anniversary Statement," sealed by nine southern Mindanao Lumad tribes, Lake Agko at the foot of Apo Sandawa, Kidapawan, North Cotabato, April 13, 1990.

17. Statement of the Lumad Mindanao Council of Elders, reprinted in *National Midweek* 4 (August 2, 1989): 35.

18. Quoted in Maria Elena Ang, "The Price of Development," *Manila Standard*, July 25, 1991.

On Mount Apo, see Legal Rights and Natural Resources Center, Special Issue on Mount Apo Geothermal Project, *Philippine Natural Resources Law Journal* 2, 2 (May, 1990); Yasmin Arquiza, "People or Power?" in Eric Gamalinda, ed., *Saving the Earth: The Philippine Experience* (Manila: Philippine Center for Investigative Journalism, 1990), pp. 33–46; Rene Agbayani, "Dayandi: 'To the Last Drop . . .'" in Ruffy Manaligod, ed., *Struggle Against Development Aggression: Tribal Filipinos and Ancestral Domain* (Quezon City: Tunay na Alyansa ng Bayan Alay sa Katutubo [TABAK], 1990); Yasmin Arquiza, "Everyday Heroes: Edtami Mansayagan," *National Midweek* 5, 1 (November 8, 1989); Bernardo Lopez, "PNOC in Mt. Apo—A Tribal Perspective," *Philippine Daily Inquirer*, May 2, 1989; and Chip Fay, "Background Paper on the Mt. Apo Geothermal Energy Project" (Washington, D.C.: Environmental Policy Institute [now Friends of the Earth], 1989).

19. On biodiversity, see Myers, "Environmental Degradation and Some Economic Consequences in the Philippines," pp. 210–11; and S. H. Sohmer (of the Bishop Museum, Honolulu), "Preservation and Maintenance of Biological Diversity," annex D, in Dames & Moore International, Louis Berger International, and Institute for Development Anthropology for the United States Agency for International Development, *Sustainable Natural Resources Assessment—Philippines: A Review of the Present Sta-*

tus with Recommendations for Future Directions, U.S. Aid Project 398-0249 (Manila: U.S. Agency for International Development, September, 1989), p. D-2.

20. Center for Environmental Concerns, "A Glance at Philippine Environmental Data," p. 2.

21. On foreign agribusiness in Mindanao, see Porter with Ganapin, *Resources, Population, and the Philippines' Future,* p. 16; and Robin Broad, "Our Children Are Being Kidnapped," *Bulletin of Concerned Asian Scholars* 12, 3 (July–September, 1980).

On the use of banned chemicals, see, for instance, Yoko Nakamura, "Philippine Workers, Japanese Consumers, and Banana Pesticides," *Global Pesticide Campaigner* 1, 1 (October, 1990).

22. The 70 percent figure was used by Maximo Kalaw, Jr.: see Testimony before Subcommittee on Human Rights and International Organizations, Committee on Foreign Affairs, U.S. House of Representatives, September 26, 1990, p. 1. On foreign markets for Philippine coral, see Porter with Ganapin, *Resources, Population, and the Philippines' Future,* p. 42.

Chapter Three: The Last Rainforests

An earlier version of parts of this chapter appeared in Robin Broad and John Cavanagh, "Marcos's Ghost," *Amicus Journal* 11, 4 (Fall, 1989).

1. Department of Environment and Natural Resources, "The Philippine Environment," briefing paper on the state of the environment, Manila, 1989, p. 29; Dames & Moore International, Louis Berger International, and Institute for Development Anthropology for the United States Agency for International Development, *Sustainable Natural Resources Assessment—Philippines: A Review of the Present Status with Recommendations for Future Directions,* U.S. Aid Project 398-0249 (Manila: U.S. Agency for International Development, September, 1989), annex D, p. D-13; and J. Honculada Primavera, "Intensive Prawn Farming in the Philippines: Ecological, Social, and Economic Implications," *Ambio* 20, 1 (February, 1991): 29.

2. Nicholas Guppy, "Tropical Deforestation: The Global View," *Foreign Affairs* 62, 4 (Spring, 1984): 949.

3. See James F. Eder, *On the Road to Tribal Extinction: Depopulation, Deculturation, and Adaptive Well-Being Among the Batak of the Philippines* (Berkeley: University of California Press, 1987).

4. The figure of 19,000 hectares cited in this paragraph is from Melanie Manlogon, "Interview with Maximo T. Kalaw, Jr.: A Million Signatures for Palawan," *National Midweek* 3 (July 6, 1988): 15. The 54 percent

figure was given by Kalaw in personal correspondence to the authors, June 23, 1989. In addition to the interviews we conducted and the *National Midweek* article, the information on Alvarez in this paragraph and the next comes from James Clad and Marites Vitug, "Philippines: The Plunder of Palawan," *Far Eastern Economic Review* (November 24, 1988): cover story; and transcript of interview with Maximo Kalaw, Jr., conducted by Dolores Flamiano, John Gershman, and Walden Bello, staff of the *Philippine Resource Center Monitor*, Philippine Resource Center, Berkeley, California, May, 1989.

5. Ruffy Manaligod, ed., *Struggle Against Development Aggression: Tribal Filipinos and Ancestral Domain* (Quezon City: Tunay na Alyansa ng Bayan Alay sa Katutubo [TABAK], 1990), p. 3. This situation is not unique to the Philippines. As a World Resources Institute study notes: "Throughout the world, governments largely determine how forests should be used. . . . According to a comprehensive FAO assessment, in the Third World over 80 percent of the closed forest area are [*sic*] public lands" (Robert Repetto, *The Forest for the Trees? Government Policies and the Misuse of Forest Resources* [Washington, D.C.: World Resources Institute, 1988], p. 1).

On the Philippines, see also Owen J. Lynch, Jr., "Colonial Legacies in a Fragile Republic: A History of Philippine Land Law and State Formation," Ph.D. dissertation, Yale University Law School, 1991; and Antonio G.M. La Viña, "Recognition of Ancestral Domains: An Imperative for Democratic Upland Resource Management," in Chip Fay, ed., *Our Threatened Heritage: The Transcript, Recommendations, and Papers of the Solidarity Seminar on the Environment* (Manila: Solidaridad Publishing House, 1989).

6. Transcript of interview with Kalaw by Flamiano, Gershman, and Bello, pp. 2–3.

7. Isagani de Castro, Jr., "Money and Moguls: Oiling the Campaign Machinery," in Lorna Kalaw-Tirol and Sheila Coronel, eds., *1992 and Beyond: Forces and Issues in Philippine Elections* (Quezon City: Philippine Center for Investigative Journalism and the Ateneo Center for Social Policy and Public Affairs, 1992); and John McBeth, "The Final Test," *Far Eastern Economic Review* (June 13, 1991): 35. See also Belinda A. Aquino, *Politics of Plunder: The Philippines Under Marcos* (Quezon City: Great Books Trading in cooperation with the University of the Philippines College of Public Administration, 1987); and Paul Hutchcroft, "Oligarchs and Cronies in the Philippine State: The Politics of Patrimonial Plunder," *World Politics* 43, 3 (April, 1991).

8. Sean McDonagh, S.S.C., *The Greening of the Church* (Maryknoll, New York: Orbis Books, 1990), p. 81.

9. Manlogon, "Interview with Kalaw," p. 16.

10. Manlogon, "Interview with Kalaw," p. 16. The budget figure was provided by a member of the Palawan provincial board.

11. See, for example, the advertisement entitled "The Truth Behind the Palawan Forest Conservation Issue," *Philippine Daily Inquirer*, November 26, 1988.

12. Transcript of interview with Kalaw by Flamiano, Gershman, and Bello, p. 2.

13. Gareth Porter with Delfin Ganapin, Jr., *Resources, Population, and the Philippines' Future: A Case Study*, WRI Paper No. 4 (Washington, D.C.: World Resources Institute, 1988), p. 13.

14. See Sheldon Annis, "Debt and Wrong-Way Resource Flows in Costa Rica," *Ethics and International Affairs* 4 (1990): 119, for an insightful distinction between the "merely poor" (who are resource optimizers and protectors) and the "very, very poor" (to whom this paragraph is referring).

15. Nestor Baguinon, "Development and Conservation of Indigenous Non-Dipterocarp Trees and Shrubs," paper prepared for National Conference on Genetic Resources and Development, Tagaytay City, September 2–6, 1987, quoted in McDonagh, *The Greening of the Church*, p. 83.

16. Norman Myers, who has been studying rainforests for decades, summed up the role and motivation of small farmers in a passage that merits quoting at length: "There is strong reason to believe the present deforestation rate will continue to accelerate for the foreseeable future unless vigorous measures are taken with due urgency to tackle the main causes of deforestation, viz. the commercial logger, the cattle rancher and the smallscale farmer. The third appears to account for much more deforestation than the other two combined, while being far less 'blameworthy.' In his main manifestation as the shifted (displaced) cultivator, the smallscale farmer is subject to a host of forces—population pressures, pervasive poverty, maldistribution of traditional farmlands, inequitable land-tenure systems, inadequate attention to subsistence agriculture, adverse trade and aid patterns, and international debt—that he is little able to comprehend, let alone to control. Thus he reflects a failure of development strategies overall, and his problem can be confronted only by a major restructuring of policies on the part of governments and international agencies concerned. Without an integrated effort of sufficient scope, there is every prospect that we shall witness the demise of most tropical forests within another few decades" (Norman Myers, *Deforestation Rates in Tropical Forests and Their Climatic Implications* [London: Friends of the Earth, 1989], p. 2). See also Myers's "Environmental Degradation and Some Economic Consequences in the Philippines," *Environmental Conservation* 15, 3 (Autumn, 1988).

17. See Clad and Vitug, "Philippines: The Plunder of Palawan."

18. Betsy Hartmann and James Boyce, *Needless Hunger: Voices from a Bangladesh Village* (San Francisco: Institute for Food and Development Policy, 1979). See also their *A Quiet Violence: A View from a Bangladesh Village* (San Francisco: Institute for Food and Development Policy, 1983).

19. David M. Kummer, "Deforestation in the Post-War Philippines," Ph.D. dissertation, Boston University, 1990, p. 236.

20. World Wildlife Federation, "First Debt-for-Nature Swap in Asia," news release, June 23, 1988, p. 1.

21. Sylvia Mayuga, "The Last Preserve," *Philippine Daily Globe*, May 30, 1989.

22. McDonagh, *The Greening of the Church*, pp. 74–106; Richard P. Tucker, "Five Hundred Years of Tropical Forest Exploitation," in Suzanne Head and Robert Heizman, eds., *Lessons of the Rainforest* (San Francisco: Sierra Club Books, 1990); Dennis M. Roth, "Philippine Forests and Forestry, 1565–1920," in Richard P. Tucker and J. F. Richards, eds., *Global Deforestation and the Nineteenth Century World Economy* (Durham, N.C.: Duke University Press, 1983), pp. 35–49; and Porter with Ganapin, *Resources, Population, and the Philippines' Future*, pp. 23–33.

23. Tucker, "Five Hundred Years of Tropical Forest Exploitation," p. 49. "Raw logs" refers to SITC category 242, "rough wood," in United Nations, *1978 Yearbook of International Trade Statistics* (New York: United Nations, 1979), p. 63.

24. Delfin Ganapin, Jr., "Environmental Crisis in the Philippines: A Challenge to the NGO Community," speech at symposium of the Philippine Rural Reconstruction Movement (PRRM), Quezon City, June 29, 1989.

25. Porter with Ganapin, *Resources, Population, and the Philippines' Future*, p. 27.

26. Guppy, "Tropical Deforestation: The Global View," p. 949.

27. See Marites Danguilan-Vitug, "Fighting for Life," *Far Eastern Economic Review* (June 13, 1991).

28. World Bank, *Philippines: Environment and Natural Resource Management Study*, A World Bank Country Study (Washington, D.C.: World Bank, 1989), p. 5.

29. Figures from Republic of the Philippines, Department of Budget and Management, *Budget of Expenditures and Sources of Financing, 1987–1991*, quoted in Jenina Joy Chavez, "Bogged Down (by) Budgeting," *Ibon Facts & Figures* 14, 1 (January 15, 1991): table 1.

30. For more on the World Bank and the International Monetary Fund, see Robin Broad, *Unequal Alliance: The World Bank, the International Monetary Fund, and the Philippines* (Berkeley: University of California Press, 1988; paperback ed., 1990). On the connection between

debt and environmental destruction, see Susan George, *The Debt Boomerang: How Third World Debt Harms Us All* (London: Pluto Press, 1992), pp. 1–33.

31. "A Brazilian Tale," *Economist* (February 18, 1989): 31.

Chapter Four: "The First Environmentalists"

1. Pedro Walpole, "The DENR Fails to Do Its Homework," *Manila Chronicle*, June 1, 1989. Subsequent to our May, 1989, research trip to San Fernando (and to initial drafts of this chapter), two excellent books have been published in the Philippines on San Fernando: Karl M. Gaspar, Redemptorist, *A People's Option: To Struggle for Creation* (Quezon City: Claretian, 1990); and Jun Jabla, *Defending the Forest: A Case Study of San Fernando, Bukidnon, Philippines* (Davao, Philippines: Kinaiyahan Foundation, 1990).

2. Alternate Resource Center, "Mindanao Economy in Brief," *Mindanao Focus*, nos. 14, 15 (April–September, 1987): 98.

3. Jabla, *Defending the Forest*, p. 7.

4. Karl Gaspar, Redemptorist, "Letter from the Mountains," from San Fernando, Bukidnon, July 15, 1988.

5. Jabla, *Defending the Forest*, p. 9.

6. Provincial environment and natural resources officer, quoted in Carol Arguillas, "Mindanao's Grim Scenario: A Desert in 10 Years," *Manila Chronicle*, December 15, 1988.

7. Yasmin Arquiza, "To Fast for Mother Earth," *National Midweek* 4, 42 (October 25, 1989): 4.

8. On PSK and the Redemptorists, see Jabla, *Defending the Forest*.

9. *Caridad C. Almendras, CCA Logging Enterprises vs. Roger Regañon et al.*, restraining order for injunction and damages, Civil Case No. 1748, July 31, 1987 (mimeographed copy).

10. *Caridad C. Almendras, CCA Logging Enterprises vs. Roger Regañon et al.*, restraining order for injunction and damages.

11. "Seven Towns Want Logging Banned in Bukidnon," *Manila Chronicle*, December 1, 1988.

12. Karl Gaspar, Redemptorist, "Letter from the Mountains," from San Fernando, Bukidnon, January 30, 1989.

13. Gaspar, *A People's Option*, p. 156; and Pedro Walpole, "Damage Has Been Done in Bukidnon," *Manila Chronicle*, January 4, 1989.

14. Gaspar, "Letter from the Mountains," January 30, 1989.

15. Walpole, "Damage Has Been Done in Bukidnon."

16. Letter from Roger Regañon et al., members of the Monitoring

Team for the Protection and Rehabilitation of the Forest of San Fernando, Bukidnon, to Secretary Fulgencio Factoran, Jr., June 13, 1989.

17. Edward M. Gerlock, "Listen to the Poor," *Scarboro [Canadian] Missions* (October, 1990): 19.

18. There are more than one hundred linguistic, cultural, and racial groups in the Philippines, with some eleven languages and eighty-seven dialects. The main language spoken by the people of San Fernando is Cebuano Visayan; by those in Manila, Tagalog or Pilipino.

19. Joy Hofer, "Bukidnon: Local Communities Lead the Way," in Eric Gamalinda, ed., *Saving the Earth: The Philippine Experience* (Manila: Philippine Center for Investigative Journalism, 1990), p. 21.

20. Ed Santoalla, "DENR Will Enforce Total Ban in Bukidnon," *Manila Chronicle*, October 5, 1989.

21. Arquiza, "To Fast for Mother Earth," p. 4.

22. Quoted in Ed Santoalla, "Environmentalists End 'Fast for Forest' Protest," *Manila Chronicle*, October 6, 1989.

23. Gerlock, "Listen to the Poor," p. 15.

24. Pedro Walpole, "The Work Begins for Bukidnon 13," *Manila Chronicle*, November 22, 1989.

Chapter Five: Life Along the Death March

1. A scientist at the Aquaculture Department of the Southeast Asian Fisheries Development Center calculated development and equipment costs per hectare of "intensive" prawn farming at about $24,000 and about an equal amount in annual operating expenses: J. Honculada Primavera, "Intensive Prawn Farming in the Philippines: Ecological, Social, and Economic Implications," *Ambio* 20, 1 (February, 1991): 31. See also table 1 of that article.

2. Matt Miller, "Philippines' Prawn Craze Boosts Exports," *Asian Wall Street Journal*, March 28, 1989. In 1988, Philippine prawn exports totaled $250 million.

3. On the environmental costs of prawn farms, see Primavera, "Intensive Prawn Farming in the Philippines"; and Tezza O. Parel, "More Bad News from Negros," *National Midweek* 4, 21 (May 3, 1989). See also "Negros Water Turning Salty," *Manila Chronicle*, November 7, 1988; Priscilla Arias, "Salt Water Found Going to Fishponds," *Manila Bulletin*, March 6, 1989; and H. Melencio, "Prawn Farms Making Negros Water Sources Salty," *Philippine Daily Globe*, July 17, 1989.

Primavera's article also discusses the environmental havoc wrought by Taiwan's prawn boom. For an analysis of the social and environmental impact of shrimp farming in Honduras, see Denise Stanley, "Capitalist Agriculture and Differentiation in Southern Honduras: A Social-Historical Analysis of the Shrimp Boom," Department of Agricultural Economics, University of Wisconsin–Madison, unpublished paper, May 9, 1990. On Bangladesh, see João P. de Campos Guimarães, "Shrimp Culture and Market Incorporation: A Study of Shrimp Culture in Paddy Fields in Southwest Bangladesh," *Development and Change* 20, 4 (1989).

4. In 1988, prawns and shrimp became the leading Philippine export to Japan, according to statistics cited in "Shrimps Lead Exports to Japan," *Philippine Daily Inquirer*, May 30, 1989.

5. David L. Llorito, "Mergers and Acquisitions: Games Big People Play," *Bantaaw: Economic and Social Indicators of Mindanao* 2, 4 (2d Quarter, 1988): 5. This is a publication of the Davao-based Alternate Resource Center.

6. Republic of the Philippines, Department of Health, Regional Health Office No. 3, Integrated Provincial Health Office, "Vital Health Statistics for 1987," Balanga, Bataan, p. 3 (mimeograph).

7. On rural credit in the Philippines, see Sagrario L. Floro and Pan A. Yotopoulos, *Informal Credit Markets and the New Institutional Economics: The Case of Philippine Agriculture* (Boulder: Westview Press, 1991).

8. Survey by Sisters of Fatima Center in Iriga, Bicol, cited in Denis Murphy, "Bad Times for Balatan's Fishermen," *Manila Chronicle*, June 10, 1989.

9. An excellent source on Manila Bay's pollution is the series of seven papers written by researchers at the Tambuyog Development Center and published by the Center as *Manila Bay Researches* (Quezon City: Tambuyog Development Center, 1990). See also Eva S. Diaz, "City's Polluted Waters Worry RP's Neighbors," *Philippine Daily Inquirer*, February 7, 1989.

Cyanide fishing also contributes to the death of the corals. On dynamite and cyanide fishing, see, in addition to the Tambuyog study, Yasmin Arquiza, "Troubled Waters," in Eric Gamalinda, ed., *Saving the Earth: The Philippine Experience* (Manila: Philippine Center for Investigative Journalism, 1990); and World Bank, *Philippines: Forestry, Fisheries, and Agricultural Resource Management Study (ffARM Study)*, Country Department II, Asia Region (Washington, D.C.: World Bank, May 16, 1988), pp. 35–36.

10. See Katherine Ellison, *Imelda: Steel Butterfly of the Philippines* (New York: McGraw-Hill, 1988).

11. Jorge Emmanuel, "The Philippine Environment and Sustainable Development," in Dolores Flamiano and Donald Goertzen, eds., *Critical Decade: Prospects for Democracy in the Philippines in the 1990s* (Berkeley: Philippine Resource Center, 1990), p. 103; Ian Victoriano, "Bataan Oil Spill Anniversary," *National Midweek* 6, 12 (February 27, 1991): 7; and

Associated Editors, "Bataan Oil Spill: Disaster Hits 5 Towns," *Philippine Daily Inquirer*, April 22, 1991.

12. Sources for information on the Philippine fishing industry in this and the immediately following paragraphs include John P. McAndrew, Alberto R. Cacayan, and Ponciano L. Bennagen, "A Critical Assessment of the Samal Island Development Foundation Experience in Davao and the Central Visayas Regional Project–1 Nearshore Fisheries Experience in Cebu and Bohol," unpublished manuscript prepared for Private Agencies Collaborating Together (PACT) and the American Jewish World Service, February–mid-April, 1989, pp. 1–5; Gareth Porter with Delfin Ganapin, Jr., *Resources, Population, and the Philippines' Future: A Case Study*, WRI Paper No. 4 (Washington, D.C.: World Resources Institute, 1988), pp. 21, 35–44; Flor Lacanilao, "Giving Small-Scale Fishermen Territorial Rights over Their Water," *Diliman Review* 36, 2 (1988); World Bank, *Philippines: Forestry, Fisheries, and Agricultural Resource Management Study (ffARM Study)*, pp. 30–42; Eduardo C. Tadem, "Modernization and Depletion: The Case of the Fishing Industry in Mindanao-Sulu," in Eduardo Tadem, Johnny Reyes, and L. Susan Magno, eds., *Showcases of Underdevelopment: Fishes, Forests, and Fruits* (Davao City: Alternate Resource Center, 1984), pp. 13–89; and Depthnews, "Tuna Glut Clouds Prospects of Fishing Industry," *Manila Times*, June 3, 1989. See also *Lundayan Magazine*, the quarterly publication of the Quezon City–based Tambuyog Development Center, and Jose Aspiras, "Towards Genuine Fishery Reforms," in Chip Fay, ed., *Our Threatened Heritage: The Transcript, Recommendations, and Papers of the Solidarity Seminar on the Environment* (Manila: Solidaridad Publishing House, 1989), pp. 126–30; and cf. the chapter by the Community Extension and Research for Develoment (CERD), "Philippine Fisherfolk Communities: Issues and Responses," pp. 146–56.

On the issue of Japanese involvement, see especially *Mindanao Focus* 2, nos. 3, 4 (May, 1984); and Riza Faith C. Ybanez, "Fattening Our Creditors," *National Midweek* 5, 42 (October 24, 1990).

The breakdown among aquaculture, commercial fishing, and municipal fishing is based on 1988 figures of the Philippine government for the value of fish production, cited in Roniel Santos and Catherine Duran, "A Fishy Predicament," *Ibon Facts & Figures* 12, 16 (August 31, 1989): 4.

A good general reference on this topic is C. Bailey, "The Political Economy of Fisheries and Development in the Third World," *Agriculture and Human Values* 5, 1 (1988).

13. Yet, as DENR Assistant Secretary Delfin Ganapin tells us, "If you factor in all the positive effects of mangroves, direct and indirect, you get less production from fishponds than from intact mangrove forests."

14. By definition, commercial fishers are those who use boats of more

than three gross tons and operate three or more nautical kilometers from shore. The final category, municipal fishers, is made up of those whose boats are under three tons and who operate within the three-kilometer limit. In practice, however, commercial fishing is sometimes done inside this limit.

15. On the history of land concentration in the Philippines, see Ibon Databank, *Land Reform in the Philippines* (Manila: Ibon, 1988), pp. 25–40; John McAndrew, "The Urban Process and Social Differentiation in a Philippine Village," paper prepared for the International Symposium on Third World Urbanization, Stockholm, Sweden, June 7–9, 1989, pp. 3–7; and Jonathan Fast and Jim Richardson, *Roots of Dependency: Political and Economic Revolution in the 19th Century Philippines* (Quezon City: Foundation for Nationalist Studies, 1979). See also John McAndrew, "From Friar Estates to Industrial Estates," Ph.D. dissertation, University of Amsterdam, 1990; Renato Constantino, *A History of the Philippines* (New York: Monthly Review Press, 1975), pp. 342–49; and Owen J. Lynch, Jr., "Invisible Peoples and a Hidden Agenda: The Origins of Contemporary Philippine Land Laws," *Philippine Law Journal* 63 (September, 1988).

16. See Walden Bello et al., *Development Debacle: The World Bank in the Philippines* (San Francisco: Institute for Food and Development Policy, 1982).

17. Ibon Databank, *Land Reform in the Philippines*, p. 15.

18. James Putzel, "The Problems of Making Agrarian Reform Dependent on ODA," *Issues and Letters* (of the Philippine Center for Policy Studies) 1, 9 (1991): 2. See also Congress for a People's Agrarian Reform, *Popular Grassroots Initiatives Toward Genuine Agrarian Reform: A Descriptive Report—with CPAR Assessment of First Year Implementation of Republic Act No. 6657* (Manila: Congress for a People's Agrarian Reform, 1989), p. 2.

19. Roy Prosterman and Timothy Hanstad, University of Washington School of Law, "Whether Failure Is Inevitable Under the New Philippine Land-Reform Law," memorandum to file, November 3, 1988, p. 1.

20. On Philippine land reform, see the work of James Putzel, including: James Putzel, *A Captive Land: The Politics of Agrarian Reform in the Philippines* (New York: Monthly Review Press, 1992); and James Putzel and John Cunnington, *Gaining Ground: Agrarian Reform in the Philippines* (London: War on Want, 1989). For an analysis of the biggest of the D.A.R. scandals, see Juaniyo Arcellana, "Garchitorena," *National Midweek* 4, 28 (June 28, 1989). See also Susan Wong, *The Making of the 1988 Comprehensive Agrarian Reform Law*, Monograph No. 2 (Quezon City: Institute on Church and Social Issues, Ateneo de Manila University, February, 1989).

21. Republic of the Philippines, Department of Health, Regional Health Office No. 3, Integrated Provincial Health Office, "Vital Health Statistics for 1987," p. 2.

Chapter Six: The Wall

1. Philippine government advertisement for BEPZ, "Remember Bataan?" *Fortune* (October, 1975): 47, quoted in James K. Boyce, "Export Agriculture," p. 29 of the 1989 draft of chapter 5 for Boyce's *The Philippines: The Political Economy of Growth and Impoverishment in the Marcos Era* (London: Macmillan, 1992).

2. Peter G. Warr, *Export Processing Zones in the Philippines*, ASEAN-Australian Economic Papers no. 20 (Canberra: ASEAN-Australian Joint Research Project, 1985), cited in Robin Broad, *Unequal Alliance: The World Bank, the International Monetary Fund, and the Philippines* (Berkeley: University of California Press, 1988; paperback ed., 1990), p. 317, note 84.

3. The Australian sand story is found in Sterling Seagrave, *The Marcos Dynasty* (New York: Harper and Row, 1988), pp. 232, 300. The number of firms in 1980 is cited from Philippine Export Processing Zone Authority, *Annual Report 1980* (Metro-Manila: EPZA, 1981), p. 24. On the goal of 150 firms, see Patria Amor, "Foreign Funds Eyed for Export Zones," *Malaya*, November 19, 1988.

4. Boyce, "Export Agriculture," p. 4.

5. See Ed. C. de Jesus, *The Tobacco Monopoly in the Philippines: Bureaucratic Enterprise and Social Change, 1766–1880* (Quezon City: Ateneo de Manila University Press, 1980); Alfred W. McCoy and Ed. C. de Jesus, eds., *Philippine Social History: Global Trade and Local Transformation* (Quezon City: Ateneo de Manila University Press, 1982); and Richard P. Tucker, "Five Hundred Years of Tropical Forest Exploitation," in Suzanne Head and Robert Heizman, eds., *Lessons of the Rainforest* (San Francisco: Sierra Club Books, 1990).

6. Alfred W. McCoy, "A Queen Dies Slowly: The Rise and Decline of Iloilo City," in McCoy and de Jesus, eds., *Philippine Social History*.

7. Shirley Jenkins, *American Economic Policy Toward the Philippines* (Stanford: Stanford University Press, 1954; reprint Metro-Manila: Cacho Hermanos, Inc., 1985). See pp. 32–34. The two bills were the United States Tariff Act and the Philippine Tariff Act.

8. For details of the garment industry, see Cornelia H. Aldana, *A Contract for Underdevelopment: Subcontracting for Multinationals in the Philippine Semiconductor and Garment Industries* (Metro-Manila: Ibon Databank, 1989). On electronics, see Roel Landigan, Jo-ann Maglipon, and Cornelia Aldana, *The Semiconductor Industry* (Metro-Manila: Ibon

Databank, 1990). For more on the lack of integration of Philippine industry, see David C. O'Connor, "Industry in a Mixed Economy," in Emmanuel S. de Dios and Lorna G. Villamil, eds., *Plans, Markets, and Relations: Studies for a Mixed Economy* (Manila: Philippine Center for Policy Studies, 1990); David C. O'Connor, "Microelectronics-Based Innovations: Strategic Implications for Selected Industries in the Second-Tier Newly Industrializing Countries (NICs) of Southeast Asia," draft report prepared for the OECD Development Centre, Quezon City, September, 1988; and World Bank, *The Philippines: Issues and Policies in the Industrial Sector*, vol. 2 (Washington, D.C.: World Bank, April 29, 1987).

9. Sixto K. Roxas, "Thirty-Seven Years of Rural Reconstruction in the Philippines," speech given at the thirty-seventh anniversary celebration of the Philippine Rural Reconstruction Movement, Nueva Ecija, July 16, 1989, p. 7.

10. On agricultural productivity, see Green Forum–Philippines, "Alternative to Crisis: Agenda for Sustainable Development," Manila, January, 1991 draft, pp. 25–26, 28–29. For a good overview of the strengths and weaknesses of the economy, see the various articles by Rigoberto Tiglao in "Focus: Philippines 1991," *Far Eastern Economic Review* (June 13, 1991).

11. Mar Supnad, "Dunlop Increases Production Level," *Manila Times*, June 3, 1991; and "R.P.-Made Tennis Balls Find Way into Wimbledon," *Philippine Daily Inquirer*, June 2, 1991.

12. On the BEPZ general strikes, see Henry Holland and Mimi Brady, "Le Nouveau Militantisme Ouvrier," *Le Monde Diplomatique* (January, 1983).

13. On the issue of "value-added," see, for instance, Aldana, *A Contract for Underdevelopment*, pp. 58, 142; Broad, *Unequal Alliance*, p. 192; and Peter G. Warr, "Export Processing Zones: The Economics of Offshore Manufacturing," *World Bank Internal Discussion Paper: Latin America and the Caribbean Region Series*, Report No. IDP-9, Trade, Finance, and Industry Operations, Country Department 1 (Washington, D.C.: World Bank, August, 1987), pp. 16–17.

Data from the Export Processing Zone Authority for 1989 show $124.3 million of imports against $79.8 million earned in exports for BEPZ. These figures are given in a memo from the Ad-Hoc MIS Group to the Administrator, "Re: Summary of 1989 Performance—Zone and Zone Enterprises," February 2, 1990.

14. Warr, "Export Processing Zones," p. 11.

15. A local labor leader we later interview believes that only 10–15 percent of the workers in the zone are from Bataan. "They don't hire workers from Bataan," he says. "They think it's too easy for you to go on strike. You'd be supported by your family."

16. Warr, "Export Processing Zones," p. 12.

17. Cayetano Paderanga, Jr., "Employment in Philippine Development," Discussion Paper No. 8905, University of the Philippines School of Economics, Quezon City, March, 1988, p. 54.

18. World Bank, *The Philippine Poor: What Is to Be Done?* (Washington, D.C.: World Bank, 1988), confidential version, p. 11 of Chapter II, and p. 2 of Summary and Conclusions.

19. In 1990, after a long fight between the two provinces that eventually was argued before the Philippine Supreme Court, the Taiwanese investors, USI Far East Corporation, decided to scrap the Philippine petrochemical project altogether. See Rigoberto Tiglao, "A Chemical Reaction," *Far Eastern Economic Review* (April 12, 1990); Rigoberto Tiglao, "No Way, Jose," *Far Eastern Economic Review* (June 21, 1990); and "USI Far East Pulls Out of Philippine Project," *Far Eastern Economic Review* (December 20, 1990).

20. Sixto K. Roxas, "Blueprint for a Banana Republic," *Philippine Daily Inquirer*, March 4, 1990. (The first part of Roxas's article appeared on March 3, 1990.)

Chapter Seven: Hearts and Minds

1. Provincial government, Bataan, untitled report on the province of Bataan, Section I, Part A, "Brief History" (mimeographed, 1989).

2. See Ed. C. de Jesus, *The Tobacco Monopoly in the Philippines: Bureaucratic Enterprise and Social Change, 1766–1880* (Quezon City: Ateneo de Manila University Press, 1980), pp. 60–62.

3. On the Huks, see Benedict Kerkvliet, *The Huk Rebellion: A Study of Peasant Revolt in the Philippines* (Berkeley: University of California Press, 1977); and Edward G. Landsdale, *In the Midst of Wars* (New York: Harper and Row, 1972).

4. Many estimates list NPA membership separately. See James B. Goodno, *The Philippines: Land of Broken Promises* (Atlantic Highlands, N.J.: Zed Press, 1991), p. 140; Richard Kessler, *Rebellion and Repression in the Philippines* (New Haven: Yale University Press, 1989), pp. 56, 100; Gregg Jones, *Red Revolution: Inside the Philippine Guerilla Movement* (Boulder: Westview Press, 1989), p. 8; and William Chapman, *Inside the Philippine Revolution* (New York: W. W. Norton, 1987), p. 14.

5. For more on the history of the Philippine legal and illegal left, see Benjamin Pimentel, *Rebolusyon! A Generation of Struggle in the Philippines* (New York: Monthly Review Press, 1991); and Goodno, *The Philippines: Land of Broken Promises*. On the Philippines' illegal left, see Kessler, *Rebellion and Repression in the Philippines*; Chapman, *Inside the Philippine Revolution*; and Jones, *Red Revolution*.

6. For more on San Juan and its history, see the three-part series by Benjamin Pimentel, "The Secret of Barrio San Juan," *National Midweek* 3, nos. 9–11 (January, 1987).

7. Task Force Detainees, Bataan Unit, "Collated and Statistical Reports of Human Rights Violations: January 3, 1990–February 6, 1990," Balanga, Bataan, [n.d.], p. 1; January to July, 1990, statistics from BAYAN-Bataan, letter reprinted in "'Salvaging': Unwritten Policy," *National Midweek* 5, 31 (July 4, 1990): 35. See also Tezza O. Parel, "Women in Prison," *National Midweek* 6, 15 (March 27, 1991).

8. Lt. Col. Enrique Galang, Bataan PC-INP, quoted in "30 Companies Operate at BEPZ," *Manila Bulletin*, October 8, 1990.

During the Aquino administration, a Philippine National Police (PNP) was created by merging the Philippine Constabulary (PC) with the Integrated National Police (INP). As a result, the Philippine Constabulary was removed from the military chain of command. The military counterpart to the PNP remains the Armed Forces of the Philippines (AFP), of which the Philippine Army is a part.

9. News report in the *Manila Chronicle*, December 16, 1990, reported in *Philippine News Digest* 2, 6 (January 21, 1991): 6.

10. See Parel, "Women in Prison."

Chapter Eight: "The Bastards of Bataan"

1. Some of the best accounts of World War II events in the Philippines are to be found in William Manchester, *American Caesar* (New York: Dell Publishing, 1978); E. Bartlett Kerr, *Surrender and Survival: The Experience of American POWs in the Pacific, 1941–1945* (New York: William Morrow, 1985); and Donald Know, *Death March: The Survivors of Bataan* (New York: Harcourt Brace Jovanovich, 1981). See also an historical novel: Ralph Graves, *Share of Honor* (New York: Harper and Row, 1989).

2. Katherine Ellison, *Imelda: Steel Butterfly of the Philippines* (New York: McGraw-Hill, 1988), p. 73.

3. Letty Jimenez-Magsanoc, "Too Little, Too Late," *Philippine Daily Inquirer*, August 3, 1989.

4. "After Bataan," *Philippines Free Press*, December 10, 1988.

5. Quoted in Arnold Molina Azurin, "War of the Raw Deal: Old Veterans' Last Fight," *Philippine Daily Globe*, July 16, 1989.

6. Frank Quesada, himself a gray-haired veteran, quoted in Azurin, "War of the Raw Deal." For the figure of $3 billion and the average age of seventy-three, respectively, see Associated Press, "WWII Veterans Seek

$3B Claim," *Philippine Daily Globe*, June 30, 1989, and Jimenez-Magsanoc, "Too Little, Too Late."

7. In March, 1992, the Philippine government signed an out-of-court settlement with Westinghouse that stipulated that Westinghouse would upgrade and operate the plant. As of mid–1992, a major debate had erupted in the Philippines over whether the Ramos administration should approve the settlement.

See Brian Dumaine, "The $2.2 Billion Nuclear Fiasco," *Fortune* 114 (September 1, 1986); Walden Bello, Peter Hayes, and Lyuba Zarsky, "500-Mile Island: The Philippine Nuclear Reactor Deal," *Pacific Research* (of the Pacific Studies Center) 10, 1 (1st Quarter, 1979); Robin Broad and John Cavanagh, "Bataan Plant," *Amicus Journal* 11, 4 (Fall, 1989): box, p. 23; Roberto Verzola, Mae Buenaventura, and Edgardo Santoalla, "The Bataan Nuclear Power Plant," in Amado Mendoza, Jr., ed., *Debts of Dishonor* (Quezon City: Philippine Rural Reconstruction Movement, 1991); Alan Robles, "Bataan Nuke Plant: A Frozen Colossus," *Manila Chronicle*, January 3, 1989; and Johanna Son, "Mothballed Nuke Workers," *Manila Chronicle*, January 4, 1989.

8. Caltex is a company jointly owned by the oil giants Texaco and Chevron. See John Blair, *The Control of Oil* (New York: Vintage Books, 1978), pp. 36–38.

9. Leonardo B. Roman, Provincial Governor, "Briefing Paper: Province of Bataan—Its Problems and Issues," Balanga, Bataan, 1988; and Leonardo B. Roman, Provincial Governor, "Bataan Province: On the U.S. Facilities," Balanga, Bataan, 1988.

10. According to article II, section 8, of the 1987 *Constitution of the Republic of the Philippines*, "The Philippines, consistent with the national interest, adopts and pursues a policy of freedom from nuclear weapons in its territory."

11. According to one researcher, "An internal [U.S.] Defense Department report reveals hazardous waste disposal problems in several overseas bases including the Philippines": Jorge Emmanuel (of the Alliance for Philippine Concerns, the Berkeley-based Philippine Resource Center, and the San Francisco Arms Control Research Center), "Environmental Destruction Caused by U.S. Military Bases and the Serious Implications for the Philippines," paper presented at "Crossroads 1991: Towards a Nuclear Free, Bases Free Philippines—An International Conference," Manila, Philippines, May 14–19, 1990.

12. Loida Nicolas Lewis, *How the Filipino Veteran of World War II Can Become a U.S. Citizen According to the Immigration Act of 1990* (New York: Filipino Reporter, 1991). See also Margot Cohen, "Fiscal Time Bomb," *Far Eastern Economic Review* (November 23, 1989).

13. Lt. Col. Angel Dayot (RMO), American Legion adjutant, to a gathering of twelve hundred veterans in Zamboanga City, Mindanao, quoted in Armand Nocum, "Veterans Call to Junk Bases," *National Midweek* 6, 23 (June 5, 1991): 31.

Chapter Nine: From Plunder to Sustainability

1. Quotes are from Caucus of Development NGO Networks (CODE-NGO), "The Right to Development: Conference Report," report of conference held at Jay-cee Resort, Barrio Pansol, Calamba, Laguna, Philippines, April 26, 1991, appendix 1, p. 1; and Caucus of Development NGO Networks, "Covenant on Philippine Development," adopted in Manila, December 4, 1991, p. 2.

The United Nations resolution is United Nations General Assembly, "Declaration on the Right to Development," adopted by General Assembly resolution 41.128, December 4, 1986.

2. The largest of these "tendencies" is the "national democrats," followed by the "social democrats" and other smaller groups.

3. For a history of peasant organizing in the Philippines, see Francisco Lara, Jr., and Horacio Morales, Jr., "The Peasant Movement and the Challenge of Democratisation in the Philippines," *Journal of Development Studies* 26, 4 (July, 1990).

4. Catholic Bishops' Conference of the Philippines, "What Is Happening to Our Beautiful Land? A Pastoral Letter on Ecology," January 29, 1988, reprinted as appendix 1 in Vincent Busch, *Hope for the Seeds* (Quezon City: Claretian Publications, 1989). See, for instance, Yasmin Arquiza, "The Vanishing Trees of Gabaldon," *Sunday [Philippine] Inquirer Magazine*, September 30, 1990.

5. Melanie Manlogon, "Interview: Rev. Jose P. M. Cunanan," *National Midweek* 6, 24 (June 12, 1991): 21.

6. See Philippine Environmental Action Network, "Founding Congress: A Conceptual Framework," three-page document, April 19–22, 1990 Founding Congress held at Oblate Missionary Center, Quezon City, Philippines.

7. Green Forum–Philippines, untitled paper, Makati, 1990, p. 1 of 5 pages.

8. Green Forum–Philippines, "Economic White Paper," Manila, June, 1991, pp. 22–23.

9. Manlogon, "Interview: Rev. Jose P. M. Cunanan," p. 22.

10. For a series of essays on democratizing both access to resources and management of resources in the Philippine context, see Chip Fay, ed., *Our Threatened Heritage: The Transcript, Recommendations, and*

Papers of the Solidarity Seminar on the Environment (Manila: Solidaridad Publishing House, 1989). See also *Philippine Natural Resources Law Journal*, a quarterly publication of the Legal Rights and Natural Resources Center.

11. Sometimes the connection between sustainable development and human rights is very direct, as with the tribal community harassed by the Consunji Logging Company in Sultan Kudarat, Mindanao, or the 1990 bombings of indigenous people in the Marag Valley in northern Luzon, in both cases purportedly because loggers covet the area's forests. See Sheilfa Alojamiento et al., "Whose Land Is It?" *National Midweek* 6, 2 (November 28, 1990); Sheilfa Alojamiento, "Intruders in Their Own Land," *National Midweek* 6, 3 (December 5, 1990); TABAK, "Bulletin Genocide—AFP's Oplan Nakilala-Salidummay at Marag Valley," *Action Alert* (1991); and Chip Fay, draft chapters of book with working title "Deforestation, Militarization, and Human Rights," Manila, Friends of the Earth.

12. See Chico Mendes, *Fight for the Forest: Chico Mendes in His Own Words*, trans. Chris Whitehouse, with additional material by Tony Gross (London: Latin America Bureau, 1989).

13. See Dan Connell, "Palawan Endangered," *National Midweek* 6, 22 (May 29, 1991).

14. Jorge Emmanuel, "The Philippine Environment and Sustainable Development," in Dolores Flamiano and Donald Goertzen, eds., *Critical Decade: Prospects for Democracy in the Philippines in the 1990s* (Berkeley: Philippine Resource Center, 1990), p. 107.

15. World Bank, *The Philippine Poor: What Is to Be Done?* (Washington, D.C.: World Bank, 1988), confidential version, p. 1 of Chapter IV, "Population Policies in the Philippines." The estimate of 2.8 percent, which ranks the Philippines number one in Asia, is given to us by University of the Philippines economist Alejandro Herrin and cited by Gareth Porter with Delfin Ganapin, Jr., *Resources, Population, and the Philippines' Future: A Case Study*, WRI Paper No. 4 (Washington, D.C.: World Resources Institute, 1988), p. 2. The United Nations puts the current population growth at 2.48 percent: cited in James Clad, "Genesis of Despair," *Far Eastern Economic Review* (October 20, 1988): 24. The Philippine government estimates the rate at 2.4. See Norman Myers, "Faltering Commitment to Family Planning in the Philippines?" *People* (quarterly journal of International Planned Parenthood Federation) 15, 2 (1988): 31. Population and density comparisons have been calculated from statistics in World Bank, *World Development Report 1988* (Oxford: Oxford University Press, 1988), pp. 222–23. The leading study of population and Philippine forests is Maria Concepcion Cruz, *Integrated Summary Report:*

Population Pressure and Migration—Implications for Upland Development, CPDS Working Paper No. 86-07 (Los Baños, Laguna: Center for Policy and Development Studies of the University of the Philippines at Los Baños College, 1986).

16. James Boyce, "Population Patrol: The Bomb Is a Dud," *Progressive* (September, 1990): 25.

17. For more on the authors' view of the Philippine population problem, see Robin Broad and John Cavanagh, *The Philippine Challenge: Sustainable and Equitable Development in the 1990s* (Quezon City: Philippine Center for Policy Studies, 1991). Geographer David Kummer's work disputes the demographic connection by demonstrating that the areas in the Philippines that historically had the greatest rates of deforestation had the lowest population density. See David M. Kummer, "Deforestation in the Post-War Philippines," Ph. D. dissertation, Boston University, 1990.

18. Marites Danguilan-Vitug, "Fighting for Life," *Far Eastern Economic Review* (June 13, 1991): 53.

19. R. Paris and I. Ruzicka, *Barking Up the Wrong Tree: The Role of Rent Appropriation in Sustainable Tropical Forest Management*, Asian Development Bank Environmental Office Occasional Paper No. 1 (Manila, May, 1991), p. 2. See this ADB occasional paper for an overall critique of reliance on increased environmental taxes as a way to solve deforestation problems.

20. For example, the basic framework document for the Green Forum–Philippines, "Creating a Common Future: Philippine NGO Initiatives for Sustainable Development," [1989]; Catholic Bishops' Conference of the Philippines, "What Is Happening to Our Beautiful Land?"; and Abe Padilla and Maria Teresa B. Guia, "Development Work and the Indigenous Peoples," *Kabalikat: The Development Worker* (quarterly publication of the Council for People's Development), no. 11 (June, 1991). In that same issue of *Kabalikat*, see the interview with Pablo Santos, secretary-general of Kalipunan ng mga Katutubong Mamamayan (KAMP, or Federation of Indigenous Peoples of the Philippines).

21. Emmanuel S. de Dios and Lorna G. Villamil, eds., *Plans, Markets, and Relations: Studies for a Mixed Economy* (Manila: Philippine Center for Policy Studies, 1990).

22. See Joel Rocamora, "Discontent in the Philippines," *World Policy Journal* 8, 4 (Fall, 1991); and Barry Gills and Joel Rocamora, eds., *Low-Intensity Democracy* (London: Pluto Press, 1992).

23. There remains, however, a creative tension in the minds of many citizen leaders between the small-scale credit, health, and livelihood projects that offer minor gains and the long-term goal of shaking up the whole power system and redistributing resources. On credit programs,

for example, Philippine Rural Reconstruction Movement vice-president
Isagani Serrano warns, "Don't just mobilize people to save, as has been
done with the very creative small-scale loan-providing Grameen Bank in
Bangladesh. Mobilize them also to go after the capitalists, the moneylend-
ers and the government, who control the unjust system."

24. Isagani R. Serrano, "A Community Empowerment Strategy for
Sustainable Development," paper presented to the International Confer-
ence on Agrarian Reform, January 28–February 3, 1991, Nueva Ecija,
Philippines, p. 3. See also Green Forum–Philippines, "Economic White
Paper," Manila, June, 1991.

25. Area development strategists are pursuing a two-level approach to
the country in their selection of areas to start the process. Some places,
such as Catanduanes province in the east, have in key government positions relatively sympathetic officials who work with the organizers. Work
in other areas, such as Bataan—more typical of the Philippines—necessarily involves confrontation with local officials who by and large have
taken sides with the military in repressing people's organizations.

26. Owen J. Lynch, Jr., "Philippine Government Policy in Forest
Zones," in Flamiano and Goertzen, eds., *Critical Decade*, p. 11. For more
on this, see Owen J. Lynch, Jr., "Invisible Peoples and a Hidden Agenda:
The Origins of Contemporary Philippine Land Laws," *Philippine Law
Journal* 63 (September, 1988); and Owen J. Lynch, Jr., and Kirk Talbott,
"Legal Responses to the Philippine Deforestation Crises," *New York Uni-
versity Journal of International Law and Politics* 20, 3 (Spring, 1988). See
also Antonio G. M. La Viña, ed., *Law and Ecology: A Compilation of Philippine Laws and International Documents Pertaining to Ecology* (Quezon
City: Legal Rights and Natural Resources Center, 1991).

27. For detailed analyses of debt, see Debt Crisis Network, *From
Debt to Development: Alternatives to the International Debt Crisis*, 2d
ed. (Washington, D.C.: Institute for Policy Studies for the Debt Crisis
Network, 1986). On aid, see Frances Moore Lappé, Rachel Schurman,
and Kevin Danaher, *Betraying the National Interest* (San Francisco: Insti-
tute for Food and Development Policy, 1987); and Teresa Hayter, *Ex-
ploited Earth: Britain's Aid and the Environment* (London: Earthscan
Publications, 1989). On investment, see Richard J. Barnet and Ronald
Muller, *Global Reach: The Power of the Multinational Corporations* (New
York: Simon and Schuster, 1974).

28. Quoted in Donald Goertzen, "Agents for Change," *Far Eastern
Economic Review* (August 8, 1991): 21.

29. World Commission on Environment and Development, *Our Common Future* (New York: Oxford University Press, 1987). The commission
is commonly referred to as the Brundtland Commission.

30. Some of the ideas in this final section of the book were grappled with in Robin Broad, John Cavanagh, and Walden Bello, "Development: The Market Is Not Enough," *Foreign Policy*, no. 81 (Winter, 1990–91).

The term *Washington consensus* is used by John Williamson in *The Progress of Policy Reform in Latin America*, Policy Analyses in International Economics No. 28 (Washington, D.C.: Institute for International Economics, 1990).

31. The term *unsustainable development* is used in, for example, Nicanor Perlas, "Sustainable Development," Center for Alternative Development Initiatives, Philippines, [n.d.], unpublished paper. See Robin Broad, *Unequal Alliance: The World Bank, the International Monetary Fund, and the Philippines* (Berkeley: University of California Press, 1988; paperback ed., 1990).

32. Susan George, *The Debt Boomerang: How Third World Debt Harms Us All* (London: Pluto Press, 1992), p. 2. See also Susan George, *A Fate Worse Than Debt: The World Financial Crisis and the Poor*, 2d ed. (New York: Grove Weidenfeld, 1990).

33. The borrowing that accompanied the free-market approach erupted into a full-scale debt crisis in the early 1980s; since 1983, more financial resources have been flowing out of developing countries as a whole in debt service than have been flowing in from new loans and aid. According to the World Bank's own figures, the net outflow from the developing world totaled an estimated $168 billion from 1984 through 1989. (Calculation based on World Bank, *Annual Report 1990* [Washington, D.C.: World Bank, 1990], p. 32, table 2.6.)

34. Alan Durning, "People Power and Development," *Foreign Policy*, no. 76 (Fall, 1989): 66.

35. See Sheldon Annis and Peter Hakim, eds., *Direct to the Poor: Grassroots Development in Latin America* (Boulder: Lynne Rienner, 1988); Fantu Cheru, *The Silent Revolution in Africa: Debt, Development and Democracy* (Atlantic Highlands, N.J.: Zed Press, 1989); Alan Durning, *Action at the Grassroots: Fighting Poverty and Environment Decline*, Worldwatch Paper No. 88 (Washington, D.C.: Worldwatch Institute, 1989); Walden Bello and Stephanie Rosenfeld, *Dragons in Distress: Asia's Miracle Economies in Crisis* (San Francisco: Institute for Food and Development Policy, 1990); Broad, Cavanagh, and Bello, "Development: The Market Is Not Enough"; and David Korten, "Sustainable Development: A Review Essay," *World Policy Journal* 9, 1 (Winter 1991–92).

36. Among others: "The Manila Declaration on People's Participation and Sustainable Development," Manila, June, 1989 (adopted at June 6–10, 1989, conference sponsored by the Asian NGO Coalition [ANGOC] and attended by representatives from thirty-one citizens' association lead-

ers from Africa, Southeast Asia, South Asia, the South Pacific, Latin America, the Caribbean, North America, and Europe); "The Managua Declaration," Managua, June, 1989 (adopted at June 5–9, 1989, conference attended by one hundred and twenty representatives from more than sixty countries and every continent); International Conference on Popular Participation in the Recovery and Development Process in Africa, "African Charter for Popular Participation and Transformation," Arusha, Tanzania, February, 1990 (adopted at February 12–16, 1990, conference attended by over five hundred participants from POs and NGOs); "Statement by the Southern NGO Delegates at the Seventh Annual Interaction Forum," Baltimore, Maryland, April 25, 1990.

On these movements across the Third World, see also Jayanta Bandyopadhyay and Vandana Shiva, "Political Economy of Ecology Movements," *IFDA Dossier*, no. 71 (May–June, 1989); and David Korten, *Getting to the 21st Century: Voluntary Action and the Global Agenda* (Hartford, Conn.: Kumarian Press, 1990). Korten's *People-Centered Development Forum* newsletter is an excellent source for information on these and other declarations.

Index

Agribusiness, 36, 85. *See also* Plantations
Agriculture, 83, 93; agrarian reform, 134–
  35, 139; Bataan, 74, 75, 82, 86; cash
  crop for export, 85, 92–93; chemicals,
  18, 36, 81, 147–48; colonization and,
  84, 92; flooding, 31, 35, 36, 61–62; and
  forests, 35, 36, 45, 142, 168n.16; industry not integrated with, 93; labor
  without pay in, 159n.4; policy (lack of),
  93; regenerative, 135; San Fernando,
  59, 61–63; shifting/"slash-and-burn,"
  45–46, 66; tenant, 84, 85; water for
  prawn farming and, 78. *See also* Plantations; Rice
Agwawan (*sitio*), 87–88
Air pollution: Manila, 20–23; from open-
  pit mining, 27
Alliance of the Peoples of the Forest, 155
ALMA-BA (Alyansa ng Magbubukid sa
  Bataan), 111, 116
Almaciga trees, 43
Almendras (Caridad C.) Logging Enter-
  prises, 64–66, 67
Alvarez, Jose "Pepito," 43–54
Amazon. *See* Brazil
Ancestral domains, 139, 151; of Bagobo
  on Mount Apo, 33–35, 144–45; de-
  fined, 164–65n.13; migration to up-
  lands and, 85; as public lands, 44, 151
Animals: endangered species, 35; work,
  41–42. *See also* Aquaculture; Fishing
Apo Sandawa, 33
Apparel sector, 93, 97, 100
Aquaculture, 41, 83–84; Bataan, 17, 74–
  81, 115, 138. *See also* Fishing; Prawns
Aquino, Benigno "Ninoy," 75, 76

Aquino, Corazon, 47, 52, 75, 108, 154;
  Bataan assessment of, 113–14; and civil
  war, 10–11, 108, 109; daughter Kris,
  106; and debt, 53–54, 152; and export
  processing zones, 92; family plantation,
  9–10; and land reform, 8–9, 85; and
  left, 108; loggers and, 53; military
  coups against, 10, 106, 109; and nuclear power plant, 80, 123; and overseas workers, 15; people power of, 87,
  114; Philippine National Police created
  during, 178n.8; San Fernando citizens
  and, 57, 63–64, 69–70; and NGO policy advocacy, 150
Asian Development Bank (ADB), 49, 144
Association of Southeast Asian Nations, 33
Australia, labor exported to, 14

Bagobo people, 33–34, 144–45
Baguio (city), 5; Cordillera Resource Cen-
  ter for Indigenous Peoples' Rights, 29,
  30, 134; earthquake (1990), 160n.9;
  Mine's View Park, 5–6
Baheli (village), 41
Balanga (Bataan capital), 101–3, 104–6
Bananas, 36, 92
Bancas (canoe-like crafts), 79, 87
Bangladesh: foreign-funded tubewells,
  48–49; Grameen Bank, 183n.23; prawn
  business, 78
Banks, multilateral development, 49,
  144. *See also* World Bank
Barangays (barrios): San Fernando, 61;
  SOTs in Bataan, 109–12
Bases, U.S. *See* United States military

Consunji, Ditas, 102–3, 128
Consunji Logging Company, 181n.11
Convergence for Integrated Community-
Based Development, 148
Convict colony, on Palawan, 40
Coral reefs, 37–38, 81, 148, 172n.9
Cordillera Mountains, 5–6, 25–27, 30,
138, 164n.12
Cordillera Resource Center for Indige-
nous Peoples' Rights, 29, 30, 134
Corn, 35, 59, 61, 62–63
Corregidor (the Rock), 90–91
Corruption, 71; and logging, 45, 64, 67–
68, 69, 70, 139–40; military, 48, 115,
116, 141
Cotton, 93
"Covenant on Philippine Development,"
132–33
CPAR (Congress for a People's Agrarian
Reform), 134–35, 139
Cruz, Jacinto, 118–19
Culture: indigenous, 144–45; U.S., 122
Cunanan, Jose "Pepz," 136, 137
Cunningham, Douglas, 129

Dambana ng Kagitingan (Altar of Valor),
120
Dam protests, 155
Davao (port), 32
David, Lydia, 77
Death March, Bataan, 73, 75, 91, 98,
119, 120, 121, 129
Debt: Bataan parents', 80; "debt-for-
nature swap," 50; Freedom from Debt
Coalition and, 1, 135, 151; and free-
market development, 184n.33; government, 14–15, 50, 53–54, 66, 123, 135,
138–39, 145, 151
"Declaration on the Right to Development" (United Nations), 73, 132
Deforestation, 18, 31–33, 35–36, 50–52,
164n.11, 168n.16; Bataan, 74, 76;
blame for, 45–46; Bukidnon, 62–72; in
DENR painting, 17; and environmental taxes, 182n.19; migration to uplands
and, 33, 85; for mining, 29; population
and, 182n.17; and poverty, 45–46, 142;
for prawn ponds, 76; San Fernando,
18, 62–72. *See also* Logging
De la Rosa, Eliodoro "Ely," 114–15, 141
Del Monte company, 36, 58, 59, 62
Delos Reyes, Oscar, 99–100
Democracy: Aquino's government and,
47, 108, 113–14; "democratic coalition
government," 108; in environment/

development issues, 108, 138, 139,
140, 144; and political left, 146–47
Department of Agrarian Reform, 85
Department of Education, Culture, and
Sports, 13–14
Department of Environment and Natural
Resources (DENR), 53; and air quality,
21, 22–23; corruption in, 67–68, 152;
on forest needed for stable ecosystem,
32; and geothermal project, 34; logging
ban in virgin forests, 151–52; logging
concession power, 44, 52, 53, 66; and
logging illegalities, 45, 67–68, 69; and
logging in Palawan, 45, 48, 49, 152;
and logging in San Fernando, 57, 65–
69; and mangroves vs. fishponds,
173n.13; Manila office, 17; and reforestation, 52; World Wildlife Fund
and, 50
Department of Labor, 48
Department of Social Welfare, 86
Department of Trade and Industry, 78
Development, 90–103, 131, 132–57;
agents of, 145, 152; area, 148–50,
183n.25; Bataan, 74, 90–103, 124–25,
128–30; cash crop, 92–93; citizens'
groups' conceptions of, 89, 130, 134–
41, 144–48; "Covenant on Philippine
Development," 132–33; environmental
protection affecting, 51, 57–58, 71; export processing zone, 92–103; four
principles, 144; free-market, 145–46,
153–57, 184n.33; and inequalities, 4,
51, 85, 127–28, 137–38, 145; international partnerships, 152–53, 156; Lumad view of, 34–35; militarization and,
103; national policy advocacy, 150–52;
organizations, 86–89, 130, 133–37,
145–53; people-to-people, 129–30; redistribution and, 138–39, 182–83n.23;
regional, 148; structural-adjustment,
153, 154, 155–56; sustainable, 90, 130,
132–57, 181n.11; United Nations on,
73, 78, 132, 153; unsustainable, 154–
55; and U.S. aid to Philippines, 74,
124–25, 128; "Washington consensus,"
153–56. *See also* Industrial development
Diarrhea, 80
Diokno, Jose W., 118, 132
Diseases: from agricultural chemicals, 36;
from air pollution, 21–22; children's,
80; in evacuation sites, 11; eye, 21–22;
from garbage, 22; respiratory, 21–22,
36; typhoid, 22

Compositor: Graphic Composition, Inc
Text: 11/13 Caledonia
Display: Caledonia
Printer: BookCrafters, Inc.
Binder: BookCrafters, Inc.

8 - tenure
14 - labor / foreign exchange
29 - Baguio center
32 - deforestation rates
34 - Mt. Apo resistance
37 - 709. (reps ?
39 - Palawan → power / poverty
45 - Alvarez $s
45 - ADB project / resource access
   - Sean McDonagh
50 - Chip Fay (Kummer)
      technical solutions / resource access
63 - Redemptorist Fathers
      Bukidnon logging — licenses cancelled
64 - DENR corruph — / fast fir trees · 1989
76 ff1 - prawn farming